Greatest Emancipations

How the West Abolished Slavery

Jim Powell

palgrave
macmillan

First published in 2008 by
PALGRAVE MACMILLAN™
175 Fifth Avenue, New York, N.Y. 10010 and Houndmills, Basingstoke,
Hampshire, England RG21 6XS. Companies and representatives throughout the
world.

PALGRAVE MACMILLAN is the global academic imprint of the Palgrave
Macmillan division of St. Martin's Press, LLC and of Palgrave Macmillan Ltd.
Macmillan® is a registered trademark in the United States, United Kingdom and
other countries. Palgrave is a registered trademark in the European Union and
other countries.

ISBN-13: 978-0-230-60592-3
ISBN-10: 0-230-60592-3

Library of Congress Cataloging-in-Publication Data
Powell, Jim, 1944–
    Greatest emancipations : how the West abolished slavery / by Jim Powell.
       p.   cm.
    Includes bibliographical references.
    ISBN 0-230-60592-3
    1. Slaves—Emancipation.   2. Slavery.   I. Title.
HT1031.P68   2008
306.3'62—dc22

                                                            2007045439

A catalogue record of the book is available from the British Library.

Design by Letra Libre, Inc.

First edition: July 2008
10 9 8 7 6 5 4 3 2 1
Printed in the United States of America.

Contents

Introduction

Every civilization seems to have had slavery. There was slavery in ancient Africa, Mesopotamia, Egypt, Persia, China, India, the Americas, and the Greek and Roman empires. The Jews had slaves. The Bible accepted slavery, as did the Koran.

The worst form of slavery was chattel slavery, in which slaves were owned by somebody and could be bought and sold. Slaveholders had complete control over a slave's life, determined what work a slave did, where a slave lived, whether a slave had any privacy, and whether a slave could have a family life. If a chattel slave had children, the slaveholder owned them, too. Slave families could be broken up and their members sold separately, as a slaveholder wished. Slaveholders had the power to determine whether chattel slaves would be tortured or executed.

For thousands of years, slavery went unchallenged in principle. Christians urged slaveholders to be kind to their slaves. Humanitarians protested the cruel treatment of slaves. In the many slave revolts throughout history, the rebels struggled to break *their* chains, not necessarily the chains of another racial or ethnic group. There were no broad movements to abolish slavery. Then came a remarkable time when people began to speak out.

In June 1787, as 27-year-old Thomas Clarkson approached Bristol, England, on horseback, he had some concern about the cause he had embraced—the abolition of the slave trade. "I now began to tremble," he said, "for the first time, at the arduous task I had undertaken, of

attempting to subvert one of the branches of the commerce of the great place which was then before me. I anticipated much persecution, and I questioned whether I should even get out of it alive."[1]

During the late eighteenth century, some people in Great Britain, America and France voiced objections to slavery, but the institution was a bulwark of Western economies. British ships carried some 50,000 slaves annually across the Atlantic Ocean, over half the trans-Atlantic slave trade.[2] From 1660 to 1810, the British accounted for 3.2 million slaves out of the 7.3 million who crossed the Atlantic during this period.[3] British ships provided slaves to Spanish, Portuguese and French colonies as well as their own colonies in the western hemisphere.[4]

Tall-masted slave ships crowded the docks at Bristol, Liverpool and London, and merchants did a lively business outfitting these ships. British firms played a key role in financing the slave trade. With deep-pocket partners, they were able to wait for two years before ships finished the triangular voyage to West Africa where slaves were bought, then to the western hemisphere where the slaves were sold and slave-produced commodities such as sugar, coffee and cotton were bought, and finally back to Great Britain where those commodities were sold.[5]

The slaves were bought in West Africa by bartering with cloth, trinkets, guns and other goods, more than a third of which were manufactured in Great Britain. Some 18,000 people in Great Britain had jobs making goods for the slave trade, which accounted for between 4 percent and 5 percent of Great Britain's total exports.[6]

Everything to do with slavery was brutal. Slaves were marched long distances to West African trading stations. Slave traders bargained for the slaves, sometimes taking many weeks to fill their ships. Thomas Clarkson noted, "the right ankle of one slave was fastened to the left ankle of another by an iron fetter; and if they were turbulent, by another on the wrists. They were placed in niches, and along the decks, in such a manner, that it was impossible for any one to pass among them, however careful they might be, without treading upon them. . . . The stench was intolerable. The allowance of water was so deficient that slaves were frequently found gasping for life. For the sake of exercise, these miserable wretches, loaded with chains and oppressed with disease, were forced to dance by the terror of the lash."[7]

Even the most respectable British citizens owned slaves. For example, the Church of England (through its Society for the Propagation

of the Gospel in Foreign Parts) owned Codrington, a 710-acre sugar plantation on Barbados that had about 270 slaves. Since about a third of the slaves died within three years because of harsh treatment and tropical diseases, the plantation had to keep buying more. To discourage slaves from running away, the plantation used hot branding irons to mark their chests. None of this appeared to bother church officials, not even the archbishop of Canterbury who was on the governing board responsible for the plantation.[8]

In May 1794, it wasn't apparent what 47-year-old Toussaint L'Ouverture could do about the French who were struggling to regain control of Saint-Domingue (modern Haiti), their richest colony in the Caribbean. Saint-Domingue was then the world's largest producer of coffee and sugar (almost as much sugar as Jamaica, Cuba and Brazil put together). Nor was it clear how Toussaint would deal with the British and Spanish, who were fighting to capture the colony. A former coachman and veterinarian, Toussaint was an educated free black man who sympathized with the island's African slaves rebelling against the French since August 22, 1791.

He was drawn into guerrilla action, but the odds against success were steep. The French, British and Spanish had well-trained armies plus fleets that could supply more men and guns, while the slaves were armed mainly with knives, sharpened sticks and swords seized from plantations.[9] When the French captured rebel leader Vincent Ogré, his arms, legs and ribs were broken while he was still alive, and then his head was cut off and placed on a stake as a warning to others. A British army officer offered this observation of Cap-Français, Saint-Domingue: "The city presents a terrible spectacle. The streets are blocked by barricades, and the squares are occupied by scaffolds on which captured Negroes are tortured—the whole forming a depressing picture of devastation and carnage."[10]

In January 1831, when 25-year-old, Boston-based William Lloyd Garrison started publishing his weekly abolitionist newspaper, *The Liberator*, he encountered fierce opposition in the North as well as the

South for urging the abolition of American slavery. Such talk threatened to disrupt business and split the Union. Many Northerners who opposed slavery didn't like blacks. Garrison was jailed in Baltimore. North Carolina indicted him for provoking slave revolts. The Georgia legislature offered $5,000 for anybody who brought him back to their state for trial and probable hanging. Six Mississippi slaveholders offered $20,000 for anyone who could deliver Garrison.[11] Slavery advocates put up a nine-foot-high gallows in front of Garrison's house. A Boston mob tried to lynch him.

Proslavery interests were politically powerful in the United States. During the American Revolution, they were well represented in the Continental Congress. They had a major presence at the Constitutional Convention, and they had considerable power in the U.S. Congress. A dozen U.S. presidents owned slaves at one time or another: George Washington, Thomas Jefferson, James Madison, James Monroe, Andrew Jackson, Martin Van Buren, William Henry Harrison, John Tyler, James K. Polk, Zachary Taylor, Andrew Johnson and Ulysses S. Grant. As the Civil War and Reconstruction experience made clear, even when the federal government became supportive of blacks, it had very limited abilities to protect their civil rights from subversion by state or local officials.

Julio Vizcarrondo, a 34-year-old Puerto Rican, started the Sociedad Abolicionista Espanõla (Spanish Abolitionist Society) on December 7, 1864. He recruited friends, wrote newspaper articles, produced pamphlets, organized rallies and other events aimed at winning support for the abolition of slavery.

His goal seemed unrealistic because Cuba, another of Spain's colonies, was the world's largest sugar producer, and the business as it was then set up depended on slavery.[12] The overextended Spanish government desperately needed the customs tax revenue from sugar exports, and it suppressed abolitionist activity. Vizcarrondo helped achieve a first step toward emancipation: Spain's 1870 Moret Law liberated slave children and slaves over 60. But slaveholders had enough political clout to thwart the law.

For decades there had been talk about abolishing slavery in Brazil, but little was done about it. In 1879, 30-year-old Joaquim Nabuco, who had been elected to the Brazilian Chamber of Deputies (the lower house of their National Congress) the previous year, decided he must commit himself to abolition. He began introducing bills to abolish slavery. He helped launch the Sociedade Brasileira a Escravidão (Brazilian Anti-Slavery Society), which issued *O Abolicionista,* the leading publication of the Brazilian abolitionist movement. Nabuco gave antislavery talks around the country, and he proved to be a powerful orator.

The obstacles to abolition were overwhelming. African slavery in Brazil was a tradition going back more than three centuries. More African slaves—3.5 million—had been shipped to Brazil than to any other place in the Western world.[13] Great fortunes were made from coffee and sugar plantations, and slaveholders were the most powerful interest group in Brazil. They dominated the national as well as provincial and local governments. The national government needed revenue from export duties on slave-produced commodities. Everybody in Brazil was convinced there was no alternative to slaves as a source of labor.

In 1902 the 29-year-old journalist Edmund Dene Morel began working full time to promote the abolition of a slave system that Belgium's King Leopold II had secretly established to collect ivory and rubber in the Congo. Morel searched out people who had been to the Congo and wrote articles and books about slavery there. In 1904 he founded the Congo Reform Association to spearhead a new abolitionist campaign, adapting methods that Thomas Clarkson and his compatriots had developed in their successful campaign against the British slave trade a century before.

But the king was a diabolical adversary. For years he had posed as a crusader against the Arab slave trade in Africa. He had cultivated good will by spending some of his loot from the Congo on buildings and monuments around Belgium. He lavishly courted politicians and members of the press, and for a long time nobody believed allegations that he could possibly be involved with slavery. Missionaries and other people who worked in the Congo dared not speak about the atrocities

they had witnessed. In addition, of course, the businessmen to whom the king awarded contracts for work in the Congo were eager to keep the money flowing.

For some 400 years, from the mid-fifteenth century to the mid-nineteenth century, Western slave traders engaged in the African slave trade. The Portuguese, British, French and Dutch handled the bulk of the business. Altogether, some 10 million slaves survived voyages across the Atlantic. About 40 percent went to the Caribbean, where Saint-Domingue (Haiti), Cuba and Jamaica were the principal destinations. An estimated 50 percent of the slaves were sold in South America—Brazil alone accounted for 40 percent of the total slave shipments. About 4 percent were delivered to the United States; the rest to the Guiana and Spanish America.[14]

The first sustained abolitionist movement began in 1787 in Great Britain. Within about a century and a quarter, chattel slavery would disappear from the West.

Americans are familiar mainly with the U.S. experience of abolishing slavery after the Civil War. One might characterize this as a military strategy for emancipation, even though the battle cry of the North had been to save the Union. Most people came to believe war was essential for ending slavery. But although slavery was abolished, Reconstruction was a mixed blessing that ended in a few years when Northern troops withdrew from the South and went home. The civil rights of blacks were subverted for another century.

While the United States employed a military strategy, elsewhere abolitionists had a greater impact—but everywhere they helped get the emancipation process rolling. They changed the hearts and minds of enough people to change history. Because of the abolitionists, slavery could no longer be taken for granted as a traditional part of life. Abolitionists convinced people that slavery was evil. They overcame objections that if slavery were abolished, colonial economies would collapse and the home countries would be devastated as well. Abolitionist movements were a unique contribution of the West.

Slaves themselves did much to help their cause. Their revolts shattered the myth that slaves were happy and forced complacent people to consider the issues. Revolts reminded slaveholders that slavery was a

risky business. Slaveholders publicly demonstrated the barbarism of slavery by torturing and executing rebels, making a mockery of claims that slaveholders were interested in saving the souls of their slaves. Slaves also promoted their cause by helping others escape. When runaway slaves educated themselves and went on the lecture circuit, they offered dramatic eyewitness testimony about the horrors of slavery. It's unlikely that emancipation would have succeeded if slaves had been passive participants in the process.

This book tells the story of emancipation in the biggest, most influential slaving centers of the western hemisphere as well as in the last Western-controlled chattel slave regime in Africa. It's a story with many heroes and villains, triumphs and tragedies.

To be sure, trafficking in persons is still with us, but the perpetrators find little if any support in Western legal systems, or in most other legal systems for that matter. Thankfully, the large-scale horrors of chattel slavery, including the torture and execution of rebellious slaves, are gone.

Could Slavery
Be Abolished?

Abolishing slavery in the West seemed like an impossible dream, because it had been around for thousands of years, hardly anybody had opposed it in all that time, and powerful interest groups—including established churches—supported it. Portugal, Spain, France, Holland and England were all deeply involved with it. The very idea of emancipation was widely viewed as a threat to the social order.

Western slavery began in ancient times, was widespread in Greece and expanded dramatically during the Roman Empire. Historians have estimated that there were as many as three million slaves in Rome—perhaps 35 or 40 percent of the population.[1] Since Roman times, a flourishing slave trade had developed across the Sahara desert, bringing slaves from West Africa to North Africa. This trade commonly involved nomadic desert peoples raiding agricultural settlements. Slaves were used to harvest gum, work in gold mines, and take care for oases in North Africa.

Slavery later declined in northern Europe, but it continued in southern Europe largely because of wars and trade between Christians and Muslims. When the Moors conquered Spain in the eighth century, they reportedly enslaved as many as 30,000 Christians. By the

thirteenth century, Christians had reconquered most of Spain and in turn had enslaved thousands of Muslims.

By the fifteenth century, Muslims dominated the African slave trade. After the fall of Constantinople and the eastern Roman Empire in 1453, there was a shortage of European slaves, who had initially come from as far away as Mesopotamia, India, Java and China. There were also Albanian, Greek, Russian and Tartar slaves in European cities.

During the Renaissance, many Europeans either defended slavery or were silent on the subject. Neither Desiderius Erasmus nor Niccolò Machiavelli seems to have written anything about it. Thomas More described his vision of an ideal world in *Utopia* (1516), with slavery "a suitable station" for those captured in a war. Martin Luther believed slavery was essential for the survival of civilization. There were slaves in Genoa, Venice and Florence when the Italian Renaissance was in its glory and as late as 1606. The French navy had slaves, and there was a slave market in Marseilles. Although slavery was prevalent in Europe, the fifteenth-century shortage led to a surge of slave trading with Africa, and black slaves were brought to Spain and Portugal.

Iberia and the Slave Trade

The Portuguese enlarged the role of Christians in the slave trade. They entered the African slave trade during the fifteenth century and continued to play a major role for more than three centuries.

Despite its small size and the appearance of being a nation of many fishing villages, Portugal was a vibrant maritime nation of capable shipbuilders and mapmakers. They had a vast knowledge of geography and navigation garnered from Middle Eastern and Genoese traders whose ships often foundered on Portugal's coasts. Portuguese explorers were the first to reach many parts of Asia by sea, sailing down the west coast of Africa and around the Cape of Good Hope. While they sought gold and spices, almost every ship returned with some slaves. The sale of slaves helped pay the costs of their lengthy expeditions. Portuguese explorers discovered the Senegal and Gambia rivers, a region where slaves could be easily seized because Africans were unprepared for the Europeans. But as Africans encountered more and more Portuguese, they developed better ways to defend themselves,

and the Portuguese had a harder time collecting their human cargo. In 1445, Captain João Fernandes began buying slaves from African kings, and this became the standard European practice. The Portuguese settled along the coast at places convenient for trading. In 1482, the Portuguese built Elmina castle, a trading depot in the Gulf of Guinea, which served as their headquarters in West Africa.

For the most part, the Portuguese purchased slaves who had been captured in African wars. By 1448, some 1,000 African slaves had been brought to Portugal. Portuguese government and religious officials began buying slaves to work on farms, serve in hospitals, build ships, operate ferries, drain marshes and perform myriad other tasks. After the Portuguese secured control of the Canary Islands from Spain, slaves were used to grow sugar cane there and on São Tomé, a 372-square-mile island off the west coast of Africa.

Prompted by the success of the Portuguese navigator Vasco da Gama, who had sailed around Africa and discovered the sea route to India from 1497 to 1499, the Portuguese government sponsored a new expedition commanded by Pedro Álvarez Cabral. But the lead ship sailed off course and headed due west. On April 23, 1500, it made landfall in the area now known as Bahia in Brazil. The Portuguese slowly began to explore the area and to build fortified coastal trading posts. Indians were enslaved to cultivate sugar cane and harvest brazilwood, but they didn't seem to work as efficiently as Africans. The Portuguese realized that producing sugar could be a much bigger business than brazilwood and began large-scale cultivation of sugar cane using slaves.

Until about 1570, Indians accounted for about 80 percent of the slave labor, but the Indian population plummeted because of European diseases, such as smallpox, tuberculosis and measles, against which they lacked resistance.[2] Consequently, in the 1530s, the Portuguese began importing African slaves, primarily from Angola (the central African region between the Bengo and Quicombo rivers). Some 2,000 slaves a year were brought into Brazil by 1580. Slaves cultivated sugar cane, raised cattle, worked in mines, did construction and were household servants. The slaves were considered indispensable.[3]

Sugar cane was planted extensively in Brazil's northeast provinces of Bahia and Pernambuco. Dutch ships, with their extensive commercial connections, began distributing Brazil's sugar production in European markets. Brazil reached its economic peak during the

mid-seventeenth century, when it had the dominant share of the European sugar market.[4]

In the century and a half that the Portuguese monopolized the Atlantic slave trade, they brought an estimated 18,000 slaves to their Atlantic islands, 75,000 slaves to São Tomé, 75,000 slaves to Spanish America, 50,000 slaves to Brazil, as well as 24,000 slaves to Europe.[5]

As Spanish explorers looked for gold, they tended to claim whatever land they saw or walked on. Naturally, this practice led to conflicts with others, particularly with native populations and the Portuguese. The Portuguese were more interested in exclusive trading rights than territorial claims. They built trading forts where local people could supply something valuable such as gold or slaves, in exchange for European goods.

To resolve escalating disputes between Portugal and Spain about possessions in the western hemisphere, Pope Alexander VI drew a line on a map—270 leagues (about 932 miles) west of the Cape Verde Islands, or 46° 37'. Everything to the west of the line was to be Spain's and everything to the east was Portugal's. This was the basis for the Treaty of Tordesillas, signed in Spain in 1494. The Spanish sometimes ignored it—for example by starting a settlement on the Brazilian coast south of São Paulo—and the French ignored it too.

The Spanish at first bought slaves from the Portuguese and later decided to enter the African slave trade themselves. Portuguese captains, angered at the competition, seized some of the Spanish ships and hanged the crews. One Spanish ship was captured by Africans, and reportedly the crew was eaten. Despite these early setbacks, the Spanish expanded their efforts to establish a position in the slave trade. There was an active slave market in Seville. King Ferdinand had slaves, as did Queen Isabella.[6]

Christopher Columbus was quite familiar with the slave trade, having worked as a sugar buyer for a Genoese bank and having visited a Portuguese fort in Guinea. He began the settlement that became Santo Domingo on the island of Hispaniola, which he had discovered in 1492. The following year, Columbus sent to Spain the first shipment of slaves, natives he had captured from the various Caribbean islands he had visited.

On Hispaniola, Spaniards enslaved the local Arawak Taino Indians, devastating their population by smallpox that the Spanish had brought with them. The Indians got a bit of revenge by giving the Spaniards syphilis. Not long after sugar cane was brought to Hispan-

iola in 1506, Nicolás de Ovando, governor of Hispaniola, ordered that 40,000 Indian slaves be brought from the Bahamas. They too quickly succumbed to Spanish diseases and cruelty. Bartolomé de las Casas, a Spanish Dominican priest, protested at such savagery and suggested that African slaves be imported instead of the Indians to perform the hard work involved in cultivating sugar cane.

Meanwhile, the earliest shipments of African slaves had begun to arrive in the Caribbean. The Spanish, like the Portuguese, concluded that Indians weren't as productive as Africans, and in 1510 King Ferdinand, hoping to find gold, authorized the shipment of 50 Spanish-born African slaves to Santo Domingo. Although no gold was found there, the conquistador Hernán Cortés found plenty in New Spain (later known as Mexico). He shipped a large quantity of gold back to Spain and started growing sugar, for which he began importing African slaves.

When substantial silver deposits were first discovered at Zacatecas in northern Mexico, it was a region with few Indians who could be exploited. Consequently, African slaves were brought in at the very beginning of development and soon outnumbered the Spaniards. (Expanding mines later attracted Indians who wanted to work, lessening the need for African slaves, and by the early seventeenth century, slaves had little to do with these mining operations.)[7]

With the population of Indian slaves falling rapidly because of harsh treatment and European diseases, Spanish colonists on Hispaniola petitioned the 18-year-old Spanish King and Holy Roman Emperor Charles V for permission to import African slaves. Judge Alonso Zuazo dismissed the king's concerns that having a lot of black slaves might risk a rebellion. "I whipped some," Zuazo explained, "cut off the ears of others and, in consequence, there are no more complaints." On August 18, 1518, the king granted his Flemish courtier Lorenzo de Gorrevod an eight-year license to ship at least 4,000 African slaves to Spanish America.[8]

By the mid-1520s, slaves were operating sugar mills in Jamaica, Mexico, Puerto Rico and Santo Domingo, and gold mines in Cuba. The Catholic church was anxious to have slaves work in gold mines, to help finance the planned cathedral in San Juan, and to perform other tasks. In 1530, the bishop of Santo Domingo appealed to the king for more slaves, saying that Cuba, Puerto Rico and Santo Domingo might not survive without slaves.

That same year, the Genoese merchant Polo de Espindola, based in Málaga, Spain, dispatched his ship *Nuestra Señora de Begoña* to take some 300 slaves from São Tomé to Hispaniola—without stopping in Portugal as had been standard practice since the beginning of the African slave trade. After this voyage, increasing numbers of slaves were shipped directly from West Africa to the Americas where slave prices were double those in Europe. African slaves were sent across the Atlantic to help the Spanish conquistadors Francisco de Montejo in Yucatan, Diego de Almagro in Chile and Juan Pizarro in Peru. These men, however, didn't introduce slavery to the Americas, because native peoples in Mexico, Peru and elsewhere on the southern continent already had slaves, many of whom had been acquired in wars.

In 1545, the Spanish discovered huge silver deposits at Potosi (now in Bolivia), which required large numbers of slaves to develop. There were Indian slaves, but as happened elsewhere, European diseases decimated Indian populations. The Spanish began to import thousands of Africans, from the area between the Niger and Senegal rivers as well as from the Congo and Angola. Alluvial deposits of gold were discovered in lowlands where there weren't many Indians, and Africans mined almost all of it.

In Peru, slaves worked in vineyards, on sugar plantations and on farms producing a variety of crops; many of these agricultural enterprises were owned by the Jesuits. Slaves were fishermen, too, and slaves served as muleteers, carrying goods through jungles with teams. In cities, slaves were metalworkers, textile workers, hat makers and shoemakers.

In 1595, the Spanish government looked for a way to extract more revenue from the slave trade. The result was the *asiento* system, which involved granting a monopoly over trade routes to one contractor who would have to pay a flat, more easily monitored fee that was much larger than what individual license holders would pay. The *asiento*-holder, in turn, sold separate licenses to traders requiring access to those routes. It was in his self-interest to maximize license revenue, as the more he could collect, the more the government might ask him to pay for his *asiento*. The first *asiento*-holder was a Spaniard, but the Spanish didn't have much of a fleet to defend the trade routes, and by the seventeenth century, the *asiento* was awarded to Dutch, French and English contractors.[9]

By 1650 between 250,000 and 300,000 slaves had been imported to Spanish America, mostly for Mexico and Peru. After 1650, there was a rising demand for slaves in Spain's Caribbean colonies, which had been neglected during the precious metals boom.

While the slave trade to Spanish America was growing rapidly, slaves were still being sold in southern Europe. Not surprisingly, there were more slaves in Portugal than anywhere else on the continent.[10] The Portuguese traveled along the rivers and estuaries of West Africa, seizing slaves or trading with Africans who did the dirty work. The Portuguese brought the slaves to slave trading centers such as São Tomé or Santiago (Cape Verde islands), where they were sold to merchants who shipped them to European slaving centers such as Lisbon or Seville—or to one of the American slaving centers such as Santo Domingo, Havana (Cuba), Vera Cruz (Mexico), Cartagena (Colombia) or Portobello (Panama). The European slave trade, however, was dwarfed by the slave trade across the Sahara to the Muslim world.

There were a few isolated voices critical of slavery. The Dominican friar Tomás de Mercado, for instance, provided some graphic descriptions of how slaves were kidnapped in Africa. Father Pedro Brandão, Portuguese bishop in the Cape Verde islands, urged that black slaves be baptized and liberated. In Brazil, Jesuit Father Miguel García refused to take confessions from slave owners.[11] Refreshing though these voices were, they were isolated and had no impact on Spanish or Portuguese support for slavery.

Holland Enters the Transatlantic Slave Trade

Although the Dutch generally didn't want slaves at home, many Dutchmen were eager to sell slaves abroad. Dutch traders sought ivory and gold in West Africa, and gradually they became involved with the slave trade. Dutch slave ships began arriving in the Caribbean in 1606. In 1619, a Dutch merchant reportedly sold 20 African slaves to English settlers in Virginia. This wasn't the first time slaves had been brought into North America—the Spanish had brought slaves when they conquered the area that became Florida and New Mexico.

The Dutch government granted the Dutch West India Company, established in 1621, a trading monopoly both in West Africa and in the Americas. By 1626, after gaining control of land in northeastern Brazil, the company was deeply engaged in the slave trade.[12] The company's soldiers captured several of the most important Portuguese outposts, especially Ft. Elmira. John Maurice, the prince of Nassau-Siegen and governor of Dutch-controlled Brazil, became convinced

that neither natives nor whites could handle the rigors of sugar cultivation as well as Africans. "It is not possible to effect anything in Brazil without slaves," he declared. "They cannot be dispensed with upon any occasion whatsoever."[13] By the mid-seventeenth century, the Dutch dominated the seas, and they had established ports in West Africa and the Americas, as well as the East Indies.

The Dutch arranged to supply Spanish American colonies with slaves. Curaçao became a base for the Dutch West India Company, where slaves were brought in its ships and transferred to slave agents or to planters. The Dutch, with their comparatively free financial markets, were in the best position to raise capital needed for the slave trade, even though Spain received huge flows of precious metals from Mexico and Peru. During the second half of the seventeenth century, the Dutch were, after the Portuguese, the second leading slave traders.

Portugal, which had been claimed by Spain's financially troubled Philip II following the death of the Portuguese heir in 1580, regained its independence in 1640 and reasserted its territorial claims in Brazil and Africa. The Dutch were driven out of Brazil in 1654 and Brazil became a Portuguese stronghold until it achieved independence during the nineteenth century.

The Dutch maintained a significant presence in the western hemisphere. They still had trading forts on the north coast of South America and in the Antilles they retained Curaçao. Slaves were shipped to this island from Africa and remained there until ready for illegal shipment to the Spanish, French or English colonies. The Dutch also established slave-based sugar plantations throughout the West Indies. During the 1640s, they turned sleepy Barbados into a respectable sugar producer, and they stimulated slave-based sugar production on St. Kitts, Nevis, Montserrat, Antigua and Guadeloupe.

Altogether, the Dutch are believed to have shipped more than 525,000 African slaves across the Atlantic.[14] Dutch slave trading declined as a consequence of war and commercial competition from the British.

The French Caribbean: The Biggest Slave Market

The French were involved in the slave trade early on, but they didn't become a major player until the late seventeenth century. They focused mainly on serving their own colonies.

The French were as aggressive as the British and the Dutch at defying the Portuguese and Spanish monopolies. French pirates began seizing Portuguese ships loaded with gold from Africa's west coast, north of the Congo river. French ships competed with the Portuguese in acquiring slaves around the Senegal and Gambia rivers. Between the 1530s and 1560s, an estimated 200 French ships sailed for Sierra Leone, presumably to participate in the slave trade.[15] French ships repeatedly traded with Spanish colonists, offering goods for less money than Spanish suppliers.

French smugglers had established themselves in the western third of Hispaniola, which was free for the taking since the Spanish king, in 1609, had ordered his people to live near Santo Domingo (eastern Hispaniola) where they could be most easily protected from pirates. The land in western Hispaniola was fertile, and after 1625 French settlers began developing plantations that needed slaves. French Protestants settled on Tortuga, an island off the northwest coast of Hispaniola, originally named by Columbus.

In 1627, the Compagnie de Iles d'Amérique (Company of the American Islands) was established to start colonizing the islands of Guadeloupe and Martinique. Settlers mainly grew crops for local consumption until the Dutch brought sugar cane plants, sugar refining equipment and slaves, and offered their services for shipping refined sugar to Europe. King Louis XIV sanctioned French slave trading in 1642—"for the good of their souls," he said.[16] Slavery and sugar cane cultivation expanded together. By the 1730s, the number of slaves had grown rapidly to about 33,000 in Guadeloupe and 55,000 in Martinique.[17] When, through the 1697 Treaty of Ryswick, France officially acquired western Hispaniola as a colony that became known as Saint-Domingue (modern Haiti), the colony had no sugar plantations.

Jean-Baptiste Colbert, the finance minister for King Louis XIV, issued the Code Noir (Black Code) for regulating slaves in 1685. Legally, slaves were personal property that could be used to pay a debt. They were forbidden to assemble, to possess weapons, to testify in court, to own property. For running away or hitting a slaveholder or his wife, a slave could be whipped, branded or killed. The Code Noir provided a few benefits for slaves; in particular, they weren't obligated to work on Sundays or religious holidays.

In 1691, Louis XIV named Jean-Baptiste du Casse as governor of Saint-Domingue. He defended it against attacks and encouraged

sugar cultivation with African slaves. He looked for opportunities to develop commerce with Spanish America, and in 1701, he gained the *asiento* for 10 years. He probably did more than anyone else to develop the French slave trade.

Saint-Domingue emerged as the biggest sugar producer and biggest Caribbean slave market of all. During the eighteenth century, almost 800 sugar plantations were developed there. Owned by whites, they were mostly in the northern part of the colony. In addition, Saint-Domingue had about 50 cocoa plantations, 800 cotton plantations, 2,500 coffee plantations and 3,000 indigo plantations. These secondary plantations were generally located in the south and west of Saint-Domingue, and many were owned by free coloreds—or "free blacks" or "mulattoes" as they were also known. There were nearly as many free coloreds as whites in Saint-Domingue at this time. By 1789, there were reportedly more than 465,000 slaves—some two-thirds of whom had been born in Africa.[18]

In addition, the French had occupied Louisiana in 1699, where some white laborers and Indian slaves were used to produce tobacco, rice, indigo and cotton with limited success. The first African slaves seem to have arrived there in 1719.

In the eighteenth century, French slave ships brought approximately 1 million African slaves to the French Caribbean, supplying about 60 percent of the slaves on those islands. Additional slaves came from the British, Dutch and Danish West Indies.[19] French sugar production was at a peak. The French Caribbean islands amounted to some 11,550 square miles, more than double the 5,413 square miles of British islands, and as more of the French islands were cultivated, they surpassed production from the British islands.

Britain and the African Slave Trade

The man who started the English slave trade was the flamboyant John Hawkyns. Born around 1532 in Plymouth, the son of a privateer and political fixer, Hawkyns killed a man when he was 20, a crime for which his family apparently bought a pardon. He seemed to have picked up skillful and daring seamanship from his father. On Hawkyns's first voyage as a slave trader in 1555, he led three

ships to the Sierra Leone coast and seized about 300 Africans. He took them across the Atlantic and sold them in Santo Domingo, the principal Spanish colony in the Caribbean at that time. He made two more voyages that resulted in the sale of some 800 African slaves. Hawkyns was rewarded for his efforts by being made a member of Parliament and was named the treasurer of the British Royal Navy.

Nearly a century after Hawkyns's first slave voyage, the British-owned Guinea Company was established in 1651 to pursue the slave trade. Two years later, the Company of Royal Adventurers was chartered for the slave trade.[20] By 1665, this company had built 18 trading forts in West Africa. Despite being granted a monopoly by the British government, the company fell into debt, and in 1672 it was acquired by the Royal African Company. The Royal African Company chartered ships for gathering slaves at various points between the Senegal River and Angola, which then sailed to the Caribbean. By 1711, when the Royal African Company lost its monopoly charter, it had shipped about 135,000 slaves to the West Indies.

During the seventeenth and eighteenth centuries, the British acquired a succession of islands in the Caribbean, starting with Barbados in 1605. Some of the British islands were suitable for growing sugar cane. Great Britain's largest Caribbean island and most important sugar producer was Jamaica, seized from the Spanish in 1655. By 1800, there were an estimated 300,000 slaves growing sugar cane on Jamaica.[21]

With good sources of African slaves, colonies where the slaves could produce sugar, a substantial commercial fleet that could handle the business and a navy that could protect it, Britain became the dominant player in the slave trade. After 1698, when Parliament permitted any British merchant to enter the slave trade, the volume of slaves transported in British ships soon soared to some 20,000 annually. By 1770 there were reportedly 192 British slave ships that handled about half of the Atlantic slave trade.

Revenue from Britain's slave colonies and the slave trade was at a peak during the late-eighteenth century. Altogether, between 1662 and 1807 (when Great Britain made it illegal for British citizens to engage in the slave trade), approximately 3.5 million Africans crossed the Atlantic in British ships.[22]

Interest groups profiting from the slave trade vigorously defended it. These included British companies that refined raw sugar from the West Indies; companies that distilled sugar into alcoholic beverages; glassworks that made bottles for wine, beer and spirits; copper and brass works that made articles to be traded for slaves; and all manner of suppliers for the ships engaged in the slave trade as well as investors who provided financing for the voyages.

Bristol sugar merchant John Cary made the familiar appeal that the slave trade created jobs. It was, he declared, "the best Traffick the Kingdom hath, as it doth give so vast an Imployment to our People both by Sea and Land." During the eighteenth century, Liverpool came to handle more slave trade business than any other British port, and its Common Council told Parliament: "Liverpool has arrived at a pitch of mercantile consequence which cannot but affect and improve the wealth and prosperity of the kingdom at large."[23]

Slavery Forever?

The prevailing view among Europeans was that people in Africa and the western hemisphere weren't entitled to the same rights as they were. Hence, although Europeans were increasingly uncomfortable about having slaves in their homeland, they believed slavery was acceptable in their overseas colonies. Europeans insisted that they were entitled to continue benefiting from the substantial investments they had made in the slave trade and in slave-based plantations. Europeans supported the suppression of slave revolts, and they used their political clout to oppose abolitionist movements wherever they arose. In 1788, Lord Penrhyn, a member of Parliament from Liverpool, offered a national security argument for the slave trade when he said that it supported crews and ships that might be needed to defend Great Britain during a time of war. He warned that "if they passed the vote of abolition, they actually struck at seventy millions of property, they ruined the colonies, and by destroying an essential nursery of seamen, gave up the dominion of the sea at a single stroke."[24]

By 1800, Europeans had been shipping African slaves to the western hemisphere for about 280 years. The colonies needed laborers, and the Africans did a better job than anybody else, perhaps because

of their superior resistance to tropical diseases. Businesses counted on the continuation of slavery. Most politicians were all for it. Organized religions supported it. Abolishing slavery seemed unthinkable because so many people would be devastated. Slavery seemed like it could go on forever. Could anyone realistically hope to abolish it?

Chapter 2

Ideas that Inspired
the Abolitionists

When Western legal systems, like legal systems elsewhere, protected slavery, it wasn't possible to make a legal argument against it. Defenders of slavery had kings, constitutions, statutes and court cases on their side.

Similarly, it was difficult to make a religious argument against slavery when major organized religions were for it. The Bible has many passages acknowledging or supporting slavery.[1] The Catholic church accepted slavery. Neither Martin Luther nor John Calvin, who both led the Protestant Reformation, rejected slavery. The American Great Awakening religious revival movement was spread in New England in 1740 by Massachusetts Congregational preacher Jonathan Edwards, who owned slaves and defended slavery.[2]

In the American South, defenders of slavery offered religious arguments to bolster their position. Albert Taylor Bledsoe, a Kentucky lawyer and Episcopal clergyman, was among the most prolific proslavery authors, and in his *Essay on Liberty and Slavery* (1856), he declared that "the very best men, whose lives are recorded in the Old Testament, were the owners and holders of slaves." Abraham, for instance, was said to own more than 1,000 slaves. Bledsoe cited many passages from the Old Testament, and he noted that nothing in the New Testament

supported the abolitionist view that slavery was always sinful. He asserted that "as the slave is under an obligation to obey the master, so the master has a right to his obedience."[3] Clearly, the moral case against slavery required something other than religion.

The antislavery case had to originate outside of a legal system and established religion. It seems to have begun as a moral argument against cruelty. Those attacking slavery often mentioned God, but they emphasized general principles rather than religious doctrines.

The French political philosopher Jean Bodin (1530–1596) might have been the first author to denounce the cruelty of slavery. In *Six Books of the Commonwealth* (1576), he referred to "the base humiliations that slaves have been made to suffer . . . the cruelties one reads about are unbelievable, and yet only the thousandth part has been told." Bodin went on to say that "by the law of God it is forbidden to make any man a slave except with his own entire good will and consent. Seeing that the experience of four thousand years has shown us the insurrections, the civil commotions, the disasters and revolutions that commonwealths have suffered at the hand of slaves and homicides, the cruelties and barbarities inflicted on slaves by their masters, it was an unmitigated catastrophe that the institution was ever introduced, and then that once it had been declared abolished it should have been allowed to persist."[4]

Natural Rights and Antislavery in Great Britain

Horrified by the cruel treatment of slaves, many people believed that slaves should be treated kindly but stopped short of advocating an end to slavery. The abolition of slavery was a very big, radical step, and most people weren't willing to go that far. Clearly, revulsion against cruelty wasn't enough. A case against slavery itself—even if slaves were treated kindly—needed something more to compel large numbers of people to alter their views.

The "something more" was the idea of individual rights, freedom from various kinds of interference. These were also referred to as natural rights, meaning that people were entitled to rights because they were human beings. Natural rights couldn't be taken away legitimately by anyone—including a king, a judge or a legislature—as long as an individual respected other people's equal rights. This idea was first articulated in mid-seventeenth-century England, even as Eng-

lish merchants were playing an increasingly important part in the slave trade. The earliest champions of individual rights were the so-called Levellers who, during the English Civil War (1642–1651), advocated secure private property, free trade, freedom of association, freedom of religion, freedom of speech, freedom of the press, a rule of law, a separation of powers and a written constitution to limit government power.

The most influential of the Levellers was John Lilburne. He was a prolific pamphleteer, and he set an example for courageous opposition to tyrants. Lilburne was the first person to challenge the legitimacy of the Star Chamber, the English royal court that had become a notorious instrument for suppressing dissent. He was the first to challenge Parliament's prerogative as a law court for imprisoning adversaries and the first to challenge the prosecution tactic of extracting confessions until defendants incriminated themselves. He challenged the standard practice of imprisoning people without filing formal charges. He challenged judges who tried to intimidate juries. Four times he faced the death penalty.[5] He endured brutal beatings and was imprisoned most of his adult life.

Among the Levellers, perhaps the most eloquent pamphleteer was Richard Overton. For instance, in October 1646, he wrote *An Arrow against all tyrants and tyranny, shot from the prison of Newgate into the Prerogative Bowels of the Arbitrary House of Lords.*[6] "To every individual in nature is given an individual property by nature," he declared, "not to be invaded or usurped by any. For every one as he is himself, so he hath a self propriety, else could he not be himself. . . . No man hath power over my rights and liberties and I over no man's . . . For by natural birth all men are equally and alike born to like propriety, liberty and freedom."[7] This idea that an individual owns himself or herself had revolutionary implications.

During the 1680s, the English physician John Locke expressed the view that government is morally obliged to serve people, namely by protecting life, liberty and property. The most fundamental kind of property, he explained, is ownership of one's body. He insisted that a man "cannot enslave himself to any one, nor put himself under the Absolute, Arbitrary Power of another, to take away his Life." He viewed slavery as a "State of War between a Conqueror and a Captive."[8]

Locke went on to explain the principle of checks and balances to limit government power. He favored representative government and a

rule of law. He denounced tyranny. He insisted that when government violates individual rights, people may legitimately rebel. These views were most fully developed in Locke's famous *Second Treatise Concerning Civil Government* (ca. 1679), and they were so radical, he never dared sign his name to it.

To be sure, Locke apparently didn't apply his natural rights ideas to African slaves. He invested some £600 in the slave-trading Royal African Company.[9] As secretary for Anthony Ashley Cooper, a leading British politician, Locke participated in the drafting of the "Fundamental Constitutions for the Government of Carolina" (1669), an American colony that Cooper had invested in. There were a number of liberal features in this document, such as a secret ballot for elections and civil rights for religious dissenters, but abolishing slavery wasn't one of those features. Clause 110 stated: "Every freeman of Carolina shall have absolute power and authority over his negro slaves, of what opinion or religion soever."

Nonetheless, Locke's natural rights ideas—particularly as expressed in the *Second Treatise on Civil Government*—took on a life of their own when they were interpreted and extended by others. They influenced the development of libertarian thinking in Great Britain and America during the eighteenth century, contributing to the antislavery movement. Locke's ideas inspired the immortal preamble of Thomas Jefferson's Declaration of Independence which, in turn, inspired William Lloyd Garrison who energized the American abolitionist movement.[10]

During the 1720s, the English radical writers John Trenchard and Thomas Gordon popularized Locke's political ideas in *Cato's Letters,* a popular series of essays published in London newspapers, and these had the most direct impact on American thinkers. Trenchard was born in 1662, the son of a Somerset landowner. He graduated from Trinity College, Dublin, after studying law. Gordon, also a lawyer, was born in the late seventeenth century in Kirkcudbright, Scotland, and may have been educated at the University of Edinburgh. "A life of slavery is," they declared, "to those who can bear it, a continual state of uncertainty and wretchedness, often an apprehension of violence, often the lingering dread of a violent death."[11]

The Scottish Enlightenment provided more intellectual support for liberty and antislavery. Francis Hutcheson, an Irish moral philosopher who taught for 17 years at the University of Glasgow, was a force-

ful character who broke with tradition and delivered his lectures in English instead of Latin. Again and again, Hutcheson denounced slavery. He declared, "Nothing can change a rational creature into a piece of goods void of all rights."[12] Hutcheson went on to say: "Strange that in any nation where a sense of liberty prevails, and where the Christian religion is professed, custom and high prospect of gain can so stupefy the consciences of men, and all sense of natural justice, that they can hear such computations made about the value of their fellow-men and their liberty, without abhorrence and indignation!"

Hutcheson influenced the thinking of other Scottish thinkers like Adam Ferguson and Adam Smith. Ferguson, a professor of philosophy at the University of Edinburgh, wrote extensively about how a free society works. In his *Institutes of Moral Philosophy* (1769), he denounced slavery: "no one is born a slave; because everyone is born with all his original rights . . . no one can [legitimately] become a slave."[13]

Hutcheson's student Adam Smith had an enormous impact. Born in Kirkaldy, Scotland, and educated at Glasgow and Oxford universities, he was a quiet, thoughtful scholar who developed libertarian ideas about morals and economics.

Smith spent four years working on his first book, *The Theory of Moral Sentiments*, about motivations other than self-interest that influenced human behavior. The book also made clear his antislavery views. For instance: "There is not a Negro from the coast of Africa, who does not possess a degree of magnanimity which the soul of his sordid master is too often scarce capable of conceiving." He called slaves "heroes" and slaveholders "refuse" and "wretches"! Smith denounced "the vilest of all states, that of domestic slavery." Published in London in 1759, *The Theory of Moral Sentiments* made Smith a literary celebrity.

Quaker Opposition to Slavery

Support for antislavery views came from a mystical Protestant sect—the Quakers. The sect had been started in 1647 by itinerant preacher George Fox who emphasized a direct relationship with God. After visiting Barbados, Fox urged better treatment of slaves.

The most famous Quaker was the Englishman William Penn whose father, Admiral William Penn, had seized the slave-based sugar producing island of Jamaica from Spain in 1655. Although young William

was to own some slaves himself, he was among the very few individuals who made major contributions to liberty in both the Old World and the New World, and he set an inspiring example for Quakers who later took a stand against slavery. Penn became the leading defender of religious toleration in England. He was imprisoned six times for speaking out courageously. While in prison, he wrote numerous pamphlets that gave Quakers a literature attacking intolerance. He alone proved capable of challenging oppressive government policies in court—one of his cases helped secure the right to trial by jury. Penn used his diplomatic skills and family connections to get large numbers of Quakers out of jail, saving many from the gallows.

Moreover, during an era when Protestants persecuted Catholics, Catholics persecuted Protestants, and both persecuted Quakers and Jews, Penn established an American sanctuary that protected freedom of conscience. Almost everywhere else, colonists stole land from the Indians, but Penn traveled unarmed among the Indians and negotiated peaceful purchases. He insisted that women deserved equal rights with men. In 1682, he gave Pennsylvania a written constitution that limited the power of government, provided a humane penal code and guaranteed many fundamental liberties. For the first time in modern history, a large society offered equal rights to people of different races and religions. Penn's dramatic example caused quite a stir in Europe. The French philosopher Voltaire, a champion of religious toleration, offered lavish praise: "William Penn might, with reason, boast of having brought down upon earth the Golden Age, which in all probability, never had any real existence but in his dominions."[14]

Despite their enlightened views on many things, Quakers couldn't decide what position they should take on slavery. Here and there, a Quaker expressed the view that Friends shouldn't engage in the slave trade. In 1688, Germantown (Pennsylvania) Quaker Francis Daniel Pastorious drafted the first known protest against African slavery, and the Germantown Quakers adopted what might have been the first resolution against slavery. They said that slavery was un-Christian. Five years later, American Quaker George Keith wrote *An Exhortation and Caution to Friends concerning the buying and selling of Negroes*, a pamphlet reporting some of the horrors he saw when he visited the West Indies. In 1698, another American Quaker, William Southeby, urged that Friends in Barbados stop sending slaves to Pennsylvania. Southeby also petitioned the Pennsylvania Assembly to abolish slavery. Appar-

ently there wasn't another piece of Quaker antislavery literature for three decades, when in 1729 Benjamin Franklin published Ralph Sandiford's pamphlet *A Brief Examination of the Practice of the Times,* attacking slavery.[15] Quakers became increasingly uneasy about the violence involved in capturing, shipping and running any kind of operation with slaves. Elihu Coleman's *A Testimony Against that Antichristian Practice of Making Slaves of Men* (1733) became the first critique of slavery to be approved by a Quaker meeting.[16]

In 1754, Philadelphia Quakers began to discuss their unease about slavery. The outstanding opponent of slavery was John Woolman, a New Jersey tailor.[17] He called on Quaker slaveholders on the East Coast to persuade them about the "inconsistency of holding slaves." Quakers in the Pennsylvania Assembly proposed a bill that would double the tax on imported slaves, which would have made further slave imports uneconomical. They didn't have enough votes for passage, but this early effort to restrict slavery was a step in the right direction.

The Seven Years' War (1756–1763) between Great Britain and France helped crystallize Quaker opinion against slavery.[18] Quakers were denounced as traitors for their refusal to fight or to pay war taxes. Quakers decided they couldn't continue to hold public office and resist the war effort, so they resigned. They began to embrace outspoken, principled opposition to slavery. In 1760 American Quakers in New England decided that they must discipline their brethren who engaged in the slave trade. London Quakers, at their 1761 yearly meeting, announced that they would disavow any Quaker who engaged in the slave trade.

The Quaker Anthony Benezet was perhaps the first person to begin agitating for the abolition of slavery. He was from a French Protestant family that had emigrated from Saint-Quentin, northern France, to London where he was educated. When he was 17, his family sailed for America and settled in Philadelphia in 1730. Benezet didn't establish himself as a merchant as others in his family had done. He became a schoolteacher in Germantown, and after three years he transferred to the Friends' English School of Philadelphia (now known as the William Penn Charter School). It was here that he wrote his first attack on slavery—*The Epistle of 1754 Presented to the Yearly Meeting of the Society of Friends.*

During the evenings, Benezet began to teach slave children at home. Then he established the Quaker Girls School of Philadelphia.

In 1759, he wrote *Observations on the Enslaving, Importing and Purchasing of Negroes with some Advice thereon Extracted from the Yearly Meeting Epistle of London for the present Year.* (Apparently Benezet didn't favor short titles.) Next, he compiled *A Short Account of That Part of Africa Inhabited by Negroes* (1762).

Four years later, Benezet quit teaching so that he could focus on writing. He moved to Burlington, New Jersey, adapted part of *A Short Account* and issued it as a 45-page pamphlet, *A Caution and Warning to Great-Britain, and Her Colonies, in A Short Representation of the Calamitous State of the Enslaved Negroes in the British Dominions* (1767).

He earned little money from his writings and returned to teaching in 1770. He established the Negro School of Philadelphia and taught there as well as at the Quaker Girls School of Philadelphia. Drawing on some of his prior work, he wrote *Some Historical Account of Guinea, Its Situation, Produce and the General Disposition of its Inhabitants with an Inquiry into the Rise and Progress of the Slave Trade* (1771). This pamphlet had an impact on the thinking of British abolitionists including Granville Sharp, John Wesley and Thomas Clarkson.

Benezet corresponded with many people to promote the idea of abolishing slavery. He recruited prominent Philadelphia physician Benjamin Rush to the cause. This was a coup since Rush came from a slaveholding family and was well connected, counting Benjamin Franklin among his good friends.[19] When Rush was a student in Edinburgh, he had gotten to know a number of Scottish thinkers and had visited imprisoned British rebel John Wilkes. Benezet persuaded Rush to contact the British antislavery litigator Granville Sharp, thus deepening connections among British and American abolitionists.

In 1772, Rush wrote *An Address to the Inhabitants of the British Settlements in America, upon Slave-Keeping,* a pamphlet that had quite an impact. He declared that "slavery is so foreign to the human mind, that the moral faculties, as well as those of the understanding, are debased and rendered torpid by it." He advocated abolishing the slave trade and he urged that slaves be educated.

Benezet appealed to reform-minded Christians with *Serious Reflections affectionately recommended to the well disposed of every religious Denomination, particularly those who mourn and lament on account of the Calamities which attend us* (1778). Benezet's last major written work was *The Case of our Fellow-Creatures, the Oppressed Africans, respectfully recommended to The Serious Consideration of the Legislature of Great-Britain, by the People called Quakers* (1784). In

many of his writings, he liked to quote from libertarian thinkers such as John Locke, Francis Hutcheson and Montesquieu.

Americans Champion Natural Rights

While Quaker opposition to slavery was focused on the violence of the practice, many Americans were inspired by the natural rights philosophy. For instance, Boston judge Samuel Sewall's early pamphlet, *The Selling of Joseph* (1700), stated: "Forasmuch as Liberty is in real value next unto Life: None ought to part with it themselves, or deprive others of it . . . all men, as they are the Sons of Adam, are Coheirs; and have equal right unto liberty, and all other outward comforts of life."

British-born Thomas Paine called for the abolition of slavery in an essay he wrote for the *Postscript to the Pennsylvania Journal and the Weekly Advertiser,* published March 8, 1775—less than four months after he arrived in America. "By wicked and inhuman ways," Paine wrote, "the English are said to enslave towards one hundred thousand yearly; of which thirty thousand are supposed to die by barbarous treatment in the first year; besides all that are slain in the unnatural wars excited to take them. So much innocent blood have the Managers and Supporters of this inhuman Trade to answer for to the common Lord of all!" Paine suggested that Americans consider "immediately to discontinue and renounce it."[20]

Paine's pamphlet *Common Sense* (1776), which reportedly sold an astonishing 500,000 copies, was about American independence and not slavery, but his stirring words for natural rights must have given heart to abolitionists: "O! ye that love mankind! Ye that dare oppose not only the tyranny but the tyrant, stand forth! . . . We have it in our power to begin the world over again. . . . The birthday of a new world is at hand."

The natural rights philosophy was most famously summarized in America by Thomas Jefferson's introductory words for the Declaration of Independence: "We hold these truths to be self-evident, that all men are created equal, that they are endowed by their Creator with certain unalienable Rights, that among these are Life, Liberty and the pursuit of Happiness.—That to secure these rights, Governments are instituted among Men, deriving their just powers from the consent of the governed,—That whenever any Form of Government

becomes destructive of these ends, it is the Right of the People to alter or to abolish it, and to institute new Government, laying its foundation on such principles and organizing its powers in such form, as to them shall seem most likely to effect their Safety and Happiness."

It seems contradictory that a man could write these words and own slaves, but we must give Jefferson credit. He chose to champion ideas on liberty, and he gave them grace and eloquence that perhaps nobody has surpassed. These ideas were to inspire abolitionists in the United States and abroad, and they helped change history.

Antislavery Ideas in France

During the eighteenth century, new ideas on liberty were emerging in France as they were in Great Britain and the United States.

In his classic work *The Spirit of the Laws* (1748), Charles-Louis de Secondat, Baron de Montesquieu, made a case that slavery caused moral and practical problems for slaveholders as well as society itself. Published in England as well as in France, the book had a significant impact on thinking about slavery. "Slavery," Montesquieu explained, "is bad of its own nature; it is neither useful to the master nor to the slave; not to the slave, because he can do nothing thro' a motive of virtue; not to the master, because he contracts all manner of bad habits from his slaves. . . . He grows proud, curt, harsh, angry, voluptuous and cruel."[21]

Montesquieu denounced religious justifications for slavery, insisting that one could not at the same time embrace Christian charity and own slaves. He said, "It is impossible for us to assume that slaves are human beings, because if we assumed they were human beings one would begin to believe that we ourselves were not Christians."[22]

Montesquieu scoffed at the idea that slavery was essential to get tough jobs done. He noted that people used to believe nobody would work voluntarily in mines, yet there were enough laborers after slavery was abolished. Writing when the eighteenth-century Industrial Revolution was in its infancy, Montesquieu displayed remarkable insight that technology could handle much of the grunt work done by slaves: "With the convenience of machines, one can replace the forced labor that elsewhere is done by slaves. The mines of the Turks, in the

Province of Timisuara, were richer than those in Hungary, but they did not produce as much because the imagination of the Turks never went beyond the brawn of their slaves."[23]

Guillaume Thomas François Raynal, an influential eighteenth-century French journalist, wrote passionate denunciations of slavery. "How little are we both in our morality and our principles! We preach humanity, and go every year to bind in chains twenty thousand natives of Africa!"[24]

During the late eighteenth century and early nineteenth century, one of the greatest champions of liberty was Gilbert du Motier, the marquis de Lafayette. He came from a wealthy French family and had personal ties to King Louis XVI, yet he played a key role in three revolutions, helping to overthrow two kings and an emperor. When the king wouldn't authorize action to suppress the French slave trade, Lafayette bought a 125,000-acre sugar plantation in Cayenne, French Guyana.[25] He called the place La Belle Gabrielle, liberated the slaves and taught them how to be independent farmers. He paid workers according to their production and established rules of conduct that were applied equally to whites and blacks.

Lafayette's work in French Guyana was much written about in France. In 1789, former colonial administrator Daniel Lescallier wrote *Refléxions sur le sort des noirs dans nos colonies,* in which he reported that Lafayette's experience showed that free labor would make plantations more profitable.[26]

On February 19, 1788, the French lawyer Jacques-Pierre Brissot de Warville established the *Société des amis des noirs* (Society of Friends of Blacks). Prominent members included the philosopher Marquis de Condorcet (Marie Jean Antoine Nicolas Caritat), the politician Comte de Mirabeau (Honoré Gabriel Riqueti), Abbé Gregoire (Henri Grégoire) and Lafayette. Within a year, the society claimed to have about 140 members, some of whom had been in touch with the British abolitionist Thomas Clarkson. He advised them to aim for the abolition of the slave trade rather than the more difficult challenge of abolishing slavery itself, but the members committed themselves to abolishing slavery. They believed that principles of liberty should be extended to people in French colonies as well as in France.

Other than showing that there were Frenchmen opposed to slavery, the society seems to have had little impact. It focused on trying to influence the elite in France, but they were soon swept away by the

French Revolution. Then came the slave rebellion in Saint-Domingue, the most important French colony.

Many years were required for ideas expressed in articles, pamphlets and books to reach enough people, influence their thinking and inspire a movement. Moreover, a movement required individuals with exceptional dedication and organizational ability, and years might pass before such individuals came along. But the ideas were the essential starting point. Nowhere else but in the Western world was there such fertile ground for antislavery ideas.

Could an Economy without Slavery Work?

Ideas about natural rights and nonviolence were morally compelling, but if they failed to help people prosper, it's doubtful they would have found much support. For thousands of years, slavery was viewed as a source of wealth.[27] Living in London, the owners of British Caribbean plantations flaunted their elegant clothes, fine carriages, palatial mansions and extravagant parties. Like the Venetians who had profited from slave-based sugar plantations on Cyprus, and like the ancient Athenians who had profited from slaves captured in foreign wars, these plantation owners were convinced their business couldn't be sustained without slavery. They didn't just view slavery as cheaper than market compensation for workers. They were convinced that nobody would do hard work unless chained and whipped. The planters believed that their way of life was at stake.

This thinking was an expanded view of government control that prevailed in the Western world from the mid-1500s until the 1700s and in the communist world and many other places during the twentieth century: that an economy required substantial compulsion, if not slavery, to work. It was thought that in the absence of government intervention, people would do all sorts of things they shouldn't do, and they would neglect things they should do. The self-interest of private individuals was viewed as a threat to the social order. Government officials were presumed to be the guardians of the public good. Government regulation seemed essential for holding the economy together and protecting national security.

Detailed government intervention developed in England under Queen Elizabeth. Her Statute of Artificers (1563) extended govern-

ment control over the English labor market.[28] The law helped keep English people in their place, starting with peasants who were actively discouraged from leaving the countryside for better prospects in towns. Entry to a trade was open only to the sons of those already in it. Guilds functioned as administrative agents for the Statute of Artificers. Although it had less and less effect after 1700, it wasn't finally repealed until 1814.

For centuries, English laws had specified how various industries were to function in excruciating detail, and this process seems to have intensified under Elizabeth. The French King Henry IV, who ruled from 1589 to 1610, was apparently impressed with how Queen Elizabeth gained power over the British economy, and he tried to do the same. His policies reached a peak under Jean-Baptiste Colbert, finance minister during the late seventeenth century. Colbert promoted government intervention in the economy as few government officials had done before. For instance, he believed that if French consumers weren't forced to buy the right kind of cloth, they might buy the wrong kind—especially printed calicoes. Many people were tortured and others hanged for violating Colbert's economic regulations.[29] But all this backfired. Colbert promoted government intervention for industry at the expense of agriculture, and agricultural output plunged about a third during the reign of Louis XIV. Because of oppressive regulations and frequent wars, when the king died in 1715, the French government was broke.

The man who did more than anyone to challenge France's oppressive regulations was Anne-Robert-Jacques Turgot. Born in Paris on May 10, 1727, the son of a government official who helped build the Paris sewage system, Turgot started studying for the priesthood. But his interests expanded as he read more widely, and he switched to law. His first published work was *Le Conciliateur* (1754), a pamphlet attacking proposals to renew religious persecution in France. His advice to fellow Catholics could have been offered to slaveholders: "Men for their opinions, demand only liberty; if you deprive them of it, you place arms in their hand. Give them liberty, they remain quiet."[30]

Turgot became a good friend of Jacques-Claude-Marie Vincent, Marquis de Gournay, a highly respected teacher of economics.[31] He absorbed the ideas of Richard Cantillon, an Irishman who moved to France and wrote the *Essai Sur La Nature du Commerce en General* (about

1734) that offered perhaps the first comprehensive view of how a free market works. Gournay has been credited with coining the expression "*Laissez faire, laissez passez*" ("Let the goods pass"), which became a battle cry for economic liberty.[32]

In 1761, Turgot was appointed an *intendant* (chief administrator) for the provinces of Angoumois, Basse-Marche and Limousin, a region in central France including the city of Limoges. Almost all the approximately 500,000 people were peasants who lived on chestnuts, rye and buckwheat.[33] According to the Marquis de Mirabeau (1715–1789), peasants dressed in rags and lived in huts made of clay with thatch roofs. Many peasants used plows that weren't much better than those of ancient Rome.[34]

Year after year, Turgot pleaded for the government to cut taxes because peasants in Limoges and elsewhere were crushed by taxes. There were some 1,600 customs houses throughout France to collect taxes on goods that passed various points along roads and rivers.[35] Altogether, these taxes increased the cost of goods as much as 30 percent.[36] Moreover, there was the *gabelle,* a tax on salt, and the *taille* (a tax levied on individuals and land that substituted for military service), which amounted to about a sixth of the income of peasants. This came on top of feudal duties and church tithes. Peasants got to keep about a fifth of their income.[37]

Turgot had the power to abolish the *corvée*—a tax hated by the peasants. A remnant of serfdom, the *corvée* originated as a feudal obligation for peasants to perform a certain amount of labor without pay. The *corvée* became a demand that peasants work as much as 14 days a year on the king's roads, breaking, carting and shoveling stones.[38] Often this came at the worst time, such as when peasants were busy with their harvest. Landlords, who stood to gain more from roads, contributed nothing. As might be expected, forced labor resulted in poor work and terrible roads.

In 1778, Turgot warned Americans that "slavery is incompatible with a good political constitution."[39] He believed Americans had more to fear from civil war than foreign enemies. Turgot fumed, "This abominable custom of slavery has once been universal, and is still spread over the greater part of the earth." He denounced "Europeans who go thither to purchase negroes for the cultivation of the American colonies. The excessive labours to which avaricious masters drive their slaves cause many of them to perish."[40]

Turgot's friend Adam Smith was the most influential writer in persuading people that an economy worked best with as much freedom as possible and a minimum of compulsion. Smith started to write his masterpiece *The Wealth of Nations* in 1764 and worked on it for a dozen years. Finally, on March 9, 1776, the firm Strahan and Cadell published the book, in two quarto (9-by–12-inch) volumes totaling over 1,000 pages. Smith was 53.

The first printing of *The Wealth of Nations* sold out in six months. A German edition appeared in 1776, a Danish edition in 1779, an Italian edition in 1780 and a French edition in 1781. The Spanish Inquisition suppressed the book for what officials considered "the lowness of its style and the looseness of its morals."

Smith dispelled the illusion that compulsion was needed to maintain an orderly society and help an economy prosper. He explained how free markets give people incentives to find ways they can profit by serving others. "It is not from the benevolence of the butcher, the brewer, or the baker that we expect our dinner," he wrote, "but from their regard to their own interest. We address ourselves, not to their humanity but to their self-love, and never talk to them of our own necessities but of their advantages."[41] He marveled at how market processes arise spontaneously: "The natural effort of every individual to better his own condition, when suffered to exert itself with freedom and security, is so powerful a principle, that it is alone, and without any assistance, not only capable of carrying on the society to wealth and prosperity, but of surmounting a hundred impertinent obstructions with which the folly of human laws too often encumbers its operations."[42]

Smith's most famous lines were "[a typical investor] intends only his own security; and by directing that industry in such a manner as its produce may be of the greatest value, he intends only his own gain, and he is in this, as in many other cases, led by an invisible hand to promote an end which was no part of his intention. Nor is it always the worse for the society that it was no part of it. By pursuing his own interest he frequently promotes that of the society more effectually than when he really intends to promote it. I have never known much good done by those who affect to trade for the public good."[43]

Smith discussed the inefficiencies and evils of slavery in *The Wealth of Nations*. He focused on the lack of incentives slaves have to work efficiently and improve the value of property, compared with

the incentives of free workers. "Freemen are capable of acquiring property," he explained, "and have a plain interest that the whole produce should be as great as possible. . . . A slave, on the contrary, who can acquire nothing but his maintenance, consults his own ease by making the land produce as little as possible over and above that maintenance."[44] In addition, Smith pointed out that slaveholders incur the costs of maintaining slaves, while free workers must maintain themselves out of their earnings. Hence, his conclusion: "The work done by freemen comes cheaper in the end than that performed by slaves."[45]

Although Smith was mainly speaking about the economic disadvantages of slavery, his language made clear his belief that slavery was reprehensible. Improvements of various kinds, he wrote, "are least of all to be expected when [plantation owners] employ slaves for their workmen. The experience of all ages and nations, I believe, demonstrates that the work done by slaves, though it appears to cost only their maintenance, is in the end the dearest of any. A person who can acquire no property, can have no other interest but to eat as much, and to labour as little as possible. Whatever work he does beyond what is sufficient to purchase his own maintenance, can be squeezed out of him by violence only, and not by any interest of his own." Smith scorned slaveholders: "The pride of man makes him love to domineer, and nothing mortifies him so much as to be obliged to condescend to persuade his inferiors. Wherever the law allows it, and the nature of the work can afford it, therefore, he will generally prefer the service of slaves to that of freemen."

Smith was correct to suggest that a free labor market would mean higher living standards for workers and more efficient production. However, Smith's analysis gave abolitionists confidence to claim that plantation owners could cut their costs and maintain production simply by replacing slaves with free workers—an oversimplification. When plantations had to pay market-rate compensation, they bore the full labor cost rather than the slaves who had been forced to work for nothing. In effect, slaves subsidized the plantations. A free labor market would end the subsidy and give workers market-rate compensation for their efforts. Having to pay the full cost of labor would spur plantations to mechanize and reorganize their operations for improved efficiency—or be forced to go out of business. Experience with emancipation led some writers to claim that Smith's views were discredited,

when in fact market processes had not been fully understood. But we're getting ahead of ourselves—more on these points later.

Although ideas about natural rights were crucial in the epic campaigns against slavery because they provided compelling arguments not found in religion or constitutional law, they probably wouldn't have prevailed if slave societies outperformed free societies. That ordinary people could be both free and prosperous proved to be an irresistible idea.

Haiti and the First Successful Slave Revolt

In the late eighteenth century, France's most important colony was Saint-Domingue (Haiti), which occupied the western third of the Caribbean island of Hispaniola. It was a way station in the African slave trade. Its slave plantations were the world's leading producers of coffee, and the colony reportedly produced nearly as much sugar as Brazil, Cuba and Jamaica combined.[1] The bankrupt French royal government desperately needed the colonial revenue from Saint-Domingue and was anxious to keep the slave system going.

The slave system was inherently unstable. In 1789, when the French Revolution began, a census showed there were 465,429 slaves in Saint-Domingue. They outnumbered whites about 20 to 1. Saint-Domingue reportedly had the highest slave mortality in the Caribbean: about 10 percent died within four years. Slaves were never given medical attention, even for work-related injuries. Their daily lives and living conditions were so intolerable that some 2,500 committed suicide annually.[2]

An elaborate Black Code imposed every imaginable restriction on slaves in the French colonies to enforce their inferiority and prevent them from gaining any weapons. The Black Code barred slaves from

medicine, law, teaching and other professions; it was even illegal for a slave to become a jeweler. Slaves were not permitted to eat, dance or sing when whites were around. They were prohibited from wearing clothes nicer than the clothes of whites. The Black Code's extensive and detailed restrictions reached into every aspect of a slave's life.[3]

Plantation owners maintained slavery through terror. Slaves could be whipped 50 times for alleged laziness, as judged by their masters who could rub salt in the wounds or do other things to make the punishment worse. Slaves could be tortured with medieval devices like thumb screws and throat rings. Woe to the slave who hit his master because he could be burned alive. Particularly sadistic slaveholders would explode some gunpowder in a slave's anus.[4]

The high death rate among slaves on Saint-Domingue meant that tens of thousands of slaves had to be imported every year just to maintain the slave labor force. Consequently, an estimated two-thirds of slaves had been born in Africa; they remembered a time—in most cases within the previous 10 years—when they had been free, and undoubtedly they cherished the memory.[5]

All this spurred slaves to rebel, which they often did by escaping into the mountains. Many of these people—referred to as "maroons"—joined communities of runaways who had settled there. Some maroons had eluded police long enough that the government gave up and recognized their independence, as long as they didn't pose a threat.[6]

The French journalist Guillaume Thomas François Raynal foresaw the inevitable. In his book *L'Histoire philosophique et politique des établissements et du commerce des Européens dans les deux Indes* (1770), he warned: "Your slaves do not need your generosity or your advice to shatter the sacrilegious yoke that oppresses them. . . .

All that the negroes lack is a leader courageous enough to carry them to vengeance and carnage. Where is he, this great man, that nature owes to its vexed, oppressed, tormented children? Where is he? He will appear, do not doubt it. He will show himself and will raise the sacred banner of liberty."[7]

French Revolution Triggers Haitian Revolution

The French Revolution occurred as King Louis XVI was paralyzed with indecision amid rising government debts and intensifying griev-

ances among many interest groups. On July 14, 1789, after escalating violence in Paris, a mob headed toward the Bastille, originally built as part of the city's fortifications and later serving as a prison. The Bastille wasn't the city's worst prison—conditions in the Bicêtre were reported to be worse—but the Bastille had come to stand for the arbitrary power of the French monarchy. At the time, the Bastille had only seven prisoners, and apparently none of them were there for political reasons. But more than 1,000 people gathered outside the Bastille, anxious to strike a blow against the monarchy and to get their hands on the weapons stored there. In the fighting, the governor of the Bastille, Bernard-René de Launay, along with many of the guards were killed. This marked the beginning of the French Revolution.

A National Constituent Assembly was formed to shape a government in response to the revolution's goals. In the process of drafting a new constitution for a monarchy with limited powers, the assembly approved the Declaration of the Rights of Man and of the Citizen on August 26, 1789. Drafted by the Marquis de Lafayette, the man who had volunteered to help defeat the British during the American Revolution, this document affirmed that "men are born free and equal in rights." All people were to be guaranteed the rights to "liberty, property, security and resistance to oppression." On September 28, 1791, the National Constituent Assembly abolished slavery in France, but slavery continued in the French colonies.

The number of slave revolts increased significantly during the eighteenth century, and new philosophical and political ideas surely had something to do with this. Ideas on liberty seem to have reached the slaves, despite the fact that most were illiterate. Slaves overheard conversations among whites in houses, on ships, on docks and elsewhere, and passed on information to others. Slaves saw the reactions of whites to news and reported their observations. That they developed higher expectations and dreamed that someday they would be free became clear when the slaves heard that the king had ordered emancipation. Local officials tried to thwart the order and would uphold it only if slaves demanded it.[8]

Meanwhile, plantation owners on Saint-Domingue maneuvered for independence from the revolutionary French government. The slaves became alarmed that if Saint-Domingue gained independence, there would be even fewer constraints on how harshly they might be treated by the plantation owners. At the same time, *gens de*

couleur (free coloreds, as ex-slaves were called) were excited by revolutionary talk about liberty and equality. They hoped to gain equal status with whites.

After visiting revolutionary France, Vincent Ogé, a wealthy free colored man, headed back to Saint-Domingue. He stopped in London to meet the British abolitionist Thomas Clarkson. Somewhere during his trip he bought guns and reached Saint-Domingue in October 1790. In his hometown of Dondon, he mobilized several hundred supporters, marched to the town of Grand Rivière and took it over. He sent letters to the Provincial Assembly demanding that *gens de couleur* receive equal political rights, especially the right to vote. He warned that he would resort to force if his demands weren't fulfilled. Although he won some initial skirmishes, his forces were crushed by government troops dispatched from Le Cap. Ogé fled to Santo Domingo (the Spanish colony at the eastern end of the island), but Spanish authorities returned him to French colonial authorities in Saint-Domingue. He and his principal associate, Jean-Baptiste Chavannes, were broken on the wheel and beheaded, and their heads were stuck on pikes for all to see. Nineteen other rebels were hanged.

Killing Ogé, however, inflamed hostilities between *gens de couleur* and whites on Saint-Domingue. During the next several months, more *gens de couleur* armed themselves against white attacks. Moreover, there were reports that Chavannes had opposed slavery and that Ogé favored recruiting slaves to fight their oppressors.

The reports from Saint-Domingue were met with skepticism in France. But as it became clear that there had been a major insurrection, politicians scrambled to accommodate *gens de couleur* and mulattoes and gave them the right to vote in local elections and to hold political office. Though humanitarian considerations were a factor in this policy, the National Assembly was also anxious to retain Saint-Domingue as a lucrative French colony.

A furious debate ensued in the French National Assembly. *Gens de couleur* wanted *equal* rights, and planters were convinced that any concessions would lead to demands to free the slaves, destroying the colonial economy. The result was a compromise that the National Assembly approved on May 15, 1791: equal political rights would be granted only to *gens de couleur* born to two free parents; all other blacks and natives would be excluded.[9] Saint-Domingue whites defied this

law, and there was talk about murdering *gens de couleur* and asking British forces to intervene.

On August 14, about 200 slaves gathered on the Lenormand de Mézy plantation, Morne-Rouge parish, in northern Saint-Domingue near Le Cap. These were the slaves most trusted by their owners who were given some freedom of movement. Supposedly the slaves, from many plantations in the north-central region, were leaving their plantations for dinner. Reportedly, somebody read a statement saying that the National Assembly in Paris had banned the use of the whip by slave owners and had ordered that slaves should have three days off a week (at the time, they had two days off). The statement said Saint-Domingue officials refused to enforce these policies and that French troops were on their way to help the slaves. None of this was true, but the statement convinced slaves an uprising would be successful.

On August 21, Pierre Mossut, a plantation manager in La Gossette, was attacked by a group of slaves. He managed to escape and, with some whites from other plantations, rounded up and interrogated some slaves, who confessed that a rebellion was underway. Later that night, slaves rebelled at several plantations in Acul parish. A man named Boukman—a driver, coachman and religious leader among the slaves—led perhaps a dozen slaves to a sugar refinery, seized a man and slashed his body apart with their swords. Another man, drawn to the scene by the screams, was shot. The band of slaves found the owner of the refinery and slaughtered him. More slaves arrived and proceeded to burn the entire plantation. This inspired slaves elsewhere to set fire to their plantations. By August 23, there were about 2,000 slaves moving from plantation to plantation, destroying houses, refineries and sugar cane fields.

An estimated quarter-million slaves quit their plantations, and some 50,000 slaves acquired weapons. National guard troops counterattacked, and Boukman was caught, tortured and beheaded. His head was displayed on a spear by the gate to Le Cap. White refugees poured into the city. Ships were ordered not to leave, so that the sailors might be available to fight. Six gallows were built in a city square to handle the anticipated executions. The rebellion took whites by surprise, and they apparently got little information from captured rebels as most refused to talk.[10]

The rebels obtained guns and ammunition from the Spanish across the border in Santo Domingo, trading jewelry, dishes, furniture

and other items seized from plantations. The rebels cultivated good relations with their Spanish suppliers by declaring that they fought in the name of the French king who, according to widely circulated rumors, had authorized emancipation in Saint-Domingue. The slaves fought more effectively than anybody expected, in part because many had experience as soldiers in African civil wars before they were captured and sold to slave traders.

Some of the slave leaders were intent on avenging the terrible treatment they had endured. The slave leader Jeannot, for instance, reportedly killed two of his white prisoners every day, to intensify the fear among his other prisoners. One prisoner was reportedly whipped some 400 times. Gunpowder was rubbed into wounds, intensifying the pain.[11]

The white plantation owners were desperate because they feared the revolutionary government in France almost as much as they feared the slaves. Although some whites appealed to the British, the British were competitors and as such were likely to be more interested in possibly adding Saint-Domingue to their empire than to helping embattled French plantation owners.

The French National Assembly sent three civil commissioners to Saint-Domingue, and they arrived in November 1791. They didn't know about the slave rebellion, so they weren't prepared to deal with it. They reported, however, that the National Assembly had rejected the compromise adopted on May 15, namely the extension of equal political rights to *gens de couleur,* who became disillusioned.

In addition, the commissioners reported that the National Assembly had adopted a new scheme for a constitutional monarchy, which the king had accepted, and had declared a general amnesty for "acts of revolution." In the Saint-Domingue assembly, representatives of the planters insisted that the slave rebellion was a crime, not an "act of revolution." They feared that an amnesty for rebels would make the rebellion legitimate, and slavery would be doomed.

The most important slave leaders, Jean-François and Georges Biassou, entered the negotiations. Jean-François was a light-skinned runaway slave. He aspired to be a king, called himself the General of the Negroes, and dressed like it. He wore a white uniform with gold epaulets (like the Bourbon kings), his boots had fancy spurs, and he rode in a coach pulled by black stallions. He had acquired some education and was able to speak Spanish and speak and write French. Bi-

assou was much less impressive. He was short and stout, and his face suggested much suffering.[12]

Jean-François and Biassou explained that they would try to convince the rebellious slaves that it was time for peace, but the Saint-Domingue assembly must promise to "take care of their situation."[13] These leaders warned that failure to reach a satisfactory agreement for the slaves would surely result in more bloodshed. Planters vaguely suggested that if the slaves returned to work on the plantations, they might be forgiven. The planters, however, had no intention of accepting conditions dictated by their slaves. They insisted that before there could be serious talks, the slaves must release all their prisoners, surrender their guns and go back to work on the plantations.

Meanwhile, thousands of slaves were losing their patience. Jean-François and Biassou, who had initially focused on amnesty and some limited "liberties," such as giving slaves three days off a week, began taking a harder line. They demanded significant reforms before slaves would go back to work on the plantations. Slaves complained that their masters provided no medical care when they were sick, masters arbitrarily took away free time, and masters were executioners. Jean-François and Biassou demanded that the *cachots*—plantation prisons—be abolished. Overall, Jean-François and Biassou tried to reform slavery, not abolish it. The reforms they proposed, however, had been discussed for years and rejected by the planters who continued to resist. Slaves became increasingly suspicious: They wouldn't return to the plantations under any conditions.

Jean-François and Biassou resumed attacks on white strongholds. Planters blamed the *Société des Amis des Noirs* (Society of the Friends of Blacks) for the slave rebellion, and they urged that French soldiers be sent to suppress it. But as the French government became more radical, its members again concluded that the only way to save Saint-Domingue as a colony was to give the *gens de couleur* equal political rights. This the National Assembly did on April 4, 1792. Henceforth, there would be only two classes in Saint-Domingue: free people and slaves.

This deal failed to resolve the situation. A substantial number of whites had fled Saint-Domingue, some for France and others for America. When a few whites returned to their plantations, the slaves made clear that they weren't welcome. In many cases, *gens de couleur* took over management of plantations without any authorization from the

absent owners. Slaves asserted their prerogative to decide whom they would work for. The colonial government had its hands full dealing with violent slave resistance and couldn't be drawn into disputes about who should manage plantations.

In 1792, the slave rebellion spread from the northern province to the south, as slaves seized control of plantations there. Increasingly *gens de couleur,* who had avoided allying with slaves, concluded that they might prevail only if they joined forces with slaves. Many whites responded by freeing slaves who agreed to become soldiers and fight the *gens de couleur.* Thousands of slaves fought each other.

The *gens de couleur* and their slave allies defeated the whites. The next question was what would happen to the slaves. The *gens de couleur* freed several hundred slave leaders and wanted the rest of the slaves to return to work the plantations. The *gens de couleur* wanted slave leaders to become part of police units responsible for maintaining order among the slaves. In the southern province, many slaves wouldn't return to the plantations.

One of the slave leaders, Armand, had been promised liberty by his master, and the two men met to discuss a settlement. Armand asked that slaves have three days off a week, and he demanded that there be no more whipping. Incredibly, he didn't ask for the emancipation of all slaves. His owner, like others, refused to negotiate. Armand withdrew to the Platons, a mountainous area, and consolidated his slave forces.

The governor of Saint-Domingue, Philibert François Rouxel de Blanchelande, offered an amnesty for all slaves who returned to their plantations. The slaves burned more plantations. Blanchelande dispatched soldiers to pursue the slave forces into the mountains, but the soldiers retreated after taking big losses. The slaves escalated their demands: freedom for all rebels and three days off per week for all slaves in the region. The whites refused, but when Armand threatened to attack the city of Les Cayes and burn it down, the Provincial Assembly offered to emancipate several hundred slaves.

There was a catch. The emancipation papers weren't signed by slave owners, so they could be invalid. In addition, emancipation was extended only to about 700 slaves armed by *gens de couleur,* not those armed by whites or those who joined various slave bands. Reportedly half the qualified slaves accepted the offer for whatever it might be worth. The remaining slaves stayed in the Platons and

fortified their positions. More recruits found their way to the mountain camps. Periodically the slaves ventured out to plunder and burn plantations. By late 1792, an estimated one-third of the plantations in the south were seriously damaged if not destroyed. Soldiers brought in from France had occasional success against the rebels, but they didn't last long. They weren't prepared to deal with guerrilla fighters in the mountains, and many French soldiers succumbed to tropical diseases.

Conflict in the north took a radical turn. The established slave leaders Jean-François and Biassou as well as an emerging slave leader, Charles Belair, sent a letter to the Colonial Assembly declaring that slave resistance was justified by the Declaration of the Rights of Man and of the Citizen, which the French had adopted. Accordingly, Jean-François, Biassou and Belair demanded "general liberty for all men retained in slavery" and "general amnesty for the past." These leaders proposed trying to get everybody back to work as free workers, not slaves.[14] For the first time, general emancipation became an agenda item in Saint-Domingue. The proposal didn't go anywhere, but the authorities couldn't end the rebellion because there were too many rebel groups, they were well armed, and they controlled much of the colony.

While all this was going on, the French National Assembly sent three new commissioners—Léger Félicité Sonthonax, Etienne Polverel and Jean Antoine Ailhaud—to govern Saint-Domingue. Ailhaud soon bailed out, but Sonthonax and Polverel carried on. Both had been trained in law and, as members of the Paris Jacobin Club, they had met French abolitionist Jacques Brissot de Warville. Sonthonax and Polverel spoke out against slavery. Their top priority was to enforce the National Assembly's law granting equal political rights to *gens de couleur.* They arrived in Saint-Domingue on September 17, 1792.

The white population was alarmed that the men would try to abolish slavery, and the commissioners replied that their aim was equal rights for *gens de couleur,* in the hopes of saving slavery. They said that only colonial assemblies had the power to abolish slavery. The whites feared the evolving republican government in France and turned against it, pledging their support for the king. They took heart from developments in the French Caribbean islands of Guadeloupe and Martinique, where plantation owners had forced republican officials out of power.

Then came news from Paris that all men were to have the right to vote, and that the National Assembly would be succeeded by a new National Convention, which would displace the power of the king. France was officially a republic. The Jacobins, who gained control of the National Convention, faced the prospect of war with the European monarchies. The Jacobins believed that protecting the French republic required suppressing dissidents, and this became the responsibility of the Committee on Public Safety. Accordingly, Sonthonax and Polverel were granted powers to dismiss any government officials who opposed them. They dismissed the governor and suspended colonial assemblies. Recognizing the struggles they faced, Sonthonax governed in northern Saint-Domingue, while Polverel ruled in the south and west.

Sonthonax tried to establish a biracial army. He appointed a free black officer in each army unit, but the local unit—Regiment du Cap—balked. Members of the unit refused to take an oath pledging to uphold the policy of equal political rights for *gens de couleur*. Sonthonax ordered the entire unit expelled from the country. The Regiment du Cap seized an arsenal and attacked free black soldiers. Sonthonax appealed to loyal white soldiers who helped secure his authority in the town and proceeded to establish new regiments of *gens de couleur*.

Sonthonax didn't have as much luck with the rebels. Although his troops chased them back to the mountains, as opportunities arose the rebels resumed their raids on plantations and towns. Sonthonax appointed Etienne Laveaux to lead the offensive against rebels, and his free black soldiers destroyed camps built by slaves who had run away from their plantations. Laveaux destroyed banana trees and other plants that might provide food for the slaves. Thus, the struggle in Saint-Domingue escalated between *gens de couleur* and runaway slaves, and Sonthonax, who had become an abolitionist, emerged as an enemy of the slaves.

The struggle was taking perverse turns in Polverel's region, too. In January 1793, he ordered an attack against a rebel camp on low ground. The men fled to higher ground, leaving behind women, children and sick men. They were all slaughtered, giving Polverel a great victory. His soldiers—former slaves—had been led by Jean Kina, a slave who had allied himself with the whites and helped defend slavery!

Such victories as Sonthonax and Polverel claimed never seemed to last long. New rebel leaders quickly emerged to replace those who had

been killed. The rebels communicated continually with each other, seemed to have no trouble obtaining the supplies they needed and operated freely throughout much of Saint-Domingue.

In an effort to avoid trouble, whites generally abandoned the countryside for the cities. It was difficult to harvest crops at plantations that hadn't been burned, because most slaves had run away to join one side or another in the ongoing struggle. Plantation owners tried to sell their properties, without much luck.

After King Louis XVI was executed in January 1793, war broke out between the French republic and Britain, Spain and Austria-Hungary. The conflict extended to the colonies, complicating matters on Saint-Domingue. It was a tantalizing prize that had been a big producer of valuable crops and could be again. Spain hoped to regain the colony it had lost to the French back in 1697, and it found allies in the rebel slaves. Jean-François and Biassou, who by this time commanded some 10,000 soldiers, were mainly interested in obtaining Spanish provisions. Jean-François and Biassou also captured women, children, and some men and sold them to Spanish slave traders.[15] The whites hoped that the British could be persuaded to help restore slavery in Saint-Domingue, but by dealing with the British, they became traitors against France.

Faced with an uncontrollable insurgency and conflict with European rivals, Sonthonax realized he had to win over the slaves for France. He was slow to take action, however, until a new governor was appointed in Saint-Domingue. François-Thomas Galbaud du Fort, who owned a plantation there, turned out to be an adversary of the French republican government and its commissioners. He cultivated the many enemies Sonthonax had made, denouncing Sonthonax for having a "black soul." Sonthonax ordered his soldiers to capture Galbaud and take him to a prison ship in Le Cap harbor. But many of the crew as well as the prisoners viewed Sonthonax as a tyrant, and Galbaud recruited many supporters on the ship. They hatched a scheme to raid Le Cap and depose Sonthonax and opened the town jails to release hundreds of slaves.

On June 21, 1793, after having spilled so much blood trying to defend slavery, Sonthonax announced that any slave who fought for the French republic would be free.[16] Ironically, this policy amounted to a revival of an edict issued by the king in 1784 but never implemented because the planters had too much political clout. The new

policy convinced the slaves to side with Sonthonax, and he regained control of Le Cap. Galbaud and his supporters, as well as many terrified, whites fled to the ships. Many people left Saint-Domingue never to return.

This success enabled Sonthonax to focus on defeating the Spanish who were advancing in western Saint-Domingue. He had a harder time recruiting for this campaign because the Spanish offered liberty to slaves who joined their side. On July 11, Sonthonax extended his offer of freedom and citizenship to the wives and children of slaves who fought for the republic.[17] Polverel made the same offer to slaves in the west and south, where he governed. He ordered the emancipation of slaves who would work on plantations rather than fight. He further promised cultivators a portion of the land they worked, though he didn't provide any details about how or when this would happen. He did say that nothing would happen until all the fighting was over.

On August 29, Sonthonax issued a decree that emancipated all slaves in the northern province. They were to "enjoy all the rights attached to the quality of French citizenship." On October 31, Polverel issued a decree emancipating all Africans and descendants of Africans, men and women, as well as those who might arrive or be "born in the future."[18] The ex-slaves, however, had to continue working on their plantations for at least a year, for which they were to receive a salary. After a year, they could apply for a transfer to another plantation. Unless a man enlisted in the army, it wasn't possible to leave a plantation to live in a city, in the mountains, or elsewhere. Anyone found to have moved away from a plantation without authorization was subject to imprisonment.[19]

Despite these restrictions, the emancipations on Saint-Domingue were remarkable. Most important was the granting of the political rights of citizenship along with emancipation. Fortunately, the decisions were upheld by the government in Paris.

Independence and Reconciliation

Although Sonthonax and Polverel made giant steps toward full emancipation, the Spanish and English were gaining ground on Saint-Domingue, and the economy had collapsed amidst the fighting,

destruction and emigration. Somehow, the invaders had to be expelled, peace secured and people brought back to work.

A new rebel leader, Toussaint L'Ouverture, rose to the situation. He was born a slave on a plantation not far from Le Cap. Various sources suggest he might have been born between 1739 and 1746.[20] According to one of his sons, Isaac L'Ouverture, who wrote a memoir in the mid-nineteenth century, Toussaint's father had been a prince of Arada, one of the West African tribes, before being captured as a prisoner of war and shipped across the Atlantic. He converted to Catholicism, and his master gave him some land to cultivate. Toussaint was his oldest son. After his parents died, he was educated by his godfather, Pierre Baptiste, a free black who had been educated by missionaries, with whom Toussaint studied French, a little Latin and some geometry. Toussaint helped take care of cattle, served as a coachman and displayed enough ability that he was given some responsibility for managing the plantation. In 1777, Toussaint apparently bought his freedom. For a couple of years, he rented a small coffee plantation and owned slaves.[21] A devout Catholic, he married Suzan Simone, and they had a son, Placide. It isn't easy to separate fact from legend in Toussaint's story, but clearly he impressed people with his intelligence and ability.

To be sure, he didn't look the part. He had thin cheeks, a big chin and three battle scars on his face. His jaw was somewhat off-center. He had lost his upper teeth and he walked with a limp. He wore a madras headpiece, though, which made him look like an exotic fighter.

Toussaint emerged as a military leader during the 1791 rebellion. He seems to have acquired from the Spanish weapons that he dispersed in secret hideouts for his guerrillas around Saint-Domingue. He was the only one who had a map showing the locations of all the hideouts.[22]

He recruited about 5,000 men and put them through intensive training. He had his men practice moving quietly through a forest with weapons and supplies. He ordered his commanders to display their pistols when giving commands. Death was the penalty for disobedience. Toussaint imposed strict discipline that proved to be a key to his military success. He had his army cover as much as 80 kilometers in a day, which was better than the 70 kilometers a day Napoleon was able to move with his army.

He seems to have been very careful to maintain as much independence as possible from the various factions in Saint-Domingue.

Evidently he didn't have much confidence that the French revolutionary government would be around very long. He was not among those
who signed a July 1792 proclamation issued by Jean-François and Biassou, proposing that slavery be abolished in Saint-Domingue. Like
Jean-François and Biassou, though, when war broke out with other
European powers, Toussaint began working with the Spanish, who presumably provided guns and other supplies his soldiers needed. France
didn't seem likely to defeat the European powers allied against it.

Toussaint continued working with Spain after Sonthonax issued
his August 29, 1793, proclamation abolishing slavery in the northern
province. But more and more white planters were allying themselves
with Spain, and Spanish forces tried to reintroduce the use of the
whip on plantations, which triggered more revolts in northern Saint-
Domingue. The British, too, encountered more resistance than they
had bargained for.

By April 1794, Toussaint had concluded that the Spanish wanted to
see blacks "kill one another to decrease our numbers," then enslave
those who remained.[23] In addition, he might have been influenced by
news that the French National Convention had ordered the abolition
of slavery. He went over to the French side and began fighting the
Spanish. With him were some 4,000 soldiers and savvy officers including the free black Henri Christophe and former slaves Moïse
Dessalines and Jean-Jacques Dessalines. Toussaint recognized that the
slaves couldn't prevail in conventional battles against European forces.
The slaves were armed only with sticks, knives and a few swords seized
from plantation houses. But Toussaint had learned hit-and-run guerrilla tactics from the Spanish who had used these tactics to resist the
regime Napoleon imposed on their country.

Toussaint captured Spanish-controlled towns along with Spanish
guns and ammunition. The Spanish helped some of their supporters,
including Jean-François and Biassou, evacuate to other Spanish
colonies in the Caribbean.

Toussaint encouraged former slaves to resume working on their
plantations. In many cases, they did so, but particularly when plantations were abandoned, they cultivated land for their own use and built
their own houses on the property. They were quite industrious when
they stood to gain from their own labor.

Toussaint recognized that achieving the productive potential of
large plantations required the expertise only the white owners and

managers had. They wouldn't return to their plantations until there was peace and they felt safe. Accordingly, as Toussaint continued the offensive against his adversaries, he welcomed whites who wanted to get their plantations going again.

In practice, the policy didn't work. The whites who returned to their plantations found that they were being managed by former slaves or army officers, or the plantations were divided into many parcels worked by former slaves who refused to give up what they had. They displayed no fear of the former plantation owners and simply ignored orders. Whites complained that when they wanted food, they had to get on mules and go to market themselves. The whites sought help from local authorities who did nothing.

Because Toussaint welcomed back white plantation owners, many former slaves suspected that he was trying to reintroduce slavery. Indeed, he directed his army to force slaves back to work. Evidently, he believed that Saint-Domingue's plantations would function only with forced labor. However, the slaves seem to have been treated better—whipping was forbidden—and they received a share of plantation profits. Toussaint tried to quell black anger by emphasizing that black slaves needed to gain practical knowledge from both whites and mulattoes. The trouble was that, as a military commander, he was more familiar with giving orders than devising incentives for people to work.

Toussaint was correct, though, that the former slaves weren't likely to retain such liberty as they had for long unless the economy could be revived. Defenders of slavery would proclaim that an economy, certainly a plantation economy and such products as sugar and coffee that everybody wanted, couldn't be sustained without massive compulsion.

In 1796, Sonthonax promoted Toussaint to Général de Division and permitted him to rule the former slaves. The two men had a good working relationship for a while, and Toussaint trusted Sonthonax to arrange for his two sons to have adequate protection for their voyage across the Atlantic to attend school in Paris.

Sonthonax, however, was a Jacobin radical who wanted to exterminate Saint-Domingue's white population, which Toussaint believed was suicidal for blacks. In addition, Sonthonax was an atheist, which offended the Catholic Toussaint. Sonthonax encouraged Toussaint to demobilize his army, so the soldiers could be available to work on plantations, which Toussaint didn't dare do. His army was his security. In August 1797, he diplomatically ordered Sonthonox to leave, saying

that he had achieved "peace, zeal for work, and the reestablishment of culture," and he should inform people in France of this. Sonthonax got the hint and returned to France. As it happened, a reaction against the wild excesses of the French Revolution had occurred, bringing new people to power. Embittered, exiled planters gained more political clout, and by the time Sonthonax returned to France, he learned that he had been dismissed.

Toussaint persuaded Etienne Laveaux, an able military commander and ally, to go to Paris and represent the interests of Saint-Domingue in the French government. Laveaux did that, leaving Toussaint the unrivalled ruler of the colony.

Voennot de Vaubanc, a planter elected to the French Council of the Five Hundred, gave a vehement speech denouncing Toussaint and emancipation in Saint-Domingue. He characterized the former slaves as ignorant and violent creatures who had turned liberty into chaos. He declared that emancipation was a disaster and slavery must be reestablished. He urged the government to send a large military force that would restore order, and he wanted the government to fund the return of planters to the colony.

Toussaint replied with a letter saying that if the former slaves were ignorant, it was because their former owners had done everything possible to prevent them from getting an education. He observed that violence in Saint-Domingue was no worse than the Reign of Terror carried out by educated Frenchmen during the revolution. He suggested that a serious attempt to reestablish slavery would trigger another rebellion like that of 1791.

Toussaint issued a warning to planters who dreamed of reestablishing slavery in Saint-Domingue. He declared that slaves had endured their terrible conditions because they didn't know of anything better. Having experienced some liberty, they would never go back to the way things were.

Toussaint conducted secret negotiations with the British who had suffered horrendous casualties in Saint-Domingue. Moreover, mosquito-borne yellow fever had hit British troops hard. Former slaves who had fought for the British joined Toussaint. The British seem to have realized that the war in Saint-Domingue had cost them a lot of money and soldiers without any gains in sight. After they withdrew, the British appear to have been concerned about the safety of planters who had backed them. Toussaint provided some assurance about that.

Mindful of the desperate need to rebuild the Saint-Domingue economy, he pledged not to attack Jamaica, Britain's most important
colony in the Caribbean, and in exchange Britain offered to end its
naval blockade of Saint-Domingue, which had disrupted the colony's
trade. Toussaint wanted to make sure Saint-Domingue could export
its sugar and coffee when the plantations returned to production.
Toussaint negotiated a treaty with the British in 1798, and they were
gone that year.

All this was quite bold, considering that Saint-Domingue was still
a French colony, and dealings with other nations were supposed to be
handled by French government officials. Toussaint did more. He
wrote U.S. president John Adams, suggesting that U.S. merchants
would be able to do some profitable trading with Saint-Domingue.
Toussaint said he would provide protection for America's ships.
American secretary of state Thomas Pickering didn't see a problem if
Saint-Domingue no longer recognized French authority. Toussaint
privately agreed to turn French ships away from Saint-Domingue
ports, though saying this publicly would have provoked a serious reaction in France. He wanted his country to function as an independent
nation without inciting another war that an official declaration of independence would involve.

Toussaint had to deal with Gabriel Hédouville, a representative
from yet another French government—the Directory. He arrived in
1798 with a group of officials who openly looked forward to restoring slavery in Saint-Domingue. Although he didn't have any troops
at his disposal, he set about undermining Toussaint's authority at
every opportunity. He tried and failed to limit the size of Toussaint's army. He complained that Toussaint's army had too many
black officers, and he alleged that they were mostly illiterate. He
claimed black officers recruited soldiers from among the former
slaves working on plantations, making it harder for them to function. He was critical of the "negrophile" policies of white government officials. Toussaint tried to ignore Hédouville and focus on
his own business.

Hédouville went too far when he deposed Moïse, Toussaint's
nephew who served as a high-ranking army officer commanding
troops at Fort-Liberté (Fort-Dauphin), and installed an officer
named Grandet who was reported to have captured runaway slaves
from Santo Domingo and returned them to the Spanish. Toussaint

ordered several thousand soldiers to surround Le Cap and capture Hédouville, but he escaped to a ship bound for France.

Hédouville succeeded at one thing, however: he sowed distrust between André Rigaud, a military commander with an army largely of *gens de couleur,* and Toussaint, with his army largely of former slaves. The two men had been allies who assured that the policies of the French republic would prevail on Saint-Domingue. While Rigaud reported to Toussaint, he had ruled with considerable autonomy in the southern province since 1793. Rigaud staffed his officer corps with *gens de couleur,* and the mulattoes ended up with abandoned plantations. By contrast, most of Toussaint's officers were black. There was increasing tension between the *gens de couleur* who prospered mightily from emancipation and the former slaves who were trying to find a place for themselves.

Rigaud complained that Toussaint was abusive. Rigaud wrote, "I have chiefs, but I have no master, and never did an irritated and foul-mouthed master treat his slave in a manner as atrocious as I have been treated."[24] Toussaint branded Rigaud as a rebel against the French government, and Rigaud countered by citing a letter from Hédouville naming him as a representative of the French government.

On June 18, 1799, Rigaud ordered some of his troops to capture Petit and Grand-Goâve from Toussaint's forces, which they did. This move inspired a number of defections from Toussaint's ranks, and there were uprisings against him in the north.

Toussaint crushed the rebellion and ordered the swift execution of those involved. Then his army invaded the southern province to destroy Rigaud. He reportedly had about 45,000 soldiers versus 15,000 for Rigaud. Both sides pursued a policy of slaughtering their opponents rather than taking prisoners. Toussaint tried to corner Rigaud, but he escaped by using ships to evacuate his troops. Toussaint appealed to President John Adams, who authorized U.S. naval ships to blockade ports in southern Saint-Domingue, limiting the ability of Rigaud to out-maneuver Toussaint. Probably Adams figured Toussaint would win, and American trade relations with Saint-Domingue would be secured if Americans contributed to his victory.

Toussaint's forces undoubtedly expanded as he recruited former slaves who cultivated plantations owned by Rigaud's supporters, the *gens de couleur.* Rigaud tried but failed to recruit many of the former slaves. In June 1800, Toussaint got a boost from First Consul

Napoleon Bonaparte, the latest French ruler who proclaimed that Toussaint was the "general-in-chief" of the Saint-Domingue army—overriding Rigaud's claim that his revolt was legitimate because of Hédouville's letter. In July, Rigaud fled from Saint-Domingue like most of Toussaint's other rivals. But the brutality of the civil war made it hard to establish peaceful relations between former slaves and *gens de couleur.*

Toussaint was firmly in control, but it wasn't enough. He decided he needed to conquer Santo Domingo, which Spain had transferred to France in 1795. His expressed concern was that only by controlling all the ports on Hispaniola would he be able to deal with the constant threat of adversaries landing in Santo Domingo and making their way to Saint-Domingue. By 1801, his army occupied Santo Domingo. He promised the Spanish governor that the private property would be respected—apparently including slaves—and the governor left.

Without constraints on his power, in October 1800 Toussaint militarized the plantations to revive production. Those who worked on plantations were given orders and punished severely for failing to obey them. Former slaves were forbidden to leave their assigned plantations without permission. It was illegal for them to grow food for themselves on a small private plot of land. Although supposedly slavery had been abolished, there wasn't much freedom.[25]

Toussaint's regime of compulsion bore more than a passing resemblance to the slavery that had been abolished. While the cultivators were to be paid, they weren't free to decline whatever payment might be offered if they considered it too low. They weren't free to compare job offers from various plantations, and they weren't free to choose another line of work. After all the bloodshed, there was no free labor market. Some military officers, including Toussaint's former associates Henri Christophe and Jean-Jacques Dessalines, made a lot of money from this new plantation system.[26]

Napoleon, who was in the process of building Europe's first modern police state, noticed that his authority was disregarded by Toussaint. Napoleon appointed proslavery people to his colonial ministry. One of them was Moreau de St. Méry, who opposed granting rights to *gens de couleur* as much as he opposed emancipating slaves. To get around the French government's inconvenient commitment to liberty, Moreau suggested that there should be "special laws" for French colonies. The laws would be issued by the French government, and the

colonies would have no say in the matter—no more colonial representatives in Paris.

Napoleon realized that Saint-Domingue was a volatile place, so as
he demanded allegiance from those governing Saint-Domingue, he
promised that "the sacred principles of the liberty and equality of all
the blacks will never suffer, among you, any attack or modification."
Despite these words, Toussaint recognized danger if the French government permitted slavery anywhere in its colonial empire. He sought
"the absolute acceptance of the principle that no man, whether born
red, black, or white, can be the property of another."

On February 4, 1801, Toussaint announced that a constitutional
assembly would meet to draft a constitution for Saint-Domingue. The
members included Julien Raimond (one of Napoleon's representatives), former planters and *gens de couleurs*. Curiously, the assembly did-
n't include any former slaves. *Federalist Papers* coauthor Alexander
Hamilton recommended that the Saint-Domingue constitution authorize a president-for-life and military conscription.

The constitution announced in May was an effort to juggle con-
tradictions. It affirmed principles of the French Revolution and
Saint-Domingue's status as a French colony: "All men within it are
born, live, and die free and French." All of Hispaniola was "part of
the French empire." Roman Catholicism was to be the only "publicly
professed" religion. Although the constitution said that citizens could
choose any occupation, it also upheld Toussaint's October 1800
order that former slaves must work on their plantations because the
economy couldn't "suffer even the slightest interruption in the work
of cultivation."

The whole point of constitutions that were issued during the eighteenth and nineteenth centuries was to limit the power of government, traditionally the most serious threat to liberty. This new
constitution did very little to limit government power. On the contrary, it effectively sanctioned one-man rule, authorizing Toussaint to
serve for "the rest of his glorious life." From the standpoint of former
slaves, they were forced to do pretty much the same kind of work they
had done when they were slaves on the same plantations. As before,
slavery was sanctioned by the government. There seemed to be less
harsh treatment, and there was compensation, but that was about it.

No wonder then that slave revolts broke out in October 1801.
Toussaint ordered that they be suppressed mercilessly. Jean-Jacques

Dessalines was particularly brutal in the southern province. Toussaint summoned his nephew Moïse and accused him of encouraging the revolt. Moïse and another officer were executed. Toussaint's obsession with power seems to have deranged his mind, because in subsequent speeches he denounced Moïse and warned that others who defied him would share his fate. He blamed the revolts on parents who produced "bad citizens, vagabonds and thieves."[27] He attacked those who were "without religion" and called for strict surveillance of workers. He authorized a new system of national identification cards specifying where each individual must work; the government would enforce penalties against those found not to have an ID card. Thus, Toussaint the liberator took one step after another toward a modern police state, much like Napoleon, his adversary across the Atlantic.

According to government statistics, for whatever they might be worth, plantation production revived from virtually nothing during the worst civil war years. In 1801, coffee exports were reported to be approximately two-thirds of what they had been in 1789. Sugar plantations were harder to restore than coffee plantations, so in 1802, refined sugar exports were said to be just one-third of what they had been in 1789. These reports of one- or two-year gains, if true, probably reveal less about the success of forced labor than about what can be accomplished when wartime destruction ends and people are able to work, and when workers are given some compensation.

In 1802, Napoleon had his brother-in-law Charles Victor Emmanuel Leclerc lead a fleet of French ships and some 7,000 soldiers to Saint-Domingue, supposedly to help protect against "enemies of the Republic." Napoleon declared, "The French nation will never place shackles on men it has recognized as free." On board one of the ships were Toussaint's two sons, Isaac and Placide, who had been educated in France. When news of Napoleon's move reached Britain, the abolitionist James Stephen reasoned that France couldn't manage colonies where people were enslaved, when people were free in other colonies. Consequently, he concluded, "The true, though unavowed purpose of the French government in this expedition is to restore the old system of negro slavery in St. Domingo, and in the other colonies wherein it has been subverted."

Toussaint heard about the ships, assumed they might be aimed at him and expanded the size of his army to between 23,000 and 30,000 soldiers. He could also draw on local militias with perhaps

10,000 soldiers. He reviewed the loyalty of his top officers and ordered that his forces be prepared to prevent any warships from entering any ports.

The French ships arrived off the coast of Saint-Domingue in January 1802. Leclerc sent a message to Christophe, Toussaint's commander at Le Cap, saying he would be landing soldiers to help control "rebels." Christophe was given a letter from Napoleon: "If you are told: these forces are meant to take away your liberty, you must respond: the Republic gave us liberty, and the Republic would not accept that it be taken away from us." Leclerc warned that there would be serious consequences if there was resistance to French soldiers. When French soldiers landed, they were fired on, and Christophe's men burned Le Cap so that nothing would fall into French hands. The French captured some blacks and soon sold them into slavery. The French general Donatien Marie Joseph de Rochambeau—who had helped the Americans defeat British general Charles Cornwallis at Yorktown—overwhelmed and slaughtered Toussaint's defenders at Fort-Liberté. Some of Toussaint's officers in Port-au-Prince supported Napoleon and helped the French capture that town, and Toussaint ordered that it be burned. He ordered that wherever the French might march, everything be burned or otherwise destroyed, so "those who have come to put us back into slavery will always find in front of them the image of the hell that they deserve."

Leclerc tried to sweet-talk Toussaint. He had Toussaint's sons deliver a letter promising that Toussaint would "no longer have any worries." Lerclerc promised to respect the liberty of people in Saint-Domingue. When it became clear that Toussaint wasn't responding, Leclerc declared war.

Leclerc was aware of his weaknesses. Although he had fresh troops, they were poorly provisioned—especially not enough food or shoes. They paid a steep premium for local supplies and were beginning to feel the effects of tropical diseases such as yellow fever. Guerrilla warfare in a tropical environment posed challenges that didn't play to the strengths of conventional French forces. The French were stymied by defenders burning everything in sight as they retreated. As French forces approached Saint-Marc, where Dessalines was based, he burned his new mansion.

One atrocity led to another. Enraged at the destruction wrought by the French, Dessalines authorized indiscriminate slaughter of

whites. On one occasion he slaughtered some 800 whites rather than keep them as prisoners.

Toussaint's position was seriously undermined when Christophe, who commanded about 1,500 soldiers plus hundreds of cultivators, surrendered to the French and agreed to fight for the French. This seems to have convinced Toussaint that he couldn't hold on. He contacted Leclerc. On May 7, 1802, they signed an agreement providing that Toussaint would retire to a plantation he owned at Ennery, his soldiers would become part of the French army, and there would be no slavery in Saint-Domingue. But Leclerc perceived Toussaint's presence as a potential threat, and in June Leclerc invited Toussaint to a meeting at which his guards were overwhelmed and he was arrested. When he was grilled, Toussaint acknowledged that his holdings were substantial, including several plantations and ranches with cattle and horses. But Toussaint was cash-poor, because he had spent almost everything defending the colony.[28] He was sent to France and imprisoned at Fort-de-Joux, in the Alps. There, in a dungeon, he died on April 7, 1803, officially of pneumonia.

The French were thrilled, but their troubles mounted. Yellow fever raged among the troops. During 1802, reportedly 100 French soldiers a day died from yellow fever. In 1803, two regiments of Polish soldiers arrived to help the French, but within 10 days half of those soldiers had died from yellow fever. Although tens of thousands of European soldiers had arrived in Saint-Domingue, Leclerc had only about 10,000 capable of fighting.

Leclerc had hoped to cripple black resistance by deporting all the black generals, but European forces were so depleted by war and disease that he needed their leadership in the field. Increasingly, he came to depend on Dessalines, Christophe and other black generals. If they hadn't helped him, he would have been wiped out quickly. Dessalines was as ruthless to blacks as he had been to whites. In one raid, he captured women and children and massacred them. Leclerc hailed Dessalines as "the butcher of blacks."

Dessalines's ruthlessness won the respect of the French who assigned him the task of disarming blacks. But after he seized guns, he secretly returned many of them and kept many for himself as he stockpiled supplies for his own forces. The French policy of disarming blacks spread fear and soon inspired new revolts against the French. The black general San-Souci, who had gone over to the French side, defected and began

fighting the French again as more and more blacks joined the insurrection. The blacks were blocking roads, ambushing French soldiers and destroying whatever might be of value to the French.

Leclerc launched what he called a "war of extermination." He wrote Napoleon: "We must destroy all the blacks of the mountains—men and women." He believed the ultimate solution for Saint-Domingue was to wipe out all the blacks who had known some liberty and import black Africans who knew only slavery.[29] He ordered the execution of officers on the suspicion that they might have been supporting the rebels. Black soldiers who had fought loyally with the French were shot without a hearing or trial. Leclerc ordered the arrest of about 1,000 black soldiers in Le Cap, loaded them on ships, had a sack of flour tied to each one, then pushed them into the sea. Leclerc distrusted the black general Maurepas, so Leclerc had him and his family drowned in Le Cap harbor. He drowned the wife and children of black general Paul Louverture (who wasn't around at the time). Altogether, Leclerc was reported to have ordered the drowning of some 4,000 black officers, soldiers and family members. Such was the fear Leclerc inspired that after he captured several hundred black soldiers, almost all strangled themselves rather than be tortured or executed. Since siding with the French no longer assured safety from the French, more people went into rebellion. Leclerc died from yellow fever, on November 1, 1802.

Leclerc's comrade Rochambeau rivaled him for savagery. He had his black captives burned alive, hanged, shot and crucified. Such practices drove the *gens de couleur* into an alliance with blacks who had long been their adversaries. Large numbers of plantation cultivators, terrified of the French, swarmed into active opposition.

Further contributing to the rebellion was news that Napoleon ordered the restoration of slavery in the French island of Guadeloupe, as it had been practiced before the French Revolution. The French slave trade was revived. Then came reports about anti-black laws in France. Black soldiers weren't permitted to enter Paris or French port cities; black sailors had to stay in their ships when they anchored in French harbors. Eventually, blacks were banned from the "continental territory of the Republic." It became increasingly clear that Napoleon would restore slavery to Saint-Domingue.

In May 1803, France was again at war with Britain, which meant the end of French efforts to subdue Saint-Domingue. Because of the

high death rate in Saint-Domingue, the military couldn't persist without a continuing flow of reinforcements, but war with Britain meant that available troops would have to be deployed against Britain. In November 1803, French troops withdrew to Le Cap, where they surrendered and, shelled by rebels, they boarded British ships as prisoners. The long struggle to abolish slavery and gain independence from France had cost some 100,000 lives.[30] Napoleon was reported to have snarled: "Damn sugar! Damn coffee! Damn colonies!"

By this time, Dessalines had unified most of the rebel forces and emerged as the strongman of Saint-Domingue. He rejected a draft declaration of independence modeled after the American Declaration of Independence, instead asserting the rights of black people and their complaints against France. He accepted a declaration that railed against French barbarism.

Independence was declared on January 1, 1804. The new nation was called Haiti, the name believed to have been given the island by the indigenous Taino people. History's first successful slave revolt emancipated perhaps 450,000 slaves who survived the fighting.[31] Haiti became the second independent country in the western hemisphere.

British Abolitionists' Peaceful Campaign against Slavery

Many an Englishman made a fortune in the slave trade during the eighteenth century. In London, Bristol, Liverpool and other English ports, merchants thrived by selling the trinkets, cloth and guns that West African chiefs wanted in exchange for slaves, as well as the customary ships' supplies and slaving gear such as whips, branding irons and neck braces. Each voyage tended to be a separately financed business venture, and many English investors specialized in analyzing the opportunities and risks of proposed slave-trading voyages. In peacetime, an investor might net 8 percent, while during a war—if and when slave ships were able to get through naval blockades—profits might range from 75 to 150 percent.[1] Even a ship's doctor or carpenter might acquire a slave who could be sold for some extra money.

The world's first organized movement to abolish slavery arose from unexpected places: amidst the cauldron of natural rights ideas that had been simmering for decades, from Quakers who were most concerned about ending the violence of slavery, from some path-breaking court cases, from courageous eyewitnesses and individuals who devoted their lives to moving the abolitionist cause forward.

Granville Sharp Takes Slavery to Court

Curiously, nobody could say for sure what the legal status of slaves was in England during the early eighteenth century. There weren't any statutes that permitted or banned slavery. Some court decisions favored the slaveholder, while other court decisions favored the slave. In his *Commentaries on the Law of England* (1765–1769), the English judge and Oxford University professor William Blackstone declared that "slavery does not, nay cannot, subsist in England: such, I mean, whereby an absolute and unlimited power is given to the master over the life and fortune of the slave. And indeed it is repugnant to reason, and the principles of natural law, that such a state should subsist any where." Blackstone continued, "upon these principles the law of England abhors, and will not endure the existence of, slavery within this nation . . . And now it is laid down, that a slave or negro, the instant he lands in England, becomes a freeman; that is, the law will protect him in the enjoyment of his person and his property."[2] Nonetheless, there were an estimated 15,000 slaves in Britain during the eighteenth century.[3]

In 1767 the case of Jonathan Strong, a black slave about 17 years old who had been pistol-whipped in London by his owner, David Lisle, a lawyer from Barbados, struck a blow against slavery in England. Apparently somebody brought Strong to the Mincing Lane office of William Sharp, the king's surgeon who spent a lot of time attending the medical needs of the poor.[4] At the time, Sharp's brother Granville happened to be visiting and offered to help. Strong was admitted to St. Bartholomew's Hospital, and when he was discharged four months later, the Sharps provided follow-up care and helped Strong get a job as an errand boy for a chemist's shop on Fenchurch Street.

The Sharps, it might be noted, were members of a well-known musical family who traveled together on waterways around London on a barge-houseboat, giving concerts. William played the organ and French horn; Granville played clarinet, oboe and kettledrums. London's National Portrait Gallery has a painting by the German neoclassical painter Johan Zoffany that shows 16 members of the Sharp family on their barge-houseboat, *Apollo*.

Two years after Strong was beaten, Lisle happened to see him walking in London. Lisle arranged to have him captured and locked

in the Poultry Street jail, then sold him to plantation owner James Kerr who was headed for Jamaica. Somehow Strong got word to Granville Sharp who contacted the Lord Mayor of London. He summoned anybody claiming Strong to appear in court. Kerr's lawyer presented the bill of sale for Strong. The Lord Mayor ruled that nobody could be rightfully imprisoned unless charged with a crime. Accordingly, Strong was released. When there was an attempt outside the court to recapture Strong, Sharp threatened to file assault charges.

Lisle and Kerr subsequently filed a £200 lawsuit against Sharp for damages. Sharp's lawyer advised him to settle the dispute rather than to continue an expensive legal battle, because Lord Mansfield, chief justice of the King's Bench—roughly comparable to the U.S. Supreme Court—had previously upheld property claims for slaves. But Sharp was a stubborn, fearless, litigious man. He had spent huge amounts of time on much less important disputes. For instance, after he had been accused of failing to understand the Christian doctrine of the Holy Trinity, he learned enough Greek to research and write a pamphlet, *Remarks on the Uses of the Definitive Article in the Greek Text of the New Testament.* Sharp got into an argument with a Jew who challenged Christian doctrine, which promoted Sharp to study Hebrew.

Sharp spent about two years preparing his case. He searched through dusty records of statutes, proclamations and court proceedings, perhaps going back centuries, looking for anything that related to slavery. For instance, in a trial involving an escaped slave, around 1702, Lord Chief Justice John Holt ruled that "one may be a villeyn in England but not a slave." This view had prevailed for decades. Sharp drafted a brief arguing that slavery in England couldn't be defended based on any of the available legal records. He submitted his draft to William Blackstone himself. While Blackstone couldn't disagree with Sharp's argument, he recommended that Sharp drop the case because "it will be uphill work in the Court of King's Bench."[5] Blackstone did agree to offer advice for Sharp's defense.

Sharp decided that his best bet might be to try to sway influential London lawyers, and he circulated 20 copies of his brief. Evidently there wasn't any sympathy for Lisle and Kerr, and they decided to drop their lawsuit. They were fined triple the court costs. Sharp subsequently published his brief as a tract, *The Injustice and dangerous Tendency of tolerating Slavery in England* (1769).

Anthony Benezet, a Pennsylvania Quaker, saw the pamphlet, and the two men began to correspond. Sharp turned out more pamphlets, the most incendiary of which was perhaps *The Law of Retribution; or, a serious warning to Great Britain and her colonies, founded on unquestionable examples of God's temporal vengeance against tyrants, slave-holders and oppressors* (London, 1776).

Although Sharp won the Strong case, there wasn't any judicial decision stating general principles that would help eliminate slavery in Britain, which is why Sharp was determined to handle more cases involving slaves. His principal adversary was Lord Chief Justice Mansfield who had read his brief and evidently found it compelling and disturbing. Since Mansfield believed that private property was essential for liberty, providing a sanctuary where people could live free from outside interference, he was uncomfortable with the view that there was a conflict between liberty and private property, at least in a legal system permitting the sale of human beings. Sharp filed lawsuits with some success for former slaves Mary Hylas, Thomas Lewis and others. But judges rendered narrow decisions that didn't establish any precedents to protect former slaves who might be kidnapped in the future.

Sharp did better with his lawsuit on behalf of James Somerset who had been brought to England in 1769 by his owner, Charles Stewart, a Boston customs official. Somerset had escaped two years later but was captured in November 1771 and put on board a ship that would leave for Jamaica. Before the ship departed, Sharp obtained an order for Somerset to appear in the court of the King's Bench. The judge set a January 1772 trial date. Publicity about the case led several lawyers to volunteer their time for Somerset. Francis Hargrave played the lead role in this, his first trial. He argued that slavery was contrary to English contract law, which didn't permit an individual to enslave himself. A contract was invalid unless all parties entered into it voluntarily. Hargrave insisted that although there was slavery in British colonies, slavery was contrary to the laws of England, and there couldn't be any slavery unless Parliament passed a law making it legal, which it had not done. In an apparent effort to avoid issuing a controversial decision against slavery, Lord Mansfield repeatedly urged a settlement of the case. Since neither side was willing to compromise, he had to issue a decision.

On June 22, 1772, he ruled that "no master was ever allowed here to take a slave by force to be sold abroad because he deserted from his service, or for any other reason whatever." However, he said nothing

about enforcing his ruling. Nor did he say that slavery was illegal in England. Although this decision was carefully crafted to provide min-imal support for emancipation, it was widely publicized in newspapers and magazines, and most people—including lower-level judges—got the impression that slavery was illegal in Britain. Subsequent court rulings rejected claims to own slaves in Britain.[6] News of the decision, often oversimplified, reached America, and there were reports that some slaves ran away from their plantations and became stowaways on ships bound for England, where they hoped to be free.

Joseph Knight, an African slave, was taken to Jamaica and then went with his master to Scotland in 1769. When he heard about Mans-field's decision, he demanded that his master pay him wages for his work. When his master refused, he ran away but was caught and ar-rested. The case was heard by the sheriff of Perth who declared that Scotland didn't have slavery and that a slave brought to Scotland must be set free. Knight's master appealed to the Court of Session in Edin-burgh, in which the full panel of judges heard the case. The judges ruled that "The dominion assumed over the negro, under the law of Jamaica, being unjust, could not be supported in this country to any extent."[7] The eminent Samuel Johnson had helped Knight prepare his brief.

Johnson dominated the literary life of his time as a critic, essayist, biographer and lexicographer. He had expressed his hatred of slavery many times. Referring to Americans who proclaimed their ideals of liberty while enslaving Africans, he famously asked: "How is it that we hear the loudest yelps for liberty among the drivers of negroes?" Johnson's biographer James Boswell recalled, "Upon one occasion, when in company with some very grave men at Oxford, his toast was, 'Here's to the next insurrection of the negroes in the West Indies.' His violent prejudice against our West Indian and American settlers ap-peared whenever there was an opportunity."

Among the most interesting people Granville Sharp met in the simmering abolitionist movement was Olaudah Equiano. Born near the Niger River, Equiano had been sold into slavery when he was 11 and shipped across the Atlantic. He was purchased by Royal Navy Lieutenant Michael Pascal who renamed him Gustavus Vassa. During the Seven Years' War with France, the British needed all the help they could get, so it wasn't surprising that Equiano was given naval training and taught to read. Following the war, he was sold on Montserrat, in

the Caribbean. He was bought by Quaker merchant Robert King and, with his skills, helped in the business. King let Equiano do some trading for himself, and he managed to save enough money to buy his freedom. After attending some religious meetings, he became a Christian. While traveling on business to Georgia, he was nearly kidnapped into slavery. Equiano concluded he would be safest in England, so he sailed there, helped the abolitionist movement and wrote his memoir, *Interesting Narrative of the Life of Olaudah Equiano, or Gustavus Vassa, the African* (1789).

Wesley's Influence

Apparently spurred by news of the Somerset case, John Wesley began reading Anthony Benezet's book, *Some Historical Account of Guinea* (1771). The graphic description of slavery horrified him.

Wesley was one of the most influential preachers of his day, the cofounder of Methodism. Although he was barely five feet three inches tall, he had tremendous energy and projected great confidence. He preached at a time when the Church of England had become quite corrupt. High church officials had little to do with local parishes because they were busy hobnobbing with government officials and aristocrats. Few members of Parliament bothered going to church. Determined to energize English religion in England, Wesley founded the Methodist movement at Oxford University in 1729, embracing austere, methodical religious practices that led to "Methodism"—a term of derision given by its critics.[8]

John Wesley was born in 1703, in Epworth, England, the fifteenth child of an Anglican minister. He graduated from Christ Church College, Oxford, and worked with his father for two years. He was inspired by the religious revival of the 1730s known as the Great Awakening. In 1736, James Oglethorpe, a British general, invited Wesley to serve as a missionary in Georgia, the American colony he had founded. Wesley refused to marry or bury those he disapproved of. He wouldn't tolerate ladies dressed in fancy clothing. He urged the colonial governor to ban fishing on Sunday. He soon came to despise the white population that included many criminals expelled from Britain, and he did no better preaching among the Indians. By the end of December 1737, he fled Georgia for Charleston where he boarded a ship

sailing back to England. The one useful experience Wesley gained in Georgia was seeing plantation slavery firsthand—he detested it.

Wesley and his brother Charles, the eighteenth child in the family, cobbled together an evangelical doctrine of redemption, with elements drawn from the Anglican Church, the Moravian Brethren, the Quakers and others. They stressed the Moravian doctrine that conversion could assure redemption from sin and they traveled from town to town preaching. They tried to remain within the Anglican Church, but Anglican officials wouldn't have it, and they were forced to develop a separate Protestant denomination.

George Whitefield, a fellow Oxford graduate II years younger than Wesley, became even more influential in the development of Methodism, particularly in America. He was a charismatic figure who spoke to thousands at a time up and down the East Coast. When he preached in Philadelphia, Benjamin Franklin walked around the area occupied by the crowds and estimated that there were about 20,000 people.[9]

While Whitefield defended slavery, Wesley emerged as a passionate opponent of slavery. This was noteworthy because Wesley was a Tory (a conservative) who accepted England's aristocratic social order. During the American Revolution, he sided with King George III. He supported anti-Catholic laws in England. In 1774 Wesley wrote a pamphlet titled *Thoughts Upon Slavery.* He concluded by declaring that respectable slaveholders were responsible for the hideous crimes of capturing slaves in Africa: "It is your money that pays the merchant, and through him the captain and the African butchers. You therefore are guilty, yea, principally guilty, of all these frauds, robberies, and murders."

The *Zong* Incident and Thomas Clarkson

In 1781, an incident shocked the British people into recognizing the horrors of slavery. While the slave ship *Zong* was sailing from West Africa to Jamaica, disease spread among the approximately 400 slaves. Captain Luke Collingwood faced the prospect of a large number of deaths, and he knew the ship's insurance company didn't cover such losses. But the company would cover the loss of property thrown overboard to save the ship. Accordingly, Collingwood ordered that 132 of

the sickest slaves be pushed overboard to drown. He coached his officers to say that the ship was running out of drinking water, and the action was essential to save the rest of the slaves and the crew. When the ship returned to England, its owners filed an insurance claim for the lost slaves, but the insurance company disputed it. In the ensuing trial, in March 1783, the judge ruled in favor of the ship's owners, even though Chief Mate James Kelsal testified that the ship had plenty of water and therefore pushing the slaves overboard wasn't necessary to save the ship. The insurance company appealed.

Granville Sharp read about the case and he recognized an opportunity to strike another blow against slavery. He hired lawyers and interviewed a witness who had seen slaves being pushed overboard. He wrote angry letters to Britain's prime minister, the Earl of Shelburne, as well as to naval officials and a number of newspapers. Collingwood had succumbed to disease before the end of the *Zong*'s fateful voyage, but Sharp urged that the other responsible officers be prosecuted for murder. Sharp's old adversary Lord Mansfield presided. Mansfield maintained that the proceeding was about property loss, not about murder and he upheld the earlier trial verdict. Sharp failed in his efforts, but he wrote letters informing influential people about what happened.

Apparently Sharp stirred at least one person into action. In 1784 Dr. Peter Peckard, an Anglican priest, became vice chancellor of Cambridge University, and he announced that the topic of the university's most prestigious Latin essay competition would be the legality of slavery. One of the students who entered the competition was Thomas Clarkson, the 25-year-old son of a deceased clergyman, intent on following in his father's footsteps. Clarkson had a memorable presence—six feet tall with red hair and blue eyes.[10] Clarkson hadn't considered the issue of slavery before, but with the prodigious energy that was to be a hallmark of his career, he gathered information about slavery. Shocked at what he learned, he wrote the prize-winning essay and found his calling.

He decided he wouldn't become an Anglican minister as he had planned, and instead he would devote his life to the cause of abolishing slavery in the British empire. This was a bold decision, because he didn't have much money. He began by translating his Latin essay into English, and in 1786 it was published as *An essay on the slavery and commerce of the human species, particularly the African, translated from a Latin Dissertation, which was honoured with the first prize at the University of Cambridge, for the year 1785.*

This work brought Clarkson to the attention of many people who were concerned about ending the slave trade, among them Granville Sharp and James Ramsay who had been a naval surgeon. Back in 1759, Charles Middleton, the commander of Ramsay's ship, the *Arundel,* had asked him to inspect the *Swift,* a slave ship captured from the French. Ramsay was shocked by the barbaric treatment of the slaves. Soon afterward, he quit the navy and settled on St. Kitts where he became an Anglican priest serving two churches. He also worked as a doctor for two sugar plantations. He did everything he could to help the slaves, even inviting them to his church services, for which he was strongly disliked by the St. Kitts slaveholders. Ramsay had been living on St. Kitts for 19 years when in 1781 his former naval commander Middleton invited him to take over as priest of the Teston parish church near the Middletons' home in England. Ramsay did that and for three years worked on his *Essay on the Treatment and Conversion of African Slaves in the British Sugar Colonies.* This provoked a storm of controversy after it was published in 1784. It was perhaps the first antislavery tract to have an impact in England.

Sharp and Ramsay had joined a committee to fight slavery, started in 1783 by six Quakers—William Dillwyn, George Harrison, Samuel Hoare, Thomas Knowles, John Lloyd and Joseph Woods. The committee began to write newspaper articles and pamphlets about the horrors of slavery. Their first pamphlet was *The Case of our fellow-creatures, the oppressed Africans* (1784). The following year, the committee distributed to schools one of Anthony Benezet's pamphlets about slavery in the West Indies.

In April 1787, the Quakers and their allies formed the Society for Effecting the Abolition of the Slave Trade. Granville Sharp, their first chairman, urged that they aim to liberate slaves, but the consensus was that suppressing the slave trade was tough enough, and if they could do that, they would be in a better position to abolish slavery.[11] Clarkson was hired as a full-time researcher, organizer and publicist. He was inspired by American as well as British friends of liberty who had preceded him—Anthony Benezet, Benjamin Rush, Benjamin Franklin and others.

Clarkson recognized that to win political support for abolishing slavery, he must somehow overthrow the widely held belief that slavery was essential for British national security and prosperity. He had to counter the claim that the slave trade was a "nursery of seamen," without which the Royal Navy might not be able to find enough recruits.

On the Thames in London, he boarded a slave ship, the *Fly*, to see for himself what it was like. "The sight of the rooms below and of the gratings above, and of the equipment, and the explanation of the uses of all these, filled me both with melancholy and horror. I found soon afterwards a fire of indignation kindling within me. I had now scarce patience to talk with those on board. I had not the coolness this first time to go leisurely over the places that were open to me. I got away quickly."[12]

Clarkson embarked on an exhaustive research project that nobody had attempted before. He traveled to Bristol and Liverpool, principal centers of the British slave trade, to see how the business was conducted. Clarkson interviewed sailors who had worked on slave ships and inspected documents that revealed the shockingly large number of slave deaths on the voyages from Africa to the western hemisphere.

Clarkson brought with him letters from Quaker friends, introducing him to their friends in the respective cities, who in turn introduced him to people knowledgeable about the slave-trading business. For example, in Bristol he met Alexander Falconbridge, a surgeon who declared, "I have done with the slave trade." Falconbridge helped Clarkson deal with often hostile slave ship officers.[13]

Apparently the encounter with Clarkson led Falconbridge to write *An Account of the Slave Trade on the Coast of Africa.* He reported that "The Negroes, upon being brought onto the ship, are immediately fastened together, two and two, by handcuffs on their wrists and by irons riveted on their legs. They are then sent down below decks and placed in an apartment partitioned off for that purpose. . . . They are frequently stowed so close as to admit no other position than lying on their sides." Falconbridge told how the cramped slave quarters became filled with human waste. Slaves who refused to eat their wretched food were punished in gruesome ways. Hot coals might be forced into their mouths. Melted lead might be poured on them.[14]

Many of the survivors were seriously ill by the time they arrived in the New World, and Falconbridge reported some of the methods used to convince prospective buyers that they were healthy and valuable. For example, when a ship had slaves suffering from dysentery, a Liverpool captain

directed the ship's surgeons to stop the anus of each of them with oakum [unravelled rope fibers]. Thus prepared they were landed

and taken to the accustomed place of sale, where, being unable to stand but for a very short time, they were usually permitted to sit. The buyers, when they examined them, oblige them to stand up in order to see if there be any discharge; and when they do not perceive this appearance they consider it as a symptom of recovery . . . such an appearance being prevented, the bargain was struck and the slaves were accordingly sold. But it was not long before discovery ensued. The excruciating pain which the prevention of a discharge of such an acrimonious nature occasioned, not being able to be borne by the poor wretches, the temporary obstruction was removed and the deluded purchasers were speedily convinced of the imposition.[15]

Most slaves, Clarkson found, had been victims of African oppression or tribal conflicts, captured as prisoners-of-war. Many slaves had been sold to pay debts, others enslaved as punishment for alleged crimes, and still others household slaves resold for a profit.

What Clarkson learned about the trans-Atlantic voyages was utterly at odds with accounts offered by slave-trading interests. "The slaves who had been described as rejoicing in their captivity," he explained,

were so wrung with misery at leaving their country, that it was the constant practice to set sail in the night, lest they should know the moment of their departure. With respect to their accommodation, the right ankle of one was fastened to the left ankle of another by an iron fetter; and if they were turbulent, by another on the wrists. Instead of the apartments described, they were placed in niches, and along the decks, in such a manner, that it was impossible for any one to pass among them, however careful he might be, without treading upon them. Instead of the scent of frankincense, the stench was intolerable. The allowance of water was so deficient that the slaves were frequently found gasping for life and almost suffocated. With respect to their singing, it consisted of songs of lamentation for the loss of their country.[16]

Not surprisingly, since slaves were chained into tight spaces, lying in their own excrement, without adequate food or water, they were vulnerable to whatever disease somebody might bring on board. Tens of thousands of slaves perished on the voyages.

In the process of gathering information about the slave trade, Clarkson became aware that British seamen on slave ships were no less

vulnerable to the contagions of these voyages and often they too were subjected to cruel treatment. One of the most notorious cases involved Peter Green, a steward on a Liverpool ship who was savagely beaten for refusing to give the key for a liquor cabinet to a woman named Rodney.

The captain, Clarkson explained,

> beat him severely, and ordered his hands to be made fast to some bolts on the starboard side of the ship and under the half deck, and then flogged him himself, using the lashes of the cat-of-nine-tails upon his back at one time, and the double walled knot at the end of it upon his head or another; and stopping to rest at intervals, and using each hand alternatively that he might strike with the greater severity.
>
> The pain had now become so very severe, that Green cried out. He called upon the chief mate, but this only made matters worse, for the captain then ordered the chief mate to flog him also, which he did for some time. Green then called in his distress upon the second mate to speak for him, but the second mate was immediately ordered to perform the same cruel office, and was made to persevere in it till the lashes were all worn into threads. But the barbarity did not close here, for the captain, on seeing the instrument now become useless, ordered another, with which he flogged him as before, beating him at times over the head with the double-walled knot.
>
> The punishment, as inflicted by all parties, had now lasted two hours and a half, when a crewman was ordered to cut down one of the arms, and the boatswain the other. Green lay motionless on the deck. He attempted to utter something which was understood to be "water," but no water was allowed him. The captain said he had not yet done with him, and ordered him put in shackles. He was hoisted up and let down in a boat and left there.[17]

He was later found dead.

Clarkson copied ships' records listing all the crewmen who had been on board each voyage and what happened to them—whether they were discharged, had deserted or had died. Altogether he accumulated records on thousands of crewmen. He determined that more British seamen died on slave ships than in all other areas of British shipborne commerce combined. Clarkson concluded that far from being an essential "nursery for seamen," as proslavery interests claimed, "it

was their grave."[18] Based on this research, he wrote *A Summary View of the Slave Trade and of the Probable Consequences of Its Abolition* (1787).

Would Parliament Champion Abolition?

While the British abolitionist movement was starting to develop, it didn't have any political influence. It needed someone who could champion the cause in Parliament. The best prospect seemed to be William Wilberforce, a popular member of the House of Commons and an effective extemporaneous speaker, although he didn't look like much. He was short and thin, but he was sincere, outgoing, charming and witty.[19]

Wilberforce was born in Hull, perhaps the biggest English port that wasn't involved with the slave trade. Wilberforce's father, William, had made a fortune in the Baltic trade and was elected mayor of Hull. He died when his son was 19. Young William was influenced by George Whitefield to embrace Methodism, but his mother and grandfather were respectable Anglicans and disapproved. He was sent to Pocklington School and St. John's College, Cambridge University, where he learned to enjoy plays, drinking and other amusements frowned on by Methodists.

Wilberforce didn't want to join his father's business, so he spent perhaps £9,000 of his inheritance to campaign for a seat in Parliament. In September 1780, at age 21, he was elected as a Tory from Hull. He became a close friend of William Pitt the Younger who in December 1783, at age 24, became prime minister. Pitt was tall and thin. He seemed to be awkward outside the House of Commons, but he blossomed there and dominated it for more than two decades.[20] Parliament was dissolved in 1784, and Wilberforce decided to try for a seat in Yorkshire, the most influential constituency that traditionally had been represented by a landed aristocrat. Although Wilberforce was from a merchant family, he won and emerged as a rising star.

The following year, he began to reflect on all the time he had spent partying and gambling. He talked with Isaac Milner, a Cambridge professor who had embraced John Wesley's Methodism, and with Reverend John Newton, a former slave ship captain. Newton suggested that he use his political talent to do good. Wilberforce consulted his friend Pitt who offered similar advice: "Surely the principles as well as the practice

of Christianity are simple and lead not to meditation only, but to action."[21] Wilberforce decided to quit going to plays, dances, races and social clubs. He began to display a more independent spirit in Parliament, willing to take up an unpopular cause if it was righteous.

A number of people hoped that Wilberforce would embrace the antislavery cause. In 1783 James Ramsay had met Wilberforce and talked passionately about the evils of slavery; Newton, as a slave captain, had shared some of his shocking experiences.[22]

In 1787 Clarkson contacted Wilberforce and suggested that he consider leading the antislavery cause in Parliament. Clarkson and Wilberforce began getting together to discuss slavery. Wilberforce talked about the slavery with Pitt who advised: "Do not lose time, or the ground will be occupied by another."[23] On May 12, 1789, Wilberforce gave his first speech about abolishing the slave trade. Two years later, he introduced his first bill against the slave trade. It was defeated by a vote of 163 to 88, but he had joined the battle.

Thus, the antislavery movement that had begun with a small minority—the Quakers—became a dynamic coalition. Because Methodists had done so much evangelizing in cities, they were able to mobilize urban people. Church of England evangelicals had connections in Parliament.[24] Together, they could accomplish something.

A Glorious Campaign for Abolition

Wilberforce arranged for Clarkson to meet Pitt and present some of his voluminous findings about the shocking number of slaves and British seamen who perished in the slave trade. Clarkson recalled, "When Pitt had looked over about a hundred pages and found the name of every seaman inserted, his former abode or service, the time of his entry and what had become of him, he expressed his surprise at the great pains which had been taken in this branch of the inquiry. He confessed with some emotion that his doubts were wholly removed with respect to the destructive nature of this employ [the slave trade]."[25]

Clarkson visited Manchester and met with leaders of the Society for Constitutional Information, which believed that all men should be entitled to vote. This society embraced the idea of circulating petitions supporting the abolition of the slave trade. By the time they were

done, more than 10,000 people had signed the petitions, about half the male population of the city. Their advertisements placed in the biggest Manchester newspapers encouraged other cities to join the campaign against the slave trade.

Antislavery societies were established in Birmingham, Exeter, Falmouth, Leeds, Norwich, Nottingham, Sheffield, Worcester and York. There were large public meetings run like religious revivals. Clarkson showed the crowds devices used to control and torture slaves, such as iron handcuffs, leg shackles, neck collars, thumb-screws and branding irons—items he had acquired during his visits to slave-trading ports. In addition to Clarkson, featured speakers included former slaves such as Olaudah Equiano (Gustavus Vassa) and Ottobah Cugoano, both of whom testified about the horrors of crossing the Atlantic in a slave ship. Cugoano wrote a pamphlet attacking the slave trade and Equiano's memoir was published in 1789. Former slave ship captain John Newton gave speeches confirming the brutal treatment of slaves.

The emblem of the emerging movement was a drawing of an African slave kneeling in chains, with the motto "Am I Not a Man and a Brother?" Josiah Wedgewood, the porcelain entrepreneur, was among those producing all sorts of things, including plates, cups and jewelry, with the antislavery emblem on it.[26]

Prime Minister Pitt authorized the Privy Council Committee for Trade and Plantations to gather as much information as it could about the slave trade. Before a report was issued, Parliament began debating ways to obtain better treatment for slaves. Overcrowding was thought to be a major cause of slave mortality during transatlantic voyages, so there were efforts to limit the number of slaves that could be carried on a ship. The lower the limit, the lower the potential profits for slave traders. There was agreement on a limit of five slaves per three tons of a ship's weight, up to 200 tons, and one slave per ton above that. Accordingly, Parliament passed the Slave Trade Regulating Act (1788).[27]

Clarkson and his associates circulated petitions and held big public meetings about abolishing the slave trade. Abolitionists solicited the cooperation of churches, local governments and various private associations, so it was easy for people to find and sign an abolitionist petition. Some 400,000 people signed more than 500 antislavery petitions that were presented to Parliament in 1792. This was a high point of the antislavery campaign.[28]

In 1791 and 1792, Wilberforce introduced bills to abolish the slave trade, but they were defeated by West Indian plantation owners who were well represented in Parliament, particularly in the House of Lords, and who maintained it was wrong to undermine anything like the slave trade that was advantageous to their country. The war with France in 1793 meant that reform causes in Great Britain generally were viewed as irresponsible if not unpatriotic radicalism.

Nonetheless, Wilberforce did what he could to keep the abolition movement alive. Simply traveling from one speaking engagement to another was difficult. He arranged to have teams of fresh horses at a succession of points, so he could keep going at full speed and make as many appearances as possible.[29]

Passed as a wartime measure, the Seditious Meetings Act (1795) soon put a stop to abolitionist mass meetings as well as mass meetings for any other political cause. A political meeting of more than 50 people required government approval, and violators were subject to immediate arrest. The Treasonable and Seditious Practices Act (1795) similarly applied to speaking and writing, and antislavery articles and pamphlets ceased to be written. For about a decade, there was little antislavery activity.[30]

Wilberforce valiantly kept introducing bills to abolish the slave trade, in 1795, 1796, 1797, 1798, 1799 and 1802, but they were all defeated. He never got more than 83 votes, less than 15 percent of the House of Commons.[31] By this time Napoleon, Great Britain's dangerous adversary, was trying to restore slavery in Saint-Domingue, which meant that abolitionism could no longer be smeared as a French contagion. Moreover, the Act of Union (1800) that merged Great Britain and Ireland brought Irishmen into Parliament, and many became supportive of the abolitionist cause. In 1804 Wilberforce introduced another bill to abolish the slave trade, and it was defeated, though this time there were 124 "aye" votes in the House of Commons. Wilberforce's 1805 bill was defeated, too.

Wilberforce was anxious to show something for his efforts, and he asked Prime Minister Pitt to use his executive power over sugar-producing Dutch Guyana and French islands that Great Britain had captured in the ongoing Napoleonic wars. Accordingly, on August 15, 1805, Pitt issued an administrative decree that banned the slave trade to those places. The decree put British West Indian plantation owners, primarily the sugar producers, in an awkward political position. Undoubtedly they

were delighted to see their competitors restricted by the slave trade ban, and it was tempting to support the ban. But doing so would have made clear that they were driven by self-interest, not the high-minded ideals they claimed when they fought Wilberforce's slave trade bills.

After Pitt died on January 23, 1806, William Wyndham Grenville (Lord Grenville) became prime minister. He was more committed to abolition than Pitt had been, and because he was a member of the House of Lords, where abolitionists always ran into the most trouble, he was well-positioned to influence the proceedings. He formed a wartime coalition government that became known as the "Ministry of all the Talents." Although it wasn't able to conclude the war with France, it had better luck dealing with the slave trade.

A key man at this point was maritime lawyer James Stephen who had worked in the West Indies for a decade. He pointed out to Wilberforce that most slave ships supplying French Caribbean colonies were British ships flying neutral American flags. The ships sailed with British crews from Liverpool. Stephen noted it would be hard to argue against a bill that prohibited British citizens from trading with Britain's wartime adversary France. The effect of such a bill would be to substantially curtail the British slave trade. Accordingly, Stephen drafted the Foreign Slave Trade Bill that would make it illegal for a British citizen to trade in slaves under a foreign flag or to outfit a foreign-flag slave ship in a British port.[32] The bill quickly passed and became an Act of Parliament on May 23, 1806. It didn't affect the slave trade to British colonies.

Charles James Fox, appointed secretary of state, sought a renewed commitment to abolition of the slave trade. The great nineteenth-century historian Thomas Babington Macaulay called him "the greatest parliamentary defender of civil and religious liberty."[33] When some members proposed to maintain the slave trade by regulating it, Fox had declared that "the Slave Trade could not be regulated, because there could be no regulation of robbery and murder."[34]

On June 10, 1806, Fox offered his resolution: "this House, conceiving the African slave trade to be contrary to the principles of justice, humanity, and sound policy, will, with all practicable expedition, proceed to take effectual measures for abolishing the slave trade." As Wilberforce and Clarkson prepared for a final push for abolition, Wilberforce drafted *A Letter on the Abolition of the Slave Trade* which, published on January 31, 1807, summarized the massive evidence that had been gathered during the previous two decades.

James Stephen had a hand in drafting a new slave trade bill that Lord Grenville introduced in the House of Lords, delivering a passionate speech about the moral issues involved. The bill passed, 41 to 20, a bigger margin than anyone expected. In the House of Commons, amid tributes to Wilberforce, the bill passed by 283 to 16 on February 23. King George III assented, and on March 25, 1807, the slave trade bill became an Act of Parliament. It went into effect May 1, 1807, and provided a penalty of £100 for every slave found on a British ship. The main effect was to make the slave trade contraband, but the law was a crucial beginning.

The Illegal Slave Trade

With the British slave trade banned, the Society for the Abolition of the Slave Trade had completed its mission, and the organization was dissolved. A new organization arose in its place: the African Institution. It had three aims: (1) to make sure there was adequate law enforcement; (2) to promote slave-free commerce with Africa; and (3) to encourage other nations to withdraw from the slave trade as Great Britain had done.

Enforcement of the law against the slave trade was the responsibility of the Royal Navy. Warships were assigned to patrol the Caribbean, on the lookout for British flag slave ships that might be carrying slaves, but it soon became apparent this wasn't enough. Slave trading had to be challenged at its points of origin in Africa. Small naval patrol ships sailed slowly along the coastal shore and along rivers, creeks and lagoons so they could see any signs of slave trading.[35] The pursuit of slave traders became the task of brigs, brigantines and schooners—with 2 to 12 guns each—that could go in shallow waters and move with the often-fickle light tropical breezes. Although the Royal Navy never captured more than a small fraction of ships engaged in the slave trade, its extraordinary tenacity for more than a half-century (chronicled in the next chapter) was essential.

The African Institution tried to promote commerce by developing the West African colony of Sierra Leone. Initially, this was a destination for slaves who had gained their freedom after fighting on the British side during the American Revolution.[36] The colony was run by the Sierra Leone Company, but a substantial number of the settlers

died from tropical diseases. The company lost money, the colony was taken over by the British government, and there was corruption. Freetown, Sierra Leone, however, was a useful base for Royal Navy ships that patrolled the West African coast, looking for slave ships.

The African Institution wasn't able to persuade any other nation to withdraw from the slave trade, in part because everybody in Europe was preoccupied with the wars that raged until Napoleon's defeat and exile to the remote island of St. Helena in the South Atlantic. Then British diplomats began years of negotiations with the major Western slave-trading powers.

As the years passed after the British slave trade was officially abolished, it became apparent that slaves weren't being treated any better. Slaves reported cases of cruelty to missionaries who, in turn, contacted their superiors in Great Britain, and the cases were referred to the Colonial Office. Mindful that antislavery agents were constantly looking for evidence of cruel treatment, colonial officials seem to have become more diligent.[37] However, slavery continued to flourish, and the end was nowhere in sight.

British planters and slave traders disregarded the 1807 law, so three years later Parliament made slave trading a felony. Soon the British flag began to disappear from the slave trade. To have some assurance against seizure, British slave traders had to show a flag of another nation and have proper papers. British planters continued to import slaves from ships flying French, Portuguese, Spanish and American flags. To help stop this, in 1812 Wilberforce began drafting the Slave Registration Bill that would require slaves to be documented—an idea James Stephen had recommended. Slaves without documentation presumably would have been imported after the slave trading ban went into effect. The bill was backed by Prime Minister Spencer Percival, but after he was assassinated that year, Parliament resisted taking further action against the slave trade. By 1815, Wilberforce decided that it was time to focus on the ultimate objective of abolishing slavery.

Emancipating Slaves in British Colonies

Abolitionists had expected that the 1807 law outlawing the slave trade would hasten the end of slavery, but British West Indian planters

stubbornly defended it. They objected to any proposals aimed at emancipating slaves and similarly opposed any proposals that might improve living conditions for slaves. Planters were against giving slaves the right to purchase their freedom, insisting that they must be compensated if slaves were freed.[38]

Although there was gridlock in Parliament as far as slavery was concerned, Great Britain's Colonial Office had the power to strike down laws adopted by colonial assemblies. For example, Colonial Secretary William Huskisson struck down Jamaica's Consolidated Slave Act which, among other things, said that it was illegal for a slave to preach without his or her owner's permission. Even slaves, Huskisson ruled, were entitled to freedom of religion.

By 1821, Wilberforce was beginning to run out of steam. He and the British abolitionist movement had come a long way. When they started, very few people understood what slavery involved since it was mostly out of sight, several thousand miles away across the Atlantic. People wanted their cherished slave-produced products, especially sugar, coffee and cotton. More than two decades later, thanks to the tireless efforts of abolitionists like Wilberforce, there was widespread understanding that slavery was barbaric. Even if the end of slavery was nowhere in sight, there was widespread support for abolishing it.

The most likely successor to Wilberforce as a champion of abolition in Parliament was Thomas Fowell Buxton, who was elected from Weymouth in 1818. Buxton was born in 1786, the year before Wilberforce committed himself to fighting slavery. Although he was an Anglican, Buxton's mother was a Quaker, and he married a Quaker woman. He was impressed by how seriously the Quakers worked to make life better for people. After the slave trade was abolished in 1807, Buxton focused on abolishing slavery itself. In 1823, he helped establish the Society for the Mitigation and Gradual Abolition of Slavery Throughout the British Dominions, otherwise known as the Anti-Slavery Society. It had what seemed to be modest, realistic aims: to improve the treatment of slaves and seek gradual abolition of slavery. Immediate abolition wasn't on their agenda.[39]

Thomas Clarkson, 63, hit the road again to mobilize people for a new campaign against slavery. Within a year, the Anti-Slavery Society had about 230 local organizations, and 777 antislavery petitions were submitted to Parliament, which passed a few meaningless resolutions.[40]

In 1825 Wilberforce retired as abolitionist leader in Parliament, and Buxton agreed to succeed him. At the time, 14 members of the House of Commons and 5 members of the House of Lords—still a small minority—supported the abolition of slavery. The prevailing view was that issues relating to slaves should be left to the colonies, which of course meant that nothing would be changed.

Thwarted in Parliament, some younger members of the Anti-Slavery Society wanted to try generating support for abolition outside of Parliament. Devoutly religious, they insisted that slavery was a sin that must be abolished immediately without compensation for slave-holders. These radicals formed the Agency Committee and hired five speakers, each at an annual salary of £200, to travel around their respective districts giving talks, circulating petitions and encouraging people to form local anti-slavery organizations.[41] Perhaps the best known of the speakers was George Thompson. Apparently hundreds of British antislavery organizations were formed during the 1820s, raising enough money to be self-sustaining. In effect there were two active abolitionist groups, the one lobbying in Parliament and the other operating much like a religious revival. Those involved with the Agency Committee were more inclined to push for immediate abolition of slavery, but because of continued frustration in Parliament, more members of the Anti-Slavery Society came around to that view.

By 1830, British abolitionists had about exhausted their patience. At a May 1830 meeting of the Anti-Slavery Society, there were calls to end the apparently futile compromising and seek the outright abolition of slavery.[42] London officials ignored such demands and affirmed its policy not to "disturb by abrupt and hasty measures the present relations of society in the colonies."

Slaves were losing their patience, too. Race relations were probably worse in Jamaica than anywhere else. There were accumulated frustrations, and expectations were rising as household slaves overheard their masters discussing their concerns about slave revolts and proposals for emancipation. Rumors spread that the king had emancipated slaves, but their masters withheld the news. In 1831 some 30,000 slaves revolted in Jamaica. Sugar plantations were burned, and large numbers of whites fled to coastal ports. This shocking experience led many slaveholders to seriously consider the possibility of emancipation with compensation. They feared that emancipated slaves

might seek retribution against their former masters, but continued enslavement might cause even more bloodshed.

Parliament, however, continued resisting emancipation as it had resisted many other proposed reforms. A principal reason was opposition from members who represented so-called rotten boroughs. These were districts where few people lived, and local landholders largely determined who would represent their interests in Parliament. Such boroughs had persisted for centuries, though they didn't become known as rotten until the eighteenth century. Frustration about stifled reforms generated political pressure to abolish these boroughs and give representation to regions where towns had developed and significant numbers of people lived. The first breakthrough came with the Reform Act of 1832, spearheaded by Henry Peter Brougham, the first Baron Brougham, author, cofounder of the *Edinburgh Review* and presiding officer of the House of Lords in Lord Grey's Whig government. The Reform Act eliminated some of the rotten boroughs and extended representation to many people who had none before. Later acts continued extending the franchise until 1867, when the last rotten boroughs were abolished.

It became increasingly clear that slavery was going to be abolished in Great Britain's Caribbean colonies. But slaveholders still had enough clout in Parliament to prevent immediate emancipation, and there would be a transition period to make things easier for them. In addition, Parliament would have to compensate slaveholders for the loss of their slaves. Of course, it was the slaves who deserved compensation since they had worked long and hard for nothing. This was the position taken by members of the Agency Committee, but they had little direct influence in Parliament. Buxton and his associates on the Anti-Slavery Society supported compensation.[43] After emancipation, former slaveholders and former slaves were probably going to exist in the same society together, and the former slaveholders would still have more money and power. Consequently, the former slaves would be safer if the former slaveholders had the fewest incentives to abuse the former slaves. Parliament discussed lending the slaveholders £15 million to make the transition easier.[44] There was a political backlash against having taxpayers give this much to the former slaveholders after emancipation, and the resulting political pressure probably helped assure the cooperation of the former slaveholders.

Moreover, because emancipation would end the subsidy from slaves when they became free workers receiving compensation, Parliament agreed that sugar from the British colonies could enter Great Britain duty-free, while sugar from other places such as Cuba and Brazil would be subject to high tariffs—the tariff revenue would help fund compensation to former slaveholders. In other words, British consumers would pay a substantial part of the cost of emancipating the slaves.[45]

The ensuing elections brought to Parliament more supporters of reform. Antislavery ideas were considered with Jamaica in mind: If something could work there, probably it could work in any of the colonies. Edward Stanley, secretary of state for the colonies, introduced an abolition bill that provided slaves would be declared free but would be obligated to continue working as unpaid "apprentices" for their masters as long as 12 years, and that slaveholders would receive compensation.[46] Slaveholders complained that the proposed £15 million wasn't enough. Abolitionists opposed "apprenticeship" as slavery by another name. After some political maneuvering, the apprenticeship period was cut to six years, and as compensation the loan became a £20 million gift to slaveholders.[47]

On August 29, 1833, Parliament passed the Slavery Abolition Act, which applied to British colonies throughout the Caribbean. Lord Brougham played a key role securing passage of this law as he had done with the Reform Act. It became effective August 1, 1834. Household slaves were obligated to work as apprentices for four years and were completely free on August 1, 1838; field slaves had to work as apprentices till 1840. Planters were supposed to provide food, clothing, lodging and medical assistance when necessary. Legislatures in the various British Caribbean colonies were left to determine regulations covering the treatment of these apprentices. There was a check on the prerogative of the planters: Britain wouldn't pay any compensation until the colonial legislatures had produced regulations consistent with Parliament's Slavery Abolition Act.[48]

Emancipation affected some 800,000 slaves in Jamaica, Barbados and Britain's other 17 Caribbean colonies. In addition, the law applied to Mauritius, the Cape of Good Hope and Canada (where slavery had almost disappeared). The law didn't apply to British India or Ceylon, where as many as 8 million slaves were held by local people. There were probably another 8 million slaves held in non-British

India.[49] Such slavery went back to antiquity, often related to customs of land tenure long before Europeans arrived on the continent. British policy promoted the abolition of slavery in India and Ceylon, but industrial expansion was crucial to provide employment opportunities outside of agriculture. By ending slavery that the British had once promoted in the West, the 1833 law was a momentous achievement. Edward Stanley declared that Great Britain had embarked on a "mighty experiment." As a peaceful transition to a free society, it was an outstanding success. There was very little violence, a dramatic contrast with the experience in Saint-Domingue.

While British abolitionists had focused on slavery in the British West Indies, American abolitionists were riveted by what the British were doing. William Lloyd Garrison, the Boston-based abolitionist who began publishing the weekly *Liberator* newspaper in 1831, visited Great Britain in 1833. He shared the view of those with the Agency Committee, that slavery was a sin that should be abolished without compensation. Garrison made inquiries about the possibility that George Thompson might make a speaking tour in the United States, which he did in 1834 and 1835. His radical views infuriated so many Americans that he became concerned about his safety and returned to Great Britain. Nonetheless, the experience suggested that British abolitionists had started a movement with international implications. Indeed, Thompson played a role in the formation of two Scottish antislavery societies, one in Edinburgh and the other in Glasgow. The Glasgow Emancipation Society declared that its aim was "the Abolition of Slavery Throughout the World."

"I Bless God"

In the years after emancipation, abolitionists became alarmed at reports that some plantation owners continued to whip their apprentices as they had when the apprentices were slaves. (A new method of punishing apprentices was introduced, namely whipping them to run on a treadmill.) Plantation owners were also said to have withheld some benefits that they used to provide slaves, such as drinking water for those working in fields. In 1834 the wealthy Birmingham Quaker Joseph Sturge and Thomas Harvey, secretary of the Universal Abolition Society, went to Antigua and Jamaica so they could see what was

going on. They subsequently wrote *The West Indies in 1837*, which told how plantation owners abused apprentices to get as much work out of them as possible for as little compensation as possible. Sturge played a key role organizing a campaign against apprenticeship, essentially a rerun of the antislavery campaign that climaxed in 1833, with publicity, petition drives and touring speakers.

In February 1838 Lord Brougham introduced a motion in the House of Lords that called for the immediate end of the apprenticeship system, but it failed to carry. In the House of Commons, George Strickland proposed a similar motion that failed by a margin of 484 to 215. Abolitionists continued bombarding Parliament with petitions, and in May Eardly Wilmot reintroduced an antiapprenticeship motion in the House of Commons. The motion passed by a slim majority. By this time, plantation owners were beginning to get the hint. They concluded they would be better off abolishing apprenticeship themselves rather than waiting until Great Britain forced them to. By July 1838 the colonial assemblies of Nevis, the Virgin Islands, Grenada, St. Vincent, St. Kitts, Barbados, British Guyana, Tobago, the Bahamas, Dominica, Jamaica and Trinidad all abolished apprenticeship.

While abolitionists recognized that the struggle against slavery was far from over, they were jubilant that British West Indian slavery was gone. Thomas Buxton declared, "I bless God that He, who has always raised up agents such as the crisis requires, sent you to the West Indies."[50]

Chapter 5

British Diplomats and Commanders Struggle to Stop the Slave Trade

The British realized that their withdrawal from the slave trade would be meaningless unless other nations could be persuaded to withdraw too. The task of persuading others was left to the British Foreign Office.

The first opportunity arose with Portugal. In November 1807 Portuguese Prince Regent Dom João fled his homeland to avoid an invasion by one of Napoleon's commanders, Jean-Andoche Junot. Dom João was escorted by four British warships to Portugal's principal colony, Brazil, where he established a Portuguese government-in-exile in Rio de Janeiro. In 1810, returning the favor of British protection, Dom João opened Brazil's ports to British merchant ships. He also signed a treaty with Britain, acknowledging the "injustice and disutility" of slavery and agreeing to help adopt "the most efficacious measures for bringing about the gradual abolition of the slave trade through the whole of his dominions." This was the first time a Portuguese government had committed itself to abolishing the slave trade.[1]

Not much else could be done about the slave trade because everyone in Europe was preoccupied with the Napoleonic Wars. The French had declared war against Britain in 1793, and Napoleon had

emerged as one of the most serious threats the British ever faced. The Royal Navy was tied up maintaining a blockade of European ports, making it harder for Napoleon to replenish his supplies, but he dominated the European continent.

By 1814, the tide had turned. Devastated by his disastrous Russian campaign and overwhelmed by the nations allied against him, Napoleon abdicated as emperor on April 11. He was subsequently banished to exile on Elba, a small island off Italy's Tuscan coast. The Treaty of Paris, signed May 14, 1814, officially ended the war between France and the Sixth Coalition (Great Britain, Prussia, Russia, Austria and Sweden), rolled back French borders to where they had been in 1792 and referred other territorial revisions in Europe to the Congress of Vienna.

Representatives of Great Britain, Prussia, Russia and Austria convened the Congress of Vienna, which met from September 1, 1814, to June 9, 1815. Great Britain was represented by Foreign Secretary Robert Stewart (Viscount Castlereagh), Prussia, by its chancellor, Prince Karl August von Hardenberg, and by scholar Wilhelm von Humboldt. Tsar Alexander I and his foreign minister Count Nesselrode represented Russia. Austrian foreign minister Klemens Wenzel von Metternich presided.

After King Louis XVIII came to power in France, his foreign minister Charles Maurice de Talleyrand-Périgord joined the proceedings. The allies hoped to keep him in the background, but he asserted French interests early on. He was joined by the Spanish representative, the Marquis de Labrado, who challenged the dominance of the major allies.

Castlereagh was determined to assure the security of Great Britain by restoring the balance of power in Europe. He aimed to do this by transforming the wartime alliance against Napoleon into an ongoing alliance for peace. Accordingly, he forged the Quadruple Alliance and struggled to arbitrate conflicts that continually arose among them. Metternich, for instance, was concerned to uphold the "legitimacy" of hereditary monarchs. Alexander I wanted the alliance to defend the unlimited power of monarchs.

In Great Britain, though, there seemed to be more interest in and political support for abolishing the slave trade than for managing the European balance of power. Castlereagh was a late convert to the cause, but he knew the allies would demand concessions on other im-

portant points in exchange for going along with Britain on the issue of the slave trade.

The principal slave-trading allies were France, Spain and Portugal. French King Louis XVIII wasn't interested in abolition of the trade. With Napoleon exiled to the Mediterranean island of Elba, France was no longer dependent on Britain's naval power, and the king and Talleyrand were inclined to brush off Castlereagh's requests about the slave trade. All they would do was promise to end the slave trade "in the course of five years." Neither Spain nor Portugal was interested in suppressing the slave trade. Austria, Prussia and Russia weren't sea powers or participants in the slave trade, so any position they adopted on it didn't mean much.

As a diplomat, Castlereagh was a low-key player. He believed it didn't work to "force it [abolition of the slave trade] upon nations, at the expense of their honour and of the tranquility of the world. Morals were never well taught by the sword." He played his trump card—how much European kings owed Britain for helping to defeat Napoleon. In February 1815 he persuaded them to sign a declaration that "the commerce known by the name of the African slave trade is repugnant to the principles of humanity and universal morality."[2]

Spurred by Castlereagh, the allies agreed to meet on a regular basis, exchange information about the slave trade and discuss steps that might be taken against it. Castlereagh proposed that any European power should be able to stop and search any slave ship. In effect, this proposal gave the British the right to stop and search any other nation's slave ship, since nobody else was interested in search missions and British ships had ceased to carry slaves. The main value of the meetings was to make slave trading more visible and potentially subject to criticism.

But the allies wouldn't agree on any means of enforcing restrictions on the slave trade. Castlereagh had to negotiate treaties with each country, one by one.

The French Stall Action on Slave Trade

Before the Napoleonic Wars, France reportedly handled the second-largest volume of the slave trade (after Great Britain).[3] During the wars, the Royal Navy had been free to capture French ships, including

slavers, which had forced a decline in the French slave trade. With France no longer an adversary, the Royal Navy couldn't continue to capture French ships. The Congress of Vienna returned to France its African slave-trading colonies in Sénégal, Gorée and Bourbon, which had been seized by Great Britain during the Napoleonic Wars. Major ports in France—Nantes, Havre, Bordeaux and Marseilles—geared up for the slave-trading business again.

British abolitionists viewed this situation with alarm. "It would be shocking," remarked William Wilberforce, "to restore to Europe the blessings of peace with professions of our principles of justice and humanity and at the same time to be creating this traffic in the persons of our fellow-creatures." Wilberforce wrote letters to Alexander I, Talleyrand, Humboldt and others, appealing for political support against the slave trade. British abolitionists circulated some 800 petitions and gathered almost a million signatures, urging Great Britain to stop the revival of the French slave trade.

After Napoleon escaped from Elba and reached the French mainland on March 1, 1815, he made a bid for British public opinion by issuing a decree abolishing the French slave trade. Suddenly, Louis XVIII needed British help again and, pressed by Castlereagh, the king issued his own decree about the slave trade.[4] On November 20, 1815, he signed the Second Treaty of Paris, in which both Great Britain and France agreed to ban their citizens from participating in the slave trade. The decree wasn't published, however, so it didn't do any good.

Sensing that a French slave trader could operate without penalty, Saint-Malo shipbuilder Robert Surcouf dispatched his ship *Affriquain* to Angola on August 15, 1815. Since he was a colonel in his city's national guard, punishing him would have seemed unpatriotic, and nothing was done. Other slave traders got the hint and soon were openly back in business. Slave-trading ports in France and French Africa began to boom. The French legislature made slave-trading illegal in 1818, but the law wasn't enforced, so this prohibition, too, had little effect.[5]

Following Napoleon's final defeat at Waterloo, Belgium, and his exile on St. Helena, an island far away in the south Atlantic Ocean, the French strategy became to agree with Castlereagh when he asked for action against the slave trade but to do nothing about it. France made slave trading a criminal offense but didn't specify serious penalties. French officials replied to Castlereagh's queries with lengthy dis-

patches about human rights, yet wouldn't commit themselves to pros-
ecuting slave traders. In France, there simply wasn't much political
support for taking action against slave trading.[6]

When the Royal Navy tried to enforce the treaties France had
signed by seizing three French slave ships—*Le Hermione, La Belle* and *Le
Cultivateur*—the French were outraged. Politically connected French
shipbuilders took advantage of the situation to lobby French officials
for an agreement that they wouldn't interfere with the slave trade. In
1817 the H.M.S. *Charlotte* seized the French slave ship *Louis,* and the case
was appealed to the Admiralty Court in London. Judge William Scott
ruled, "I can find no authority which gives us the right of interruption
to the navigation of states in amity—allies like France—up on the high
seas."[7] The *Louis* was returned to its owners and resumed its role in the
slave trade.

In 1817, the French government headed by Armand-Emmanuel
du Plessis, the duke of Richelieu, authorized the seizure of any ship
caught carrying slaves into French colonies. Nothing was said about
French ships carrying slaves to places that weren't French, like Cuba or
Brazil.[8] The following year, though, it became illegal for French citizens to engage in the slave trade.

The contraband French slave trade prospered, protected as it was
by local interest groups and officials. When the French government
got around to sending four ships to Sénégal and Gorée, they inspected some French slavers, interrogated and denounced some captains, but didn't take further action. Slave ship owners and crews were
unaffected. Not surprisingly, slave ships from other nations found
that displaying the French flag would help avoid seizure by Britain's
Royal Navy.[9]

Portugal and Spain Disregard British Efforts

The Portuguese wouldn't give up the slave trade as a gesture of gratitude for British help during the Napoleonic Wars. When Castlereagh
approached Portuguese officials about helping to suppress the slave
trade, they wanted money and lots of it. Eventually Castlereagh agreed
to forgive about £450,000 of Portugal's debt to Britain and to give
Portugal £300,000, supposedly as an indemnity for slave ships the
Royal Navy might capture.[10]

In return, Portugal agreed to give up its rights to do slave trading in its colonies north of the equator, and Portugal would retain unlimited rights to do slave trading south of the equator. This meant Portugal would give up its African slave-trading port at Bissao. Portuguese ships could continue to legally buy slaves in Angola and Mozambique. Slaves could continue to be imported into Brazil, the biggest slave economy.

In other words, the offer would have left untouched most of the lucrative Brazilian slave trade.[11] After continuing pressure from the British, Portugal agreed to limit the number of slaves on board ships to five per two tons of ship weight, up to 201 tons, and only one slave per ton on larger ships. In addition, Portuguese slave traders agreed to stop using hot branding irons to mark slaves. Instead, they agreed to use metal bracelets or collars.[12]

Castlereagh negotiated with Portugal about the right of search. In July 1817 Britain and Portugal signed a treaty that permitted the navies of both countries to stop and search ships suspected of carrying slaves. Two months later, Portugal enacted a law setting punishments for illegal slave traders, while asserting that as far as it was concerned, slave trading was illegal only north of the equator. The law increased the number of slaves that a ship could legally transport.

Britain and Portugal agreed there would be "mixed courts" in London; in British West Africa, such as in Sierra Leone; and in Portugal's colony, Brazil, to adjudicate maritime seizures. Each court session had a British judge and a Portuguese judge on the bench. There was no appeal from the court. If the judges ruled against a seizure, the ship in question had to be returned to the owner. If they ruled in favor of a seizure, the ship would be auctioned off by the British.

These proceedings became a model for treaties with other nations. Sometimes there was agreement that a mixed court wouldn't function if one of the judges were absent. This seemed like a reasonable way to assure impartiality, but non-British judges often failed to show up, supposedly because of health problems, which prevented the mixed tribunals from operating. Eventually British officials persuaded the Spanish and Portuguese that the tribunals must be able to function even if one of the judges was absent.[13]

When Castlereagh began negotiating with the Spanish, they expressed as little gratitude as the Portuguese for British help during the Napoleonic Wars. So the British and Spanish dickered about money.

Spanish officials turned down an offer of £850,000 for abolishing the slave trade immediately.

In September 1816 Spain's foreign minister, Pedro Cevallos, suggested that Spain might agree to ban the slave trade immediately north of the equator and ban the slave trade south of the equator five years after ratification of a treaty. In exchange, Great Britain would pay Spain _500,000 as compensation for Spanish ships seized or destroyed by actions of the Royal Navy. Such compensation was demanded by politically influential slaveholders in the Spanish colonies of Cuba and Puerto Rico. Spain was willing to accept either money or ships. In addition, Spain sought a £700,000 loan.[14]

Although Castlereagh viewed the Spanish proposals as a "conciliatory overture," he never officially responded because the British didn't want to be seen as financing a Spanish armada to South America, where people in Spain's colonies were fighting for independence. Castlereagh proposed a ban on the slave trade with the right of mutual search—Spanish ships could stop and inspect suspected British ships, British ships could stop and inspect suspected Spanish slave ships, and cases involving detained ships would be heard by a mixed tribunal with a Spanish judge and British judge.

Castlereagh denied the Spanish loan request, as he had a French loan request, because the Napoleonic Wars had stretched British finances to the limit. Moreover, many members of Parliament didn't like Spain's autocratic government, so such a request would have been controversial there. Spanish foreign minister Pizarro insisted that without the loan it would be impossible for Spain to ban the slave trade. He lowered his loan request to £600,000; Castlereagh countered with £400,000 for compensation, which Pizarro accepted. The Spanish had already made plans to spend the money. Spanish minister of war Francisco de Eguía had signed an agreement to buy five frigates and three "ships of the line" (warships with at least two gun decks) from Russia.

Pizarro asked Castlereagh if a ban against the slave trade might be delayed until May 1820. Castlereagh agreed, provided the Spanish agreed to the enforcement terms, namely, the right of mutual search and mixed tribunals. The treaty, signed on September 23, 1817, provided that the Spanish slave trade north of the equator would be illegal immediately, and the entire Spanish slave trade would be illegal after May 30, 1820. However, there was a big loophole: A slave ship

could only be detained if there were slaves on board. This meant a ship couldn't be detained if it had just delivered slaves or even pushed them into the sea as a Royal Navy ship approached.

Pressured by outraged Cuban planters, Spanish officials petitioned the British to further delay the date when the entire Spanish slave trade would be banned. Until this issue was resolved, Spanish judges serving on the mixed tribunal in Havana decided they wouldn't uphold the seizure of a Spanish slave ship. In addition, the Spanish navy was in no hurry to capture Spanish slave ships. Between 1820 and 1842, the Spanish navy didn't capture a single Spanish slave ship. It did capture two Portuguese slave ships, but they weren't subject to the treaty between Spain and Great Britain. The Royal Navy didn't do very well either. It failed to capture a single Spanish slave ship in the Caribbean for seven years—its first capture was in 1824.[15] One reason for Britain's lax enforcement was a conflict of interest: British naval ships competed for the profitable business of carrying Cuban gold and silver—earned by selling slave-produced sugar—to European banks. Going after Spanish slavers would have meant losing the precious-metals transport business to American and French ships. By contrast, the Haitian warship *Wilberforce* as well as Colombian privateers captured a number of Spanish slave ships during this time.

The Spanish were disinclined to do much about the slave trade. Spanish naval commanders were supposed to stop ships departing from Cuba and bound for Africa and were to stop ships loaded with slaves in Cuban waters. Rewards were offered for anyone who reported slaves being landed in Cuba. Anyone found guilty of slave trading—whether crew or captain—would be sentenced to up to six years in prison. Slaves would be seized from buyers who would lose whatever they paid plus a fine of 300 pesos per slave purchased. Apparently, these measures didn't work. The British continued to seek diplomatic agreements, hoping that their counterparts would make a reasonable effort to comply, even when the counterparts subsequently disregarded the agreements.[16]

Big profits spurred slave traders to persist. For example, the *Duqesa de la Braganza* reportedly had cost $30,000 to build. The cost of a voyage from Africa to Cuba, including slaves reportedly was $60,000. After selling 860 slaves, the principals realized a profit over $200,000.

Even when a slave ship was captured and referred to a mixed tribunal, the results were often discouraging. For instance, on November 6, 1821, a Spanish ship appeared in Havana with a number of slaves rescued from a wrecked Spanish slaver. The mixed tribunal ruled that it didn't have jurisdiction. The Spanish Court of Admiralty, the auditor of war and the judge of finance discussed who should handle the case. Eventually it was transferred to Spain, by which time the slaves had been taken away by the owner of the wrecked ship.[17]

No wonder that the flow of slaves seems to have continued into Cuba throughout the 1820s. According to reports of the Havana commissioners, there were 152 landings and a total of 43,150 slaves delivered. Since it was illegal for Spanish ships to deliver slaves, contraband trade wasn't reported. Altogether more than 68,000 slaves might have been delivered in Cuba during the 1820s.[18]

Despite relentless British pressure, Cuban planters became, if anything, more adamant about slavery. Perhaps their most determined defender was Miguel Tacón y Rosique, a Spanish military officer who fought against those, such as Simón Bolívar, who were battling for independence in Latin America. Tacón believed that Spain lost when it made concessions to colonists, thus raising their expectations. He concluded the Spanish must change nothing, concede nothing. He began serving as governor of Cuba in 1834 and opposed any political reforms. When Spain adopted a new constitution three years later, Tacón lobbied successfully against having it apply to Cuba. He enforced press censorship and deported those who protested. Cuban planters hailed him as their great protector. Reportedly they rewarded him with a half-ounce of gold for every slave delivered to Cuba.

British officials were determined to play a more direct role in Cuba. In 1826 they proposed that Spain sign a new provision for their treaty to permit the Royal Navy to seize any ship with slaving equipment as evidence that the ship was in the slave trade. For instance, slavers often had extra bulkheads where slaves could be squeezed in and iron shackles for restraining slaves. Such ships carried far more food and water than would be needed to feed the crew alone.[19]

In addition to being able to seize ships with slaving equipment, British officials proposed destroying all ships found to be slavers. The officials had observed that a number of slave ships were involved more than once in proceedings before a mixed tribunal, which suggested

that if they weren't destroyed, they might find their way back into the slave trade. Diplomatic discussions dragged on for years.

Great Britain's Success against Brazil

Thanks to coffee, Brazil became the world's largest slave economy by 1830, and the number of slaves exceeded the number of free people. The coffee business increased the political clout of a wide range of interest groups that profited from slave labor, putting Brazil on a collision course with Great Britain.[20]

In an effort to suppress the Brazilian slave trade, Britain began with diplomacy. This was hard to ignore since the British had saved the Portuguese royal family from Napoleon, British investors played a key role developing Brazilian businesses, and Britain was Portugal's biggest trading partner. When diplomacy failed, Britain used the power of its Royal Navy to disrupt the slave trade on both sides of the Atlantic.

In 1826 Brazil signed a treaty with Great Britain, agreeing to stop slaves from being imported into Brazil by 1830. The Brazilian government, dominated by slaveholding interests, didn't do much to enforce the treaty. Struggles among political factions were a major distraction. Slaves continued to come in. Slave traders displayed resourcefulness in evading attempts by the British Royal Navy to enforce the treaty.[21]

Anticipating the possible end of the Brazilian slave trade, planters bought more slaves while they could still do it easily. From 1822 to 1827, some 60 slave ships annually landed about 25,000 slaves in Rio de Janeiro province. In 1828 about 110 ships landed 45,000 slaves, and that many more arrived the following year. During the first six months of 1830, 76 ships brought more than 30,000 slaves. In addition, slaves were being landed elsewhere in Brazil.[22]

After Castlereagh, who died in 1822, the British statesman who did the most to help suppress the slave trade was Henry John Temple, the third Viscount Palmerston. He dominated British foreign policy between 1830 and 1865, serving for 25 of those years as foreign secretary or prime minister. He probably had a significant impact on the history of more countries than any other British statesman.[23] Palmerston intervened abroad when a government

upset the European balance of power, violated the rights of a British citizen or sanctioned slavery.

He was detested for his arrogance in Europe as well as in Britain—Queen Victoria couldn't stand him. His abrasive manner earned him the nickname "Lord Pumicestone." But nobody did a better job projecting British power around the world. Although he was long ridiculed as Lord Cupid for his liaisons with aristocratic ladies, ordinary Britons admired him for decisively protecting British interests.[24]

Few surpassed Palmerston's eloquence about the evils of slavery. "How many millions must have been swept away from the population of Africa!" he exclaimed. "I will venture to say that, if all the other crimes which the human race has committed were added together, they could not exceed the amount of guilt incurred in connexion [sic] with this diabolical Slave Trade. Is it not the duty of every government and of every nation, on whom Providence has bestowed the means of putting an end to this crime, to employ these means to the greatest extent possible?"[25]

Born in 1784, Temple attended Harrow School and Edinburgh University, where he studied with Adam Smith's student Dugald Stewart. Then Temple went to St. John's College, Cambridge. Upon his father's death in 1802, he became Viscount Palmerston, and five years later, he was elected to Parliament. He was named junior lord of the admiralty in the Duke of Portland's ministry, responsible for naval affairs. An 1807 speech impressed members with his intelligence, and two years later he became secretary of war, handling army finances. He remained at this post until 1830 when he entered the cabinet as foreign secretary.

Aside from his continuing efforts to prevent a single nation from dominating Western Europe and posing a potential threat to Britain, his principal cause was suppressing the slave trade. He declared, "If ever by the result of overpowering enemies, or by the errors of her misguided policies, England should fall . . . I do not know of any nation that is now ready in this respect to supply our place."[26]

Palmerston promoted the expansion of Great Britain's Royal Navy, in part to help suppress the slave trade. During the 1830s, the Royal Navy nearly tripled the size of its antislavery squadron from 6 ships to about 15. There were a dozen brigs and schooners, perhaps 5 sloops with 16 to 20 guns each, and a frigate with 40 to 50 guns.[27] By

the 1840s, about one-sixth of the Royal Navy was engaged in suppressing the slave trade.[28]

This was difficult, dangerous work. One commander of a ship in the African squadron recalled, "The monotony of the blockade is killing to officers and men . . . for months at anchor, rolling terribly, thermometer 86 degrees, no change of companions, no supplies of fresh stock except at long intervals." When a naval ship tried to capture a slaver, there could be brutal fights. During the course of a year searching for slave ships, perhaps 5 percent of naval crewmen might be killed and another 10 percent wounded. Sometimes the casualties were much higher. To help make the risks worthwhile, crewmen were offered £5 for each slave liberated and £4 per ton for every empty slave ship seized.

On November 1, 1831, Britain signed another treaty with Brazil that banned the importing of slaves into Brazil, declared that any slaves brought into Brazil must be emancipated, provided serious penalties for slave traders, and exempted plantation owners from the debts they owed slave traders. Yet more slaves were imported than before.[29] The Brazilian slave trade continued because many Brazilian officials and military officers reportedly earned fortunes from illegal slave trading.[30] During the 1830s, a Brazilian navy captain was fired for having seized a slave ship.[31]

When Britain pressed Brazil to uphold the terms of their treaty, Brazilian officials stalled as long as possible. In 1845 British prime minister Robert Peel secured passage of the Aberdeen Bill, which defined the slave trade as piracy. This meant British sea captains could capture slave ships as pirates and earn big profits. In addition, the cases would be brought before a tribunal with a British judge, rather than a tribunal with British and Brazilian judges, increasing the likelihood that British policy would be upheld.[32] The result was more vigorous action against the slave trade.[33]

The Brazilian government, headed by the Conservative Marquis of Olinda, tried to regain some initiative by passing a law that banned the Brazilian slave trade. Resourceful as ever, slave traders continued to flourish in Brazilian waters.[34] Brazil imported about 50,000 slaves a year during the 1840s. Efforts to suppress the slave trade had reduced the number of slaves reaching Brazil every year by two-thirds by 1850.[35]

The British were anxious to finish the job. James Hudson, Britain's diplomatic representative in Rio de Janeiro, viewed Brazilian govern-

ments as "vicious, corrupt and abominable." He reckoned that the time was ripe for Britain to step up the pressure. In June 1850 the steamer *Sharpshooter* joined the Royal Navy's squadron assigned to patrol Brazilian waters looking for slave ships. The *Sharpshooter* soon captured two, the *Malteza* and the *Conceição*. The *Malteza* was destroyed. The *Conceição* was dispatched to St. Helena, the South Atlantic island that the Royal Navy used as a base, where Napoleon had been banished in 1815. Then the *Sharpshooter* captured the brigantine *Polka*.

Meanwhile, the H.M.S. *Cormorant* cruised down Brazil's coast to Paranaguá, and Captain Herbert Schomborg was directed to inspect and seize all ships suspected of being involved in the slave trade. On July 1, 1850, he burned the *Leonidas* and the *Sereia*. Both of the ships had landed about 800 slaves, at Dois Rios and Macaé respectively. Schomborg captured the *Lucy Ann*, an unusually big slave ship capable of carrying some 1,600 slaves, and had British sailors take it to the naval base at St. Helena. The crew of the *Astro*, another slave ship, sunk it to keep it out of British hands.[36]

Brazilians were outraged at British disregard of their sovereignty. Brazilian officials were also concerned about how the Royal Navy might adversely affect Brazil's coastal trade. But in the Brazilian government, a number of representatives were critical of the slave trade. Denouncing Royal Navy actions against slave traders, in effect, would mean defending the slave trade, and fewer Brazilians were inclined to do that.

When slaveholder interests protested that the Brazilian government could handle things itself, the Britain's Royal Navy ceased Brazilian operations for about six months. But when the Brazilian government didn't take any action to enforce the ban on the slave trade, the Royal Navy resumed operations. The H.M.S. *Cormorant* sunk the tugboat *Sarah*, which was headed for the slave ship *Valarozo*, near Rio de Janeiro. The H.M.S. *Plumper* sank the *Flor do Mar*, which was bringing slave equipment to the *Valarozo*. Finally, the H.M.S. *Sharpshooter* seized the *Valarozo*. The *Sharpshooter* subsequently captured and destroyed *Piratinim*, a ship that traded slaves along the Brazilian coast. The H.M.S. *Locust* sailed down the Brazilian coast past Paranaguá, attacked a secret base for slave trading and destroyed a substantial amount of slaving equipment. Brazilian politicians protested.[37]

By 1852, the British decided to curtail their naval operations along the Brazilian coast, satisfied that the flow of African slaves there

had virtually stopped. The previous year, only a reported 3,200 African slaves from nine landings were brought into Brazil. Slave trading continued within Brazil. Palmerston acknowledged that the Brazilian government was at last fulfilling its agreement to enforce the ban against new slaves coming into the country.

Palmerston's Feisty Persistence

Palmerston negotiated the Anglo-Spanish Treaty, which Spain signed on June 28, 1835. It authorized the British to stop and search suspected slave ships flying the Spanish flag. The ships could be seized if they had equipment used in the slave trade. Suddenly, after two decades, the Spanish flag ceased to protect slavers from the Royal Navy. Perhaps most slave ships switched to flying the American flag, since there wasn't any treaty permitting the Royal Navy to stop American flag ships—whether or not they were actually American.

Altogether, Palmerston negotiated the right of British naval commanders to search potential slave ships flying the flags of France, Holland, Denmark and Sweden as well as Spain. He put pressure on Prussia, Russia and Austria to lend their moral support to anti-slavery efforts.[38]

But the impact of the navy was limited by treaty loopholes and the failure of mixed tribunals to enforce such restrictions as there were. Although the British navy had succeeded in liberating some 116,000 slaves, the slave trade seems to have increased between 1810 and 1849. Perhaps a million slaves were transported from West Africa to the Caribbean during this period.[39]

Frustrated by Portugal's refusal to agree that slave trading should be suppressed like piracy, Palmerston pushed through Parliament a bill authorizing the Royal Navy to seize Portuguese ships equipped for the slave trade. The cases were to be heard not by a mixed tribunal that, because of deadlocked judges, tended to release the ships, but rather by a British court, as if they were British ships. The law remained in effect for three years, during which time the Royal Navy virtually wiped out slave trading that involved ships with Portuguese flags. Portugal capitulated in 1842, agreeing that slave trading could be suppressed like piracy. No longer needed, the act of Parliament was repealed.[40]

Palmerston encouraged British naval commanders to enforce the treaties, even if they had to violate technicalities. For instance, when in 1840 Captain Joseph Denman was patrolling Africa's west coast for slave ships, he was informed that some British sailors had been captured and held at a slave-trading station on the Gallinas river (in the southern part of what is now Sierra Leone). Denman directed three British 16-gun brigs—*Wanderer, Sarascen* and *Rolla*—to find the men. They did and liberated 841 slaves, and burned barracks where the slaves had been chained together awaiting shipment to Cuba. Palmerston remarked, "Taking a wasp's nest is more effective than catching the wasps one by one."[41] He recommended Denman for a promotion.

Since Brazil was the largest slave market and refused to help suppress the slave trade, Palmerston authorized British naval ships to pursue slavers into Brazilian territorial waters and destroy them. Slavers weren't safe from the Royal Navy in the harbor at Rio de Janeiro.[42]

What to do about slave captains who flew the Portuguese flag, taking advantage of Portugal's refusal to uphold its treaty commitments and help suppress the slave trade? In the House of Commons, Palmerston introduced a bill permitting the Royal Navy to stop any ship flying the Portuguese flag. Many viewed this as an act of war, even though Portugal was Britain's oldest ally, since the Treaty of Windsor (1386). Palmerston defied the Portuguese to declare war. The bill became law, and Portugal didn't declare war.[43]

Palmerston needled the Americans who wouldn't enforce their ban against slave trading. He declared that if they didn't do it, Britain would do it. He publicly expressed his impatience with American officials who permitted slave traders to protect themselves by "hoisting a piece of bunting with the United States' emblem and colors upon it." Palmerston noted the hypocrisy of members of Parliament like Robert Peel and William Ewart Gladstone who earned fortunes from businesses involving cotton produced by American slaves.

But again the additional measures didn't reduce the volume of slave trading. While the British West Africa squadron tripled the average number of slave ships captured annually during the 1830s to 35, very few slave ships were put out of commission in the Caribbean. This was due to the quiet refusal of the Spanish to cooperate and enforce the treaty terms. Many Spanish slave traders flew the Portuguese

flag, others flew the U.S. flag, and Great Britain didn't have a treaty with either country permitting it to seize slave ships.

At the very least, naval patrols increased the risks and enforced some limits. For example, British ships kept their eye on one of the largest slave ships, the *Fama de Cadiz*, which could carry about 1,200 slaves. Consequently, it had to wait around the African coast, hoping for an opportunity to load slaves without being observed. Unfortunately, after the *Fama* had acquired some 980 slaves, a smallpox epidemic killed more than half the crew and two-thirds of the slaves. Eventually, its captain decided to give up slave trading and become a pirate who looted other slave ships.[44]

Better Strategies for Abolition?

British abolitionists, who had focused throughout the 1820s on abolishing slavery in British Caribbean colonies, were shocked by reports that despite all the treaties and naval search operations, the total number of slaves crossing the Atlantic had actually increased.

Among the disillusioned was Thomas Buxton, who had been elected to Parliament in 1818 and who founded the Society for the Mitigation and Gradual Abolition of Slavery, which later became known as the Anti-Slavery Society. He became the leading abolitionist in the House of Commons after William Wilberforce retired in 1825. He came to the conclusion that the prevailing strategy—negotiate treaties with other countries and try to have the Royal Navy enforce them—was worse than a failure. Buxton believed that the number of slaves crossing the Atlantic each year had doubled since the late eighteenth century when the British abolitionist movement began. He documented the situation in his bleak book *The Slave Trade* (1838).

He believed that the best hope for ending the international slave trade was to abolish slavery in part of Africa, then develop a free-labor market that could flourish on Africa's rich soil and mineral resources. Once legitimate commerce got underway in Africa, it could expand. "It may sound visionary at the present time," he wrote, "but I expect that at some future, and not very distant day, it will appear, that for every pound she now receives from the export of her people, a hundred pounds worth of produce, either or home consumption or foreign commerce, will be raised from the fertility of her soil."[45]

The trouble was that such ideas had been tried before. Back in the 1780s, abolitionists had envisioned establishing some kind of model society that could help displace the slave trade. The most ambitious attempt involved the Sierra Leone colony. In 1787, some 400 settlers arrived on the Sierra Leone peninsula. They bought land from Temne tribal leaders and started the Province of Freedom. But most of the settlers died from tropical diseases within a year. In 1792, John Clarkson led some 1,100 settlers who tried again, establishing Freetown approximately where the Province of Freedom had been located. Administrative tasks were handled by the Sierra Leone Company. In 1800, the original group was joined by some 500 free blacks from Jamaica. The company had financial problems, and the colony was taken over by the British government in 1808. The problems were blamed on poor soil, the proximity of swamps that seemed to promote tropical fevers and a jungle that blocked access to the African interior.[46]

Buxton proposed an ambitious scheme that involved building up the Royal Navy's Africa squadron and negotiating treaties with tribal chiefs who agreed to give up the slave trade. He acknowledged that coastal tribes, who had plenty of experience negotiating with slave traders, would be tough to deal with. He hoped for better luck with tribes in Africa's interior. All this meant more government spending, when the government was looking to cut expenses. It was apparent that Buxton was describing what had been tried before, only on a larger scale.

Buxton's stature as a valiant crusader against slavery was a principal reason his scheme got any serious consideration. Another reason was that the Whigs (as early classical liberals were called) were struggling to maintain their political support. They needed the legions who viewed Buxton as a guiding light. They doubted that his scheme would work, so they didn't want to risk much trying it. They announced that they would back some exploration of the coastal region near the mouth of the Niger River, but there wouldn't be any effort to penetrate Africa's interior, and there would be no special buildup of the Africa squadron.

Although the Whigs proposed doing much less than Buxton thought was needed, it was as much as he could get. To help promote and fund the Niger expedition, he established the Society for the Extinction of the Slave Trade and for the Civilization of Africa—also known as the African Civilization Society.

Early on they encountered snags. For instance, the government didn't have any shallow-draft ships that could operate safely on the Niger River. Three flat-bottom steamboats had to be built. They left London in 1841. Antislavery trade treaties were negotiated, but two of the ships were soon out of action because their black crews were overcome with tropical fevers—a cause for concern since it had been thought that blacks had some natural immunity to tropical diseases. The third ship managed to get an estimated 320 miles upstream, but when the water became increasingly shallow, the explorers, not wanting to risk running aground, headed back.

A model farm was set up to show local people how they could live better without the slave trade, but many of the participants were soon incapacitated with fevers. Most of the survivors decided to leave while they were still alive. Altogether, 41 of the participants died from tropical fevers. No one knew how to deal with the hostile environment.

After the model farm had been set up, the African Civilization Society decided to send another ship the following year, to evaluate the farm's progress. Despite the treaties, it was apparent that the natives continued to engage in slave trading. The superintendent of the farm had been murdered. Not much work was being done. Some of the settlers were exploiting natives, even using a whip to enforce discipline like plantation overseers. The model farm was abandoned.

The British government announced it wasn't accepting sovereignty for the land that had been explored, and if anybody wanted to settle on it, they would have to make their own arrangements with tribal chiefs. In January 1843, Buxton dissolved the African Civilization Society. He reportedly remarked, "I feel as if I were going to attend the funeral of an old friend."

The principal alternative to the campaign against the slave trade was the campaign to abolish slavery itself. Abolitionists like Joseph Sturge, a Gloucestershire farmer's son who became wealthy financing the grain trade, suggested that the slave trade couldn't be abolished as long as slavery continued: Abolitionists must "lay the axe to the root," a phrase Thomas Clarkson had used when attacking the slave trade. Active in the Anti-Slavery Society, both the British and foreign organizations, and the Central Negro Emancipation Committee, Sturge believed the abolitionist movement had to become international. His supporters went on to establish the Universal Abolition Society.

Sturge helped organize abolitionist rallies and meetings around Great Britain, the best known of which was the World Anti-Slavery Convention. Invitations went out to abolitionists in 35 countries to attend a two-week meeting in June 1840. Almost all the important British abolitionists attended. Buxton spoke about the Niger expedition; Daniel O'Connell came from Ireland; William Lloyd Garrison and Wendell Phillips were among the 53 Americans who attended. There were six Frenchmen, led by Hippolite de St. Anthoine. Others included William Knibb and Henry Beckford from Jamaica, Robert Anderson from Trinidad, Samuel Prescod from Barbados, Donald McGregor from the Bahamas, Richard Musgrave from Antigua, R. H. Schombergh from British Guyana, Joseph Ketley from Demerara, Richard Seaborn from Berbice, A. V. Hittie from Mauritius, Thomas Rolph from Canada. There were individuals from Haiti, Spain and Switzerland. Altogether, more than 5,000 people packed Freemasons' Hall, Great Queen Street, London.[47]

It was certainly a good thing to bring together abolitionists with such a wide range of experience to help inform and inspire one another. But such well-attended events didn't seem to have much impact on societies where slavery was most stubbornly rooted, such as the United States, Cuba and Brazil. Slavery persisted in the western hemisphere for nearly a half-century after the World Anti-Slavery Convention, so slavery was no easier target than the slave trade. The abolitionist movement was a crucial part of the solution to the problem of slavery, but all efforts, including Great Britain's tireless diplomacy and the power of the Royal Navy, were needed for this great cause.

Britain Presses America to Stop the Slave Trade

Article 1, Section 9 of the U.S. Constitution prevented Congress from abolishing slavery before 1808. On March 2, 1807, President Thomas Jefferson signed a bill to abolish the slave trade that took effect January 1, 1808.

Perhaps because Americans were outraged at the seeming arrogance of the British who seized American ships trading with France during the Napoleonic Wars, the U.S. government refused to accept British proposals to search American flag ships suspected of being slavers.

Although the United States, maintaining its policy of neutrality advocated by presidents Washington and Jefferson, wasn't represented at the Congress of Vienna, the British did try to enlist American co-operation. Despite the 1808 U.S. law against importing slaves, ships continued to bring slaves into the country, particularly through ports around Louisiana and East Florida. An estimated 50,000 slaves were brought into the U.S. between 1807 and 1860.[48]

President James Monroe suggested that European representatives gather for a conference to discuss ways of ending the slave trade. Europeans, however, were weary of conferences, and viewed skeptically one led by the United States, which never did become a party to a treaty aimed at helping to suppress the slave trade. Apparently, U.S. officials didn't want to be exposed as hypocrites for disregarding their own laws.

In 1819 Congress passed a bill, which President Monroe signed, that empowered the president to authorize the U.S. Navy to patrol Africa's west coast, looking for slave ships. Congress appropriated $100,000 for the mission. At the time, though, few naval ships were sent, and during the next several years appropriations were cut.

By 1839 the United States was the only slave power that had refused to sign a treaty with Great Britain to abolish the slave trade. An increasing number of slave ships were built in American ports and flew the American flag.[49] The U.S. government insisted that under no circumstances should foreigners board a ship flying an American flag, a policy that encouraged scoundrels from all nations to sail under the stars and stripes. By this time, the trade seldom involved delivering slaves to the United States, since the 1808 law made the importation of slaves illegal. Often the ships weren't American. Rather, the slavers bought American papers in Havana or other slave-trading ports to protect against seizure by the Royal Navy. There wasn't much risk of being stopped by a U.S. naval ship—which would have seized a slaver flying an American flag—since the United States wasn't actively trying to suppress the slave trade. American flag protection of slave ships contributed to the continuing slave trade that brought some 600,000 Africans to Cuba, Brazil and other destinations in the western hemisphere.[50]

Furthermore, American officials objected to the seizure of any U.S. ship unless it had slaves. In practice, this meant a ship couldn't be seized if a slave trader had his human cargo pushed into the sea or

had offloaded them to a nearby beach. Many seizures were overruled by the mixed courts because slaves weren't found on board.

That there was considerable American support for *not* enforcing U.S. law against the slave trade was apparent in the famous *Amistad* case. In February 1839 Portuguese slavers seized more than 50 Africans in Sierra Leone and sent them to Havana, Cuba. The surviving 54 were purchased by Spanish planters Pedro Montez and Jose Ruiz, who transferred the Africans to the Cuban schooner *Amistad* and sailed for Principe, near their sugar plantations. On July 1, 1839, the Africans rebelled and gained control of the ship. The captain and cook were killed. The Africans demanded that the planters—the only men on board who knew how to sail the ship—return to Africa. But the planters thought their prospects would be better if they reached the United States. They tricked the slaves into believing they were crossing the Atlantic, when actually they were heading north. The *Amistad* ended up in Long Island Sound where, on January 23, 1840, it was captured near Montauk Point by the U.S. surveying brig *Washington*. The 45 Africans on board were brought to the nearest port, New London, Connecticut, and subsequently charged with murder and jailed in New Haven. The planters were freed. While the Africans were cleared of the murder charges, they continued to be held when multiple claims were filed in the case.

Lieutenant Thomas R. Gedney and others on the *Washington* filed a salvage claim for the *Amistad*. He asserted that when the *Washington* came upon the *Amistad*, it was near shore, and slaves appeared to be in the process of getting off, that is, abandoning ship. Consequently, his crew played a role in salvaging the ship, and therefore they were entitled to whatever might be recovered, including the slaves.

The Spanish ambassador contacted the U.S. State Department, declaring that the *Amistad* and everything on board was the property of Spanish subjects and should be returned to them. President Martin Van Buren thought the Africans should be sent to Cuba, where they would be enslaved. But American abolitionists Roger S. Baldwin, Simeon Jocelyn, Joshua Leavitt and Lewis Tappan got involved in the case and used it to publicize the evils of slavery.[51]

The U.S. attorney on the case seems to have had conflicting views. On the one hand, he said that the Spanish ambassador's claim was "well founded," and perhaps the court should order that the *Amistad*, the Africans and other contents must be returned to Cuba, enabling

the United States to fulfill its treaty obligations to Spain. Apparently he was referring to a 1795 treaty (whose terms were continued in treaties of 1819 and 1821) that dealt with situations in which property belonging to citizens of one country was seized in the other country. The U.S. attorney went on to say that if it turned out that the Africans were shipped in violation of U.S. laws against the slave trade, they should be free to return to Africa.

The Africans responded that they had been born free, and they were entitled to remain free. They had never lived in Cuba or any other Spanish territory, so Spanish law shouldn't apply to them. They described how they had been kidnapped by slave traders and treated cruelly and sold as slaves for life. They asserted their right to regain their liberty, hence justifying the revolt on board the *Amistad,* and their desire to return to their homes and families. They described how they had approached land (Long Island) and a number of them had gone ashore to find food. Since Long Island is in New York State, where slavery was against the law, they should have been free.

At the Federal District Court in Connecticut, a judge ruled that the Africans had been illegally detained as slaves. The case was appealed and came before the U.S. Supreme Court in January 1841, where former president John Quincy Adams argued the case for the Africans. He insisted on their right to be free. Justice Joseph Story delivered the opinion of the court that the Africans should be set free. Subsequently 35 sailed back to Africa. A number of U.S. senators thought the government should indemnify the planters for the loss of their slaves, but their view did not prevail.[52]

The United States didn't make a serious effort to help suppress the slave trade until 1842, when it signed the Ashburton Treaty with Great Britain. During the next 15 years, the United States maintained 4 or 5 ships, with a total of 77 guns, patrolling Africa's west coast. Because the United States didn't have a base in Africa, the ships spent most of their time sailing to Madeira or the Cape Verde Islands for supplies. Even so, this was a more consistent contribution than the United States had made before, and apparently the Navy men hated what they saw of the slave trade.[53]

The American slave trade ended with the outbreak of the Civil War. When the South seceded from the Union, the North was free to enforce the law banning the slave trade. The government began pros-

ecuting offenders, starting with those in New York, which had been a lively slave trading center. Slave trader Nathaniel Gordon was hanged in accord with the 1820 law against slave trading. Finally, in 1862, the North signed an Anglo-American treaty providing for the mutual right to search each other's ships suspected of being slavers, based on equipment found on board. Mixed tribunals were established to hear cases involving seized ships. With Americans out of the slave trade, and the American flag no longer protecting a ship from seizure, the American slave trade virtually disappeared.[54]

Britain's Valiant Campaign

Great Britain's campaign to suppress the slave trade of other nations was far more difficult than anticipated by antislavery crusaders like William Wilberforce and Thomas Clarkson at the beginning of the nineteenth century. They underestimated the resistance from other nations, particularly those that had been Britain's allies against Napoleon. And, they underestimated the years of diplomatic negotiations for treaty terms that other nations refused to enforce.

The slave trade turned out to be the most time-consuming issue for one British foreign secretary after the other, as evidenced by the greater volume of correspondence, dispatches and records related to the slave trade than to anything else. Yet for all the treaties that had required seemingly endless negotiations, the British were the only ones who had made a consistent, serious effort to suppress the trade.[55]

Unfortunately, despite these monumental efforts, the slave trade actually grew bigger than it was before the British began their epic campaign. Slave populations expanded, especially in Cuba, Brazil and the United States. Without doubt, if the British had done nothing, even more Africans would have been shipped across the Atlantic.

Although the British campaign wasn't enough by itself to abolish the slave trade, it was nonetheless essential. Nations with whom the British signed treaties conceded the moral high ground, acknowledging that the slave trade should be abolished. The whole process helped keep the slave trade in the public eye. The actions of the Royal Navy increased the risks and costs of the slave trade. The British campaign

had to have given some hope, even if only a little, to the miserable slaves. It was vitally important that somebody took the initiative against the slave trade, and British abolitionists, diplomats and naval crews did more than anybody could have possibly imagined at the dawn of the nineteenth century.

The United States and the Military Strategy for Abolition

That an effective abolitionist movement took a long time to develop in the United States indicates how enormously difficult it was to free the slaves.

The pioneering pamphleteer Anthony Benezet realized that abolishing slavery would require more than publications, and he decided to try establishing an antislavery organization. There had been business associations to lobby for their slaveholding interests, and organized religions had helped the poor while helping themselves, but a secular philanthropic effort on behalf of the slaves hadn't been tried before. In part, this was probably because few could spare time or money for other people's problems, especially when something as complex as slavery was involved. What could any individual possibly do about it? In April 1775 Benezet and fellow abolitionist John Woolman invited other Philadelphia Quakers to meet at the Rising Sun Tavern and help to form the Society for the Relief of Free Negroes Unlawfully Held in Bondage. Twenty-four men showed up. They aimed to focus on litigation, but the organization folded after four meetings. Perhaps they didn't find enough support in American law to do much good for illegally enslaved blacks.

In 1784, six original members of the earlier society tried again. They formed a new antislavery organization, the Pennsylvania Society for Promoting the Abolition of Slavery and the Relief of Free Negroes Unlawfully Held in Bondage. Again the focus was on litigation. This organization outlived Benezet, who died on May 3, 1784, but it folded after two years. Evidently the men didn't know how to go about abolishing slavery, but at least they started a crucial discussion.

The direct influence of the Quakers was limited because they were considered outsiders, even kooks. Quakers didn't have a clergy or churches. Instead, they held meetings where participants meditated silently and spoke up when the spirit moved them. They addressed people as "thee" and "thou" to convey greater humility than the conventional "you." Quakers dressed plainly in undyed wool clothing. They removed their hats only when praying or preaching. They viewed popular amusements such as music and novels as frivolous. Quakers had a reputation for being serious, methodical, persistent and businesslike. They disapproved of war, including the succession of wars that England had fought with France. While Quakers played a crucial role in launching the abolitionist movement, they needed mainstream allies.

In 1787 there was a third effort to establish a Philadelphia-based antislavery organization. This time it was called the Philadelphia Society for Promoting the Abolition of Slavery. As the name suggested, opponents of slavery were becoming more radical, focusing on agitation to abolish slavery rather than litigation to help blacks who were already free. Benjamin Franklin was persuaded to become its president. Although he had owned a few slaves, he was probably the most well-known American because of his business success, his inventions, his publications, his diplomacy during the Revolutionary War and the many influential friends he had made on both sides of the Atlantic.

Whether because of Franklin's practical experience or his knowledge of the activities of British abolitionists, the Philadelphia Society for Promoting the Abolition of Slavery pursued two strategies. First, it gathered signatures for antislavery petitions. Its initial petition encouraged Congress to promote the abolition of slavery, for which the members were denounced by representatives from Georgia and North Carolina. The society maintained legal aid services for runaway slaves and helped find apprenticeship positions for former slaves. It also began establishing schools for former slaves.

Franklin corresponded with many people, encouraging an interest in abolishing slavery. Because the institution was so aggressively defended, attempts to abolish it would intensify social conflicts. Franklin warned that "Slavery is such an atrocious debasement of human nature, that its very extirpation, if not performed with solicitous care, may sometimes open a source of serious evils."

A number of antislavery societies were formed in the American colonies, but many were structured more like social clubs. The New York society, for instance, required a substantial financial commitment from prospective members. They also had to know some members before joining—one member had to be willing to propose a new person and another member had to serve as a second, vouching for the respectability of the applicant. Such societies were a long way from a popular movement.

In 1790 Franklin presented Congress with a petition urging emancipation for "those unhappy men who alone in this land of freedom are degraded into perpetual bondage." Georgia congressman James Jackson countered with the claim that the Bible approved of slavery. Franklin responded with a parody of Jackson's arguments, published in the *Federal Gazette,* a local newspaper. The parody was supposedly written by a Sidi Mehemet Ibrahim, an Algerian, denouncing efforts to end the enslavement of European Christians. "If we cease our Cruises against the Christians," the author wrote, "how shall we be furnished with the Commodities their Countries produce? If we forbear to make Slaves of their People, who in this hot Climate are to cultivate our Lands? Who are to perform the common Labours of our City, and in our Families? Must we then be our own Slaves?" This might have been Franklin's last blast; he died in April 1790.

A Legal Fortress Around Slavery

Unfortunately, the labors of Franklin and other abolitionists were overwhelmed by the political power of American slaveholders who prevailed in 1787 at the Constitutional Convention. The Constitution discreetly didn't mention the word slavery, but three provisions related directly to it.

Article I, Section 2 provided that for purposes of determining congressional representation, each slave counted as three-fifths of a

free person. This assured that the slaveholding South would have more political clout in the U.S. House of Representatives—perhaps 30 percent more at the time—than would have been the case if representation had been based only on the population of free people.

Article 1, Section 9 provided that "The migration or importation of such persons as any of the states now existing shall think proper to admit, shall not be prohibited by the Congress prior to the year one thousand eight hundred and eight." This clause was a compromise that both extended the slave trade for 20 years and acknowledged that it could be limited after that. Abolitionists made repeated efforts to move up the date when the slave trade would end, but none of their efforts succeeded.

Congress passed a bill banning slave imports after January 1, 1808, and President Thomas Jefferson signed it into law, but it affirmed that slavery was lawful. Moreover, American slavers continued to operate. Two years later, President James Madison told Congress, "it appears that American citizens are instrumental in carrying on a traffic in enslaved Africans equally in violation of the laws of humanity, and in defiance of those of their own country." It wasn't clear what anybody could do about it.

The third of the Constitution's clauses relating to slavery, Article 4, Section 2 (the "fugitive slave clause") provided: "No person held to service or labor in one state, under the laws thereof, escaping into another, shall, in consequence of any law or regulation therein, be discharged from such service or labor, but shall be delivered up on claim of the party to whom such service or labor may be due." This was perhaps the most important section of the Constitution that dealt with slavery, because if it were easy for slaves to run away, slavery would collapse. The clause meant that to gain freedom, it wouldn't be sufficient for a slave to escape from his or her home state, nor even to escape from the South. A runaway slave could be captured in New York, Massachusetts, Maine or anywhere else in the Union and be returned to the plantation.

This provision wasn't enough for the slaveholders. At the end of George Washington's first term, in 1793, Congress passed the first federal fugitive slave law. It empowered any federal or state judge to approve the capture of a runaway slave without a jury trial. In many cases, slaveholders hired private slave hunters to track down their runaways, but in some states this was viewed as kidnapping. Moreover, Congress blocked proposals to stop those who kidnapped free blacks. In 1801 Congress nearly passed a law requiring that any employer hir-

ing a black person must publish a physical description of the individual in two newspapers. No wonder American abolitionists had little confidence that slavery could ever be abolished.

Many state laws supported slavery—for instance, some states had laws restricting manumission, the ability of slaves to buy their freedom. As the proslavery Illinois senator Stephen A. Douglas later admitted, "Slavery cannot exist a day or an hour anywhere, unless it is supported by local police regulations." Slaveholders feared that the larger the population of free blacks in an area, the easier it would be for slaves to escape. In addition, slaveholders were concerned that manumitted slaves might help incite a slave rebellion. Slaveholders, apparently having little confidence in their ability to sustain slavery on their own, successfully convinced state governments to support it with myriad laws. It was illegal for a slave to leave a plantation without a pass. Slaves were forbidden to carry weapons. Fearing that slaves might try to communicate with one another and organize a rebellion, states made it illegal for slaves to blow a horn, beat a drum or learn to read and write. Similarly, it was illegal for slaves to gather with other slaves unless a white person, such as an overseer, was present. Perhaps to remind slaves that they must stay in their place, slaves were forbidden from enjoying pleasures available to whites, such as gambling, smoking or riding in a carriage (except as a servant).

Massively protected from abolitionist attack, slavery flourished in the United States. Working conditions weren't as harsh as they were in the Caribbean and in South America, and as a result the birth rate of slaves in the United States was high enough to increase the population without further slave imports. Between 1800 and 1860, the number of slaves in the United States quadrupled to nearly 4 million, increasing the political clout of the slaveholding South.[1]

Rebirth of American Abolitionism

The next phase of the American abolitionist movement began with the founding of the American Colonization Society in 1816. Championed by New Jersey Presbyterian clergyman Robert Finley, its goal was to send free American blacks to Africa. This approach won much support in the South because the society never actually challenged slavery. Among those who embraced colonization were President

James Madison, Kentucky senator Henry Clay and Harvard president Edward Everett. Although some in the society hoped their efforts would encourage slaveholders to let more slaves buy their freedom, society members did what they wished with their slaves.[2] Furthermore, few blacks were interested in moving to Africa. Most were born in America and wanted to be free in America. Nonetheless, colonization remained a widely held idea for many years.

The popular movement to abolish American slavery began with William Lloyd Garrison. His gospel was the Declaration of Independence.[3] Garrison vowed that "As long as there remains a single copy of the Declaration of Independence, in our land, we will not despair."[4]

He had a big bald head and blue eyes behind steel-rimmed glasses. Essayist Ralph Waldo Emerson described him as "a virile speaker."[5] British abolitionist Harriet Martineau wrote: "Garrison had a good deal of the Quaker air; and his speech is deliberate like a Quaker's but gentle as a woman's. . . . Every conversation I had with him confirmed my opinion that sagacity is the most striking attribute" Garrison's associate Wendell Phillips avowed: "Such is my conviction of the soundness of his judgment and his rare insight into all the bearings of our cause, that I distrust my own deliberate judgment, when it leads me to a different conclusion from his."[6]

Garrison was born in Newburyport, Massachusetts, on December 12, 1805. His father, Abijah Garrison, was a red-bearded, hard-drinking sea captain who was seldom at home. His mother, Frances Maria Lloyd, struggled to make ends meet as a nurse, and she did the best she could to instill moral values. She taught her children that slavery was wrong.

In 1821 Garrison met Caleb Cushing, the son of a local merchant who opened his eyes to the moral outrage of slavery. For example, newspaper advertisements told how to identify runaway slaves: "will no doubt show the marks of a recent whipping taken . . . stamped N.E. on the breast and having both small toes cut off . . . has a scar on one cheek and his left hand has been seriously injured by a pistol shot . . . from being whipped, has scars on his back, arms and thighs . . . has an iron band around his neck . . . branded on the left cheek, thus 'R' . . . has a ring of iron on his left foot . . . has a large neck iron." Such advertisements included the names and addresses of the slaveholders who sought the slaves' return, so clearly they were not perturbed by such cruelty to slaves. South Carolina lawmakers suggested

that cruelty was often much more shocking when they made it illegal "willfully to cut out the tongue, put out the eye, castrate or cruelly scald, burn or deprive any slave of any limb or member."[7]

Garrison got a job as an apprentice with the *Newburyport Herald*. His strong antislavery views became evident early on, as in this commentary about a South Carolina law that made it illegal to teach slaves how to read or write: "There is something unspeakably pitiable and alarming in the state of that society where it is deemed necessary, for self-preservation, to seal up the mind and debase the intellect of man to brutal incapacity."

In 1826 Garrison became editor of the *Newburyport Free Press*. One highlight of his tenure there was a poem he published by shy, 18-year-old John Greenleaf Whittier from Haverhill, Massachusetts. Whittier was proud of his Quaker heritage: German Quakers from Philadelphia had organized the first protest against slavery back in 1688, and no Quakers had owned slaves since 1777. Whittier was inspired by John Milton's *Areopagitica* (1643), the eloquent early case for freedom of the press, and by the poems of Lord Byron who had died fighting for Greek independence.

By 1828 Garrison had accepted an offer to edit *The Genius of Universal Emancipation*, a Baltimore-based newspaper that promoted colonization. Garrison hid a runaway slave who had been lashed 37 times for failing to load a wagon fast enough. He made friends among blacks and realized that they just wanted to enjoy freedom in America. If they were colonized, it would be against their will. Consequently, he abandoned the colonization idea and embraced immediate emancipation—the right "to make contracts, to receive wages, to accumulate property, to acquire knowledge, to dwell where he chooses, to defend his wife, children, and fireside."[8]

Garrison wasn't the first to support immediate emancipation. The Virginian George Bourne had advocated it in *The Book and Slavery Irreconcilable* (1816), as had the Kentucky writer James Duncan in *Treatise on Slavery* (1824) and the English Quaker Elizabeth Heyrick in the pamphlet *Immediate Not Gradual Emancipation* (1824). Garrison was the first to run with the idea.

Meanwhile, Southerners were becoming more anxious about the federal government's support for slavery. Although the U.S. Senate was evenly divided—12 free states and 12 slave states—the North had more votes in the U.S. House of Representatives because population

growth was much higher in free states. Many Southerners concluded they must aggressively defend slavery and promote its expansion. Virginia senator John Randolph did much to transform "state's rights" into a defense of slavery: He ridiculed the Declaration of Independence as "a fanfaronade of metaphysical abstractions." South Carolina senator John C. Calhoun, perhaps the most vehement defender of slavery, declared: "Many in the South once believed that slavery was a moral and political evil. That folly and delusion are gone. We see it now in its true light, and regard it as the most safe and stable basis for free institutions in the world."9

Garrison decided that he must launch his own antislavery newspaper. He obtained financial backing from Boston lawyer Ellis Gray Loring and Quaker merchant Arthur Tappan, and Garrison served as editor. His penniless childhood friend Isaac Knapp was the publisher, and another friend, Stephen Foster, did the printing. They took on a black apprentice, Thomas Paul. Garrison rented an 18-square-foot office in Merchants Hall. It had just enough room for a desk, a table, two chairs and a mattress where Garrison could rest. He bought a cheap little press and borrowed type during the night when another publisher wasn't using it.

He began publishing *The Liberator* on January 1, 1831. A four-page weekly appearing every Friday, each page was 14 by 9¼ inches with four columns per page. In his editorial, Garrison declared: "I will be as harsh as truth, and as uncompromising as justice. On this subject, I do not wish to think, or speak, or write, with moderation. No! No! Tell a man whose house is on fire, to give a moderate alarm; tell him to moderately rescue his wife from the hands of the ravisher; tell the mother to gradually extricate her babe from the fire into which it has fallen;—but urge me not to use moderation in a cause like the present. I am in earnest—I will not equivocate—I will not excuse—I will not retreat a single inch—AND I WILL BE HEARD."10

The Liberator was always a shoestring venture. After a year, it had only 50 white subscribers; a year later, just 400. Three-quarters of subscribers were free blacks. Total circulation never exceeded 3,000. *The Liberator* lost money, but Garrison was to continue publishing it for 35 years without missing a single week—1,820 issues altogether.

In August 1831 the slave Nat Turner led a rebellion against slaveholders in Southampton County, Virginia, and about 60 whites were killed. Because this rebellion occurred months after Garrison

launched *The Liberator*, his radical rhetoric was blamed for stirring insurrection. Indeed, he wrote after the killings: "If we would not see our land deluged in blood, we must immediately burst the shackles of the slaves."[11]

Southern states suppressed freedom of the press, making it illegal to speak or write about abolition. Several Northern governors expressed their support. New York governor William L. Marcy, for example, said: "Without the power to pass such laws, the states would not possess all the necessary means for preserving their external relations of peace among themselves." The governors of Virginia and Georgia urged the mayor of Boston to take action against *The Liberator*. South Carolina senator William G. Preston warned, "Let an abolitionist come within the borders of South Carolina, if we catch him, we will try him, and notwithstanding all the influence of all the governments on earth, including the Federal Government, we will hang him." In Mississippi, men merely suspected of being abolitionists were hanged. Worried that Garrison might be kidnapped since he often worked till midnight at his Merchants' Hall office, neighborhood blacks formed patrols to follow him on his three-mile walk home and make sure he was safe.

American Abolitionists Face Stubborn Opposition

On November 13, 1831, 15 men gathered at Samuel Sewall's State Street law office to hear Garrison propose an organized campaign against slavery. He talked about how British abolitionists were crusading for immediate emancipation. Nine of the men joined him. The New England Anti-Slavery Society held its first meeting January 1, 1832, in the basement schoolroom of the African Baptist Church on Joy Street. The first president was Arnold Buffum, a Quaker hatter. Later, as other states formed abolitionist societies, the name was changed to Massachusetts Anti-Slavery Society.[12]

Garrison was convinced that as long as colonization was considered a respectable cause, it would paralyze the antislavery movement. He wrote a pamphlet, *Thoughts on African Colonization* (1832), which drew on publications of the American Colonization Society and statements by its supporters. He attacked it as a "handmaid of slavery."[13] He showed that many supporters of colonization were slaveholders. He

insisted blacks had the right to choose where they would live and made
clear that many blacks were opposed to colonization. Each year some
15,000 slaves were smuggled into the United States, and about
45,000 were born, but during the past 16 years the American Colonization Society had sent only about 2,160 slaves back to Africa.[14] As a
consequence of Garrison's work, colonization ceased to be a factor in
the abolitionist movement.

Garrison borrowed money to visit Great Britain and speak about
the evils of slavery. He met the aging British abolitionist heroes
William Wilberforce and Thomas Clarkson. He saw Daniel O'Connell, the great champion of Irish freedom. He got to know the young,
eloquent agitator George Thompson who played a major role in abolishing slavery in the British West Indies (1833).[15]

Garrison arranged for Thompson to help promote the abolition
of slavery in the United States. A year older than Garrison, he was
about 5 feet 10 inches tall and had a powerful build. He was a passionate and provocative speaker, and a phenomenal organizer.[16] During
the next two years, he would organize 328 antislavery societies
throughout the North.[17]

In December 1833, 62 abolitionists from nine states (including
21 Quakers) gathered in Philadelphia and established the American
Anti-Slavery Society to operate in the Northern states. Meetings were
held during the day because the mayor announced that police would
be unable to provide adequate protection at night. Nantucket abolitionist Lucretia Mott was among the speakers. Expenses were met by
the British Quaker Joseph Sturge and several New Yorker businessmen. Garrison drafted the Society's Declaration of Sentiments. "All
persons of color who possess the qualifications which are demanded
of others," he wrote, "ought to be admitted forthwith to the enjoyment of the same privileges, and the exercise of the same prerogatives, as others."[18]

Garrison faced stubborn opposition throughout the North. The
most respectable mainstream thinkers were against both slavery and
the abolitionist movement. In *Slavery* (1835), the influential, Harvard-educated Unitarian minister William Ellery Channing insisted
that emancipation was up to Southerners, and Northerners should
mind their own business. Presbyterians refused to preach against
slavery, as did a majority of Baptist ministers. In 1836, the General
Conference of the Methodist Church ordered members "wholly to

refrain from the agitating subject which is now convulsing the country." Garrison despaired that "I am forced to believe that, as it respects the greater portion of professing Christians in this country, Christ has died in vain."[19]

Repression against abolitionists and free blacks escalated. Bills to restrict abolitionist literature were introduced in the legislatures of Connecticut, Maine, New Hampshire and Rhode Island. The president of Amherst ordered that the college antislavery society be disbanded because it was "alienating Christian brethren, retarding and otherwise injuring the cause of religion in the College, and threatening in many ways the prosperity of the institution." Free blacks were banned from settling in Illinois, Iowa, Indiana or Oregon.[20] A Marblehead, Massachusetts, mob wrecked the printing press and home of publisher Amos Dresser, who had previously suffered a public lashing for abolitionist agitation in Nashville.[21] In New Canaan, New Hampshire, local people used oxen to drag a school into a nearby swamp because the teacher was educating black children. Philadelphia abolitionists raised $57,000 to build Pennsylvania Hall on Sixth Street between Race and Arch Streets, providing a bookstore, offices for the Pennsylvania Anti-Slavery Society, offices for the *Pennsylvania Freeman,* which John Greenleaf Whittier edited, and an auditorium accommodating about 3,000 people. The next day, a proslavery mob burned the place down, and the day after that they burned down an orphanage for black children that had been built by the Society of Friends.[22]

The Boston Female Anti-Slavery Society announced that on October 21, 1835, George Thompson would be speaking at their annual meeting, Anti-Slavery Hall, 46 Washington Street. Proslavery goons posted some 500 notices around Boston saying, "A purse of $100 has been raised by a number of patriotic citizens to reward the individual who shall first lay violent hands on Thompson, so that he may be brought to the tar kettle before dark."[23] After Garrison appeared at the hall, a lynch mob turned on him, and he escaped through a back window and hid in a carpenter's shop in Wilson's Lane. The mob found Garrison, threw a noose around his neck and dragged him away. Fortunately, several big men intervened and took him to the Leverett Street Jail, about a mile away, where he might be safe.[24]

One who witnessed this attempted lynching was 24-year-old Wendell Phillips, who watched from his law office on Court Street. Reportedly his oratorical career began at age 5 when he began giving speeches

about the Bible to his family. He attended Boston Latin School, Harvard College and Harvard Law School. Phillips's professor of rhetoric and oratory, Edward T. Channing, criticized the fashionable flowery style used by speakers such as Daniel Webster and urged the value of plain talk.[25] Phillips took it to heart.

A tragic event in Alton, Illinois, propelled Wendell Phillips to the front ranks of the abolitionist movement. Elijah P. Lovejoy, a Presbyterian minister from Maine, had moved to St. Louis where he edited a religious newspaper. He saw Garrison give a speech, and it convinced him to abandon his gradualist views and support immediate emancipation. After he condemned the lynching of a black man, a proslavery mob broke into his offices, destroyed his printing press, and nearly tarred and feathered him. He moved about 30 miles north to Alton, Illinois, where he ordered a new printing press. But as the boat arrived with it, a proslavery mob seized it and threw it into the Mississippi. Lovejoy ordered two more printing presses, and they too were thrown into the river. On November 7, 1837, local people learned that a fourth printing press had been delivered to Lovejoy's house. They broke in, destroyed it and shot him.[26]

News of his murder outraged people in Boston. There were petitions to hold a meeting at Fanueil Hall, which could accommodate about 5,000 people. The building had been given to the city in 1742 by Peter Faneuil, a merchant who had prospered in the slave trade, as a forum for discussing issues of the day. It had become known as the Cradle of Liberty because during the American Revolution, Samuel Adams, John Hancock and James Otis had given speeches there. Initially, city officials denied permission to use the hall, but after protests, the officials gave way. Although motions were presented to uphold freedom of speech and freedom of the press, there wasn't any reference to slavery. Then Massachusetts Attorney General James Trecothick Austin denounced Lovejoy as "presumptuous and impudent." Austin compared the murderers to heroes of the American Revolution.

Phillips climbed onto the speaker's platform. He ridiculed Austin's efforts to associate the mob with revolutionary heroes. He attacked "the tyranny of this many-headed monster, the mob, where we know not what we may do or say, till some fellow-citizen has tried it, and paid for the lesson with his life." Phillips was greeted with tumultuous applause. Linking emancipation with freedom of speech and

freedom of the press proved a breakthrough. Garrison gained his most important associate, and the abolitionist movement gained its greatest orator.

Another abolition stalwart was Theodore Weld. In 1832 Garrison had heard about how he had emerged as a premier abolitionist speaker and organizer in Ohio. Born two years before Garrison, Weld was the son of a Harvard-educated Connecticut Congregational minister, and he went on to Hamilton College. There he encountered the spellbinding Presbyterian evangelist Charles Grandison Finney, who preached about the horrors of eternal damnation and the glory of salvation.[27] Weld began preaching, too, and met British captain Charles Stuart, a preacher who got him interested in temperance, manual-labor education and emancipation. Compared to Garrison, Weld was a moderate, since he believed that *gradual* emancipation should begin immediately, but for most people this was a radical view.

Weld displayed his organizing ability when he attended Lane Seminary, Cincinnati. Although seminary regulations prohibited students from getting involved with issues like slavery about which Christians disagreed, Weld organized well-attended debates and ended up converting students to abolition. Pressured to stop their agitating, almost the entire student body quit the place. Weld was blamed, left the seminary and became a full-time agent for the American Anti-Slavery Society.

Garrison invited him to speak at the annual meeting of the Massachusetts Anti-Slavery Society. Supported by Garrison's benefactors Arthur and Louis Tappan, Weld subsequently organized the Ohio State Abolition Society. He promoted emancipation at the General Assembly of the Presbyterian Church. A tireless speaker like popular evangelists, Weld spoke for a couple of hours at a time. He spoke in churches, barns, stores, homes and any other place that might accommodate a crowd.[28] The number of local antislavery societies in Ohio soared from 38 in 1835 to 133 the next year. Among Weld's converts to emancipation were a young lawyer named Edwin M. Stanton, who later became Abraham Lincoln's secretary of war; Joshua R. Giddings and Ben Wade, both of whom became U.S. senators; and Gerrit Smith, one of New York's wealthiest philanthropists who abandoned colonization and supported emancipation.

Weld joined Garrison to help train new agents in New York. "Weld," recalled Garrison, "was the central luminary around which

they all revolved." Weld remained in New York, helping the American Anti-Slavery Society. He became a good friend of Whittier, who was working for the society and was able to win over many liberal clergymen who were turned off by Garrison's militant views.

Weld married Angelina Grimké who, together with her sister Sarah, was working with Garrison. They were ardent feminists as well as abolitionists. "The great self-evident principles of human rights could be invoked in behalf of women as well as slaves," Sarah insisted.[29] The daughters of a Charleston planter, they had been outraged by slavery and wrote antislavery pamphlets that the Charleston postmaster had burned. They liberated the slaves they had inherited, moved to Philadelphia, became Quakers and embraced Christian reform. Garrison invited them to Boston, and soon they were popular, passionate speakers on the antislavery circuit.

Among the most dynamic of all abolitionists was the former Maryland slave Frederick Douglass, who escaped to freedom in 1838 when he was about 20. He discovered *The Liberator,* which he called "my meat and potatoes." He wrote, "My soul was all set on fire. Its sympathy for my brethren in bonds—its scathing denunciations of slaveholders—its faithful exposures of slavery—and its powerful attacks upon the upholders of the institution—sent a thrill of joy through my soul, such as I had never felt before!"

On March 12, 1839, Douglass spoke against colonization at a church meeting and his remarks were reported in *The Liberator.* About a month later, Garrison gave a talk in New Bedford, Massachusetts, where Douglass lived, and the two met.[30] Garrison invited Douglass to attend a meeting on Nantucket, a prosperous whaling port and abolitionist stronghold. There he met the Massachusetts Anti-Slavery Society's general agent John A. Collins, Wendell Phillips, Lucretia Mott and other key figures in the movement. Before the assembled crowd, Douglass stood up and told his personal story: how he suffered as a slave, how he taught himself to read, to speak well and seize his destiny. Garrison remarked, "Patrick Henry, of revolutionary fame, never made a speech more eloquent in the cause of liberty, than the one we had just listened to from the lips of that hunted fugitive."[31]

Soon the Massachusetts Anti-Slavery Society bought Douglass a small house in Lynn, Massachusetts, a Quaker town, and he went on the lecture circuit. He spoke out for the abolition of slavery and the repeal of Northern laws discriminating against blacks, such as laws

mandating segregated seating on railroad cars. These laws were referred to as Jim Crow, a derogatory reference to blacks from a popular
song of the 1830s.[32]

By 1840, an estimated 200,000 people belonged to antislavery
organizations, but the movement was splintering. Those insisting on
women's rights as well as black rights stuck with Garrison, and mem-
bership plunged.[33] Lewis Tappan broke with the American Anti-
Slavery Society over the issue of women's rights and formed the
American and Foreign Anti-Slavery Society; it endured for 13 years
but never had much impact.

Kentucky-born James Birney liberated the slaves he had inherited
and became an advocate of trying to abolish slavery through political
means. He led the Liberty Party, but he didn't do well in the 1840 and
1844 elections. The main consequence in 1844 was to divert 62,000
votes from one slaveholding candidate, Henry Clay, assuring the election of another slaveholding candidate, James K. Polk.[34] In 1848, the
Free Soil Party was formed to stop the expansion of slavery into new
U.S. territories. It appealed to people who didn't want to do anything
about slavery and to people who feared competition from slave labor.

In 1843 Garrison conceived a blitz campaign of a hundred gath-
erings in Indiana, Ohio, Pennsylvania, New York, Vermont and New
Hampshire, and Douglass was a big attraction. He began one morning in Syracuse with an audience of just five people, Booker T. Washington reported, and "so powerful was his appeal that in the
afternoon he had an audience of five hundred and in the evening he
was tendered the use of an old building that had done service as a
Congregational church. In this house the convention was organized
and carried on for three days. The seeds of Abolition were so well
sown in Syracuse, that thereafter it was always hospitable ground for
anti-slavery advocates."[35]

Douglass proved his mettle in Richmond, Indiana. More than 50
thugs tore down the lecture platform as he was speaking and then went
after him. He was so badly beaten that they gave him up for dead. He
was nursed back to health by Mrs. Neal Hardy, a local Quaker, but he
never regained the full use of his right hand. He went back to speak in
Indiana again and again.

When Douglass wrote his *Narrative of the Life of Frederick Douglass, an
American Slave* (1845), it included an enthusiastic foreword by Garrison
and a letter by Phillips. "I was glad to learn, in your story," Phillips

wrote, "how early the most neglected of God's children waken to a sense of their rights, and of the injustice done them."[36]

Douglass and Garrison traveled to Great Britain for a speaking tour in 1845. Douglass appeared many times with Daniel O'Connell, who always introduced him as the "Black O'Connell." The beloved Irish orator thundered: "No matter under what specious term it may disguise itself, slavery is still hideous. It has a natural, an inevitable tendency to brutalize every noble faculty of man."[37] Douglass called on pioneering British abolitionist Thomas Clarkson.[38] He joined Richard Cobden and John Bright as they campaigned for repeal of the "corn laws," which restricted food imports, thus harming poor people.

Douglass gained considerable notoriety because of his book and widely reported public appearances, and abolitionists worried that he would be targeted by Southern slave hunters. "It would have been regarded as little less than a calamity to have had Frederick Douglass, the incomparable orator, the man in whom almost for the first time, the silent, toiling slaves had found a voice, dragged back into bondage," explained Booker T. Washington.[39] Accordingly, John Bright kicked off a campaign to raise $1,250, the price asked by Douglass's Maryland owner.[40] The manumission was arranged by attorney Ellis Gray Loring, an original backer of The Liberator.

Long indifferent to the slavery issue, literary lion Ralph Waldo Emerson was much impressed by Douglass, and he became an abolitionist. Garrison wrote Emerson: "You exercise a strong influence over many minds in this country which are not yet sufficiently committed to the side of the slave. . . . You are not afraid publicly and pointedly to testify against the enslavement of three million of our countrymen."

Although Garrison had made himself the greatest American champion of abolition, he alienated some of his backers, was hounded by creditors and nearly bankrupt. Garrison raised his subscription price from $2 to $2.50. One benefactor, Gerrit Smith, sent money to keep Garrison "above want . . . having his own mind unembarrassed by the cares of griping poverty, he may be a more effective advocate of the cause of the Saviour's enslaved poor." Several more benefactors—merchants Francis Jackson, Edmund Quincy and William Bassett—stepped forward to pay Garrison's debts, and they agreed to manage The Liberator's finances.[41]

Garrison tried petition campaigns as British abolitionists had done so effectively. He circulated petitions to abolish slavery in the District of Columbia but that proposal was defeated in the House of Representatives.[42] The House banned discussion of antislavery petitions in its chamber.[43] South Carolina Senator John C. Calhoun denounced Garrison's petitions as "a foul slander on nearly one-half of the states of the Union."[44] Despite the best efforts of John Quincy Adams and his compatriots, Congress adopted gag rules that blocked petitions. President Andrew Jackson asked Congress for a law prohibiting the mailing of "incendiary publications intended to instigate the slaves to insurrection."[45]

A Turning Point

Suddenly, the Compromise of 1850 made slavery touch the lives of complacent Northerners as nothing had before. According to this legislation, California was admitted to the Union as a free state, but people in the Utah and New Mexico territories would decide whether or not to allow slavery. The slave trade was outlawed in the District of Columbia, although not slavery itself. The shocker was the Fugitive Slave Act, which provided for federal commissioners to be appointed to issue warrants and force citizens to help catch runaway slaves. Alleged runaways were denied a jury trial and couldn't testify in their own defense. The law put the burden of proof on blacks to show they weren't runaway slaves. Any Northerner could be accused by a slave hunter of helping an alleged runaway slave, brought before a federal commissioner and imprisoned down South. Federal commissioners who decided cases were paid $5 if they freed the accused and $10 if they ordered him or her sent South. A principal deal maker for the Compromise of 1850 was Henry Clay, who had remarked: "I am myself a slaveholder, and I consider that kind of property as inviolable as any other in the country."[46]

The Fugitive Slave Act angered Cincinnati housewife Harriet Beecher Stowe, who began writing about slavery. In March 1852 her novel *Uncle Tom's Cabin* was published, and it was a sensation. It chronicled the suffering and the dignity of black slaves. The book sold a million copies in the United States and another million in Great Britain. Translated into 22 languages, it was considered the second

most popular book (after the Bible). Wendell Phillips observed: "If the old antislavery movement had not roused the sympathies of Mrs. Stowe, the book had never been written; if that movement had not raised up hundreds of thousands of hearts to sympathize with the slave, the book had never been read." Garrison, however, was dissatisfied with the humility of the hero: "Talk not to them of peacefully submitting to chains and stripes—it is base servility! Talk not of servants being obedient to their masters—let the blood of the tyrants flow. . . . Is there to be one law of submission and nonresistance for the black man and another law of rebellion and conflict for the white man?"[47]

In an August 26, 1852, Senate speech, Charles Sumner of Massachusetts denounced the Fugitive Slave Law. He declared that it "offends against the Divine law. No such enactment is entitled to support. As the throne of God is above every earthly throne, so are his laws and statutes above all the laws and statutes of man. To question these is to question God himself. . . . I AM BOUND TO DISOBEY THIS ACT."[48]

On July 4, 1854, at an outdoor meeting of the Massachusetts Anti-Slavery Society in Framingham, Garrison staged one of his most dramatic events. The runaway slave Anthony Burns had recently been caught and returned to Virginia in chains. Garrison had his platform draped in black, and the American flag was hung upside down and bordered in black. After several speakers, including Henry David Thoreau, had denounced slavery, Garrison got up. He spoke about the promise of the Declaration of Independence and lit a candle. Then he burned a copy of the Fugitive Slave Law, and the audience said "Amen." He burned a copy of the orders sending Burns back to Virginia, and again the audience said "Amen." Finally, he burned a copy of the Constitution, with its provisions supporting slavery, and he described it as "a covenant with death, an agreement with hell. . . . So perish all compromises with tyranny." The audience said "Amen."[49]

This was the year the Free Soil party evolved into the Republican Party, and many of its recruits came from the ranks of the abolitionist movement. Few Republicans criticized Garrison for his campaign against the Union. The Illinois lawyer Abraham Lincoln attacked only Southern critics of the Union.

Garrison's dire warnings were borne out by subsequent events. The Kansas-Nebraska Act (1854) established two new U.S. territories

and let them decide whether to permit slavery—which meant that it could extend north of latitude 36° 30', essentially repealing the 1820 Missouri Compromise. In 1857, Supreme Court Chief Justice Roger B. Taney issued his notorious *Dred Scott* decision. He ruled that blacks were not citizens, they could not become citizens, and Congress couldn't ban slavery in any new U.S. territory. Increasing numbers of Southerners demanded that the slave trade, outlawed since 1807, be legalized again. For a while, John Brown's October 1859 raid on the federal arsenal at Harper's Ferry, intended to stir a slave rebellion, triggered a backlash against blacks and abolitionists. When a letter from Frederick Douglass was found among Brown's papers, Douglass fled to Canada and went on a speaking tour through England and Scotland.[50]

Conquest and Destruction

Six weeks after Lincoln was elected president in 1860, South Carolina seceded from the Union, and Garrison urged that it be permitted to go peacefully. "All Union-saving efforts are simply idiotic," he wrote.[51] The April 12, 1861, Confederate assault on Fort Sumter in Charleston's harbor convinced Garrison that it was no longer possible to free the slaves peacefully. "The one great cause of all our national troubles and divisions is SLAVERY; the removal of it, therefore, is essential to our national existence."

Lincoln wanted war to save the Union, not to abolish slavery. While he hated slavery, he wasn't an abolitionist. He became preoccupied with military and political issues of the war. Among other things, he was afraid of losing the support of the slave-holding border states. His December 1861 annual message didn't say anything about emancipating slaves.

Lincoln initially wanted to resolve the slavery conflict by gradual emancipation and colonization. He had talked with speculators about developing the Chiriqui plantation in Panama where free blacks might be sent. Antislavery Union generals Benjamin Butler and David Hunter issued emancipation orders in regions they recaptured from the South, but Lincoln struck them down. On August 30, 1861, John C. Fremont, commander in Missouri, issued an emancipation order, but Lincoln was worried about Kentucky leaving the Union, and he

struck it down, too. In March 1862 Lincoln floated a plan for gradual emancipation with compensation for slaveholders.

These gradualist schemes were opposed by the Radical Republicans. The leading Radical in the U.S. Senate was Charles Sumner. Born in Boston, he had attended the Boston Latin School and graduated from Harvard. After he traveled for three years in Europe, where he learned French, German and Italian, he returned to America in 1840 and lectured at Harvard Law School, edited court reports and wrote law articles. A tall man of six feet four inches, he proved to be a persuasive orator. He was elected to the U.S. Senate in 1851. He attacked the Supreme Court's *Dred Scott v. Sandford* (1856) decision supporting slavery. That Sumner stirred strong emotions became clear in 1856 when enraged South Carolina congressman Preston Brooks beat him so savagely on the Senate floor that Sumner didn't return to for about three years. During the 1860 presidential election campaign, he delivered his famous "Barbarism of Slavery" speech that, among other things, reflected on the epic campaigns to abolish slavery. He noted the contributions of John Locke, Adam Smith, Thomas Jefferson, Benjamin Franklin, Lord Mansfield, John Wesley, Samuel Johnson, Thomas Clarkson, William Wilberforce, William Lloyd Garrison, John Quincy Adams and others.[52] True, Sumner's speeches didn't seem to affect legislative proceedings, but he did inspire more mainstream support for the abolitionist cause. Sumner's principal Senate allies were Benjamin Franklin Wade of Ohio and Henry Wilson of Massachusetts.

In the House, the leading Radical was Thaddeus Stevens of Pennsylvania who had been called "a perfect brigand, a rude jouster in political and personal warfare."[53] Born in Vermont, he suffered many hardships, including a club foot and an alcoholic father, but he did well enough in school to enter and graduate from Dartmouth College. He became a lawyer, starting his practice in Pennsylvania. He emerged as a vigorous champion of Jews, Indians, Chinese, women and others who had been badly treated, as well as black slaves. He was one of only three congressmen who voted against the July 1861 Crittenden-Johnson Resolution, which stated the aim of the war was to save the Union—the resolution was intended to help retain the loyalty of slave states remaining with the North. Stevens supported the August 1861 Confiscation Act permitting Union troops to seize any property, including slaves who helped the Confederate cause.

Stevens declared that saving the North required the destruction of the South: "one party or the other must be reduced to hopeless feebleness and the power of further effort shall be utterly annihilated." After the war, he insisted that the South should be treated as harshly as necessary. He believed the federal government should confiscate plantations and assure the destruction of the old slaveholding aristocracy. Thaddeus Stevens's principal allies included George W. Julian of Indiana and James M. Ashley of Ohio. For these men, abolishing slavery and extending equal rights to blacks, including the right to vote, were top priorities.

The war wasn't going well, and Lincoln was desperate for an advantage. There had been talk about emancipating slaves, but Lincoln didn't want to issue such a proclamation from a position of weakness or have it appear as of desperation. After Union forces prevailed in the Battle of Antietam (September 17, 1862), Lincoln issued a preliminary emancipation proclamation that he made official on January 1, 1863. A tactic for encouraging slave rebellion in the South, it declared that slaves there were free. The Emancipation Proclamation didn't apply to slaves in border states that were still part of the Union, but it did establish that freeing the slaves was a war aim. It also permitted emancipated slaves to join the Union Army, and some 200,000 did.[54]

The Union army began enforcing the North's antislavery policy throughout Southern territory it controlled. In Tennessee, the army began enforcement in middle and western Tennessee, where most of that state's slaves were. Unionists appointed themselves representatives at a state convention that proposed amending Tennessee's constitution to abolish slavery. This was ratified by some 25,000 white Tennesseans permitted to vote in February 1865.[55]

The Union army occupied much of Louisiana, including the port city of New Orleans and the sugar parishes in the southeastern part of the state. Louisiana's Free State Association supported giving free-born blacks the right to vote, but this was opposed by the Union general Nathaniel P. Banks. Lincoln wrote Louisiana governor Michael Hahn about permitting some blacks to vote, but Lincoln added "this is only a suggestion." There was a constitutional convention that abolished slavery and gave some blacks the right to vote. While General Banks was for abolishing slavery, he didn't see how the South could function without the plantation economy, so he forced former slaves

to continue working on their plantations. They received wages, food and medical care, and although they wouldn't be subjected to corporal punishment, they would be punished for refusing to work.

Garrison, Lincoln and just about everyone else underestimated the consequences of war. It split society apart in both the North and South. Military conscription in the North led to the New York draft riots that occurred from July 13 to July 16, 1863. Thousands of people, mostly Irish, attacked draft offices and police stations, but the rioters soon directed much of their fury against blacks. Major General John E. Wood was dispatched to suppress the riot, but he didn't have enough troops. The army used artillery against the rioters and eventually brought the violence to an end, destroying a number of buildings in the process. In the South, there were reportedly over 100,000 deserters from the Confederate army. A high proportion of these were poor conscripts who lived in the Southern upcountry—people who didn't own any slaves.

Stalemated for three years, the war became ever more brutal. Union general Ulysses S. Grant adopted a "policy of pounding": relentless attacks aimed at beating the enemy into submission. But Grant incurred massive casualties, as many as 60,000 in a month.[56] Essayist Ralph Waldo Emerson remarked, "'Tis far better that the Rebels have been pounded instead of negotiated into a peace."[57]

After Union general William Tecumseh Sherman realized his adversaries included civilians as well as soldiers, he concluded he must wage total war. He growled that he must make "old and young, rich and poor, feel the hard hand of war."[58] Sherman destroyed supplies his army didn't need to prevent them from falling into enemy hands. He vowed to "make war so terrible . . . generations would pass away before they would again appeal to it."[59] In Georgia he destroyed rail lines, roads, houses, food, everything. He ordered people to evacuate an area some 60 miles wide that his army passed through on his way to the Atlantic Ocean, where he anticipated meeting up with Union warships. Eliza Andrews, a white woman, described what she saw in the wake of Sherman's army: "I almost felt as if I should like to hang a Yankee myself. There was hardly a fence left standing all the way from Sparta to Gordon. The fields were trampled down and the road was lined with carcasses of horses, dogs, and cattle that the invaders, unable either to consume or to carry away with them, had wantonly shot down, to starve out the people

and prevent them from making their crops. The stench in some places was unbearable."[60]

Confederate general Robert E. Lee's Army of Northern Virginia had endured a nine-month siege at Richmond and Petersburg, Virginia, then tried to escape. But his men were pursued and cornered by General Grant. On April 9, 1865, Lee surrendered at Appomattox Court House, Virginia. Confederacy president Jefferson Davis urged his people to pursue guerrilla warfare against the Yankees, but the Confederates had had enough.

Lincoln had hoped that a firm but generous settlement might ease the transition toward a peace without slavery. After Union forces occupied New Orleans and other Louisiana parishes in 1862, and then occupied Arkansas and Tennessee, he had appointed military governors for those states and had subsequently announced there would be amnesty for most Southerners who swore their loyalty to the Union. He proposed what came to be called the Ten Percent Plan. After federal troops occupied a Southern state, when one-tenth of white voters swore their loyalty to the Union, they could establish a state government provided that slavery was abolished.

In Lincoln's Second Inaugural Address, March 4, 1865, he declared: "With malice toward none, with charity for all, with firmness in the right as God gives us to see the right, let us strive to finish the work we are in to bind up the nation's wounds." These were noble thoughts, though it was too much to expect that many people would be forgiving after the whirlwind of violence.

Though Thaddeus Stevens's ally George W. Julian was the son of a Quaker, he snarled: "As for [Confederacy president] Jeff Davis, I would indict him, I would convict him and hang him in the name of God; as for Robert E. Lee, unmolested in Virginia, hang him too. And stop there? Not at all. I would hang liberally while I had my hand in."[61]

Radical Republicans were skeptical that if only 10 percent of white voters were loyal, there might be efforts to bring back slavery. The Radicals insisted that a majority of white voters must swear their loyalty to the Union. In addition, the Radicals wanted former Confederate officials barred from voting. These proposals became the Wade-Davis bill that Lincoln refused to sign. On December 18, 1865, Congress ratified the Thirteenth Amendment to the Constitution, banning slavery. Some 3.9 million American slaves were free at last.[62]

Revolts, War and the Collapse of Cuban Slavery

After Saint-Domingue was convulsed by slave rebellion during the 1790s and its sugar production collapsed, many French planters fled to Cuba and began building sugar plantations there. Soon Cuba emerged as a major exporter of sugar. One historian referred to the sudden prosperity as the "dance of the millions."[1]

When in 1811, the Cortes, Spain's national legislature, followed Great Britain's lead and introduced a bill to abolish the Spanish slave trade, Cuban planters became hysterical. They warned that abolishing the slave trade would be an economic catastrophe. They warned it could incite slaves to rebellion—another Haiti. Cuban planters suggested they might have to consider seeking immediate independence from Spain. Patterning their strategy after that of planters in the British Caribbean who for years stalled proposals to abolish the slave trade, they demonstrated the strength of their political opposition.

In 1815, Cuba produced only about half as much sugar as Jamaica. A quarter-century later, Cuba produced 60 percent more sugar than Jamaica and all of Britain's Caribbean colonies put together, and double Brazil's production.[2]

In the process, many plantations grew quite large and their own-ers, quite rich. By the late 1820s, sugar was produced on about 1,000 plantations that averaged about 160 acres of sugar cane fields and per-haps 750 acres of woods and pasture. An average plantation with ap-proximately 70 slaves might have produced about 70 tons of sugar annually.[3]

Initially, sugar plantations were located around Havana. When these were expanded and more sugar plantations were developed by burning the forests, slaves and oxen were brought in to do the work. Sugar cane was planted on the same soil year after year, without adding manure or anything else to enrich the soil. After planting, sugar cane had to be cut by hand when the amount of sucrose in the juice was highest. The harvested cane was hauled on carts to a planta-tion sugar mill. Since the sugar had to be extracted within 24 to 48 hours before it spoiled, and Cuban roads were poor, it wasn't possi-ble to carry the harvested cane very far. Every plantation had to have its own mill. Harvesting cane and extracting sugar required large numbers of people at the peak time, and there wasn't always much for all these people to do the rest of the year. It was seasonal work, yet the planters had to maintain the slaves year-round—an inherent ineffi-ciency of the slave system.[4]

The planters didn't have strong incentives to upgrade the effi-ciency of their mills. Having built the mills, the planters seemed con-tent to have them last as long as possible before spending more money on them. Rather than invest in steam-driven rollers for pressing the sugar cane, for instance, many plantation owners continued to rely on the oxen-driven rollers. No surprise, then, that not one improve-ment in sugar milling technology was developed in Cuba. Cultivating more land for sugar cane appeared to be the principal method to im-prove the productivity of a mill.

The solution to every major issue involving sugar production seemed to be buying more slaves, who essentially subsidized the plan-tations since they did not get market-rate compensation. Slaves con-tinued to come into Cuba even after Great Britain negotiated treaties with Spain to stop the slave trade. According to British consul David Turnbull, each slave brought into Cuba cost the importer a gold dou-bloon: a quarter went to bribe Cuba's captain-general (governor), a quarter to bribe the coast guard, a quarter to the harbor master and a quarter to the custom's officer. The more slaves came into Cuba, the

more money these officials made, so they had a direct stake in the slave trade. For decades, they stubbornly resisted internal and external assaults on the slave trade in Cuba. Naturally, it was in the interest of these officials to suppress any slave revolts that might disrupt their racket. Spain maintained 25,000 to 30,000 soldiers in Cuba throughout most of the nineteenth century.

To be sure, sugar wasn't everything in Cuba. There were several thousand cattle ranches, but Cuba wasn't noted for the quality of its beef. Although there were some efforts to introduce better breeds like Hereford or Durham as well as Guinea or Para grass, the results were disappointing. Perhaps 10 percent of the people working on cattle ranches were slaves. Many of the French planters who fled the revolution on Saint-Domingue settled in eastern and central Cuba where they grew coffee. There were reportedly as many as 2,000 coffee farms achieving peak production during the 1830s, and for many years coffee farms had about as many slaves as sugar plantations. But the return on investment in sugar production was double that in coffee production. Cuban coffee production declined after the 1840s. As coffee production declined, tobacco production went up, especially in eastern Cuba. The number of black slaves involved with tobacco growing increased, but most of the work was done by free blacks and whites.[5] So sugar production dominated the Cuban economy and the demand for slaves.

As the sugar planters became wealthy, they often moved off the plantations and bought houses in towns such as Havana, Santiago or Matanzas. Many of the planters were anxious for respectability and paid large sums to acquire aristocratic titles from the Spanish government, which was always in need of cash: A count might cost $25,000 and a marquess might cost $45,000.[6] In addition to respectability, such titles were also convenient since a title-holder couldn't be arrested for debt or many other crimes. The planters liked to live lavishly on their slave labor. One sugar planter was said to have installed at his estate a fountain of gin for men and a fountain of cologne for women, another had his dining room floor lined with gold doubloons. Marble staircases, renaissance ceilings and luxurious touches abounded in the houses where planters attended one costume or masked ball after another.

Partially to hedge the risk of a slave revolt that might destroy their Cuban plantation assets, planters often invested some of their money

in overseas properties, including New York townhouses and French chateaus. Many Cuban planters invested in Spain, building factories, banks and other properties. Naturally, such Cuban planters acquired political clout, influencing Spain's policies about Cuba and slavery. In addition, captains-general (governors) of Cuba usually returned to Spain with a fortune in bribes, further expanding Cuba's influence on the mother country. It was no wonder the British had a hard time getting Spanish officials to crack down on Cuban slavery.

Fear of Slave Revolts

Cuban plantation owners lived in fear of a slave revolt, which implied there was a limit to how far slavery could safely go. As the number of black slaves in Cuba increased by the thousands every year, Cuban creoles as well as white planters and merchants were more mindful of the large populations of free blacks in nearby Haiti and Jamaica and of what might happen in Cuba.

A succession of slave revolts broke out in 1843. At the Alcancia plantation in Cárdenas, slaves destroyed a sugar mill, then moved to the Luisa, Trinidad and Moscú plantations, recruiting rebels and causing much destruction. Slaves revolted on a horse-breeding ranch at Ranchuelo and on the Cárdenas railroad. Many of the slaves fled to Cuba's interior, and the authorities used bloodhounds in an effort to track down the runaways.

The government announced new regulations for slaves. Slaves were forbidden to leave their plantations without permission. Slaves would be liberated and given $500 if they tipped off authorities about a planned revolt. In an effort to discourage further revolts, Captain-General Gerónimo Valdés dispatched troops around Cuba.

This wasn't enough of a deterrent. A slave revolt at the Triunvirato sugar mill occurred in which some 400 slaves seized control of the mill, burned sugar cane and destroyed five other sugar mills on neighboring plantations before they were cornered and slaughtered. Fearing a large-scale revolt, the government arrested some 2,000 free blacks, more than 1,000 slaves and about 70 whites. Many were tied to ladders and whipped to extract confessions. A hundred were whipped to death, and another 78 were shot. Black militia regiments were dissolved since authorities feared blacks with guns.[7] Stricter slave regula-

tions ensued. African religious ceremonies, for instance, were out-lawed, since slaves communicated with each other at such events and drums were apparently used to communicate with slaves farther away. Planters who didn't go along with all this were exiled. Although the repression seemed to work, planters began to fear that there would be a full-scale slave revolt if they didn't make some concessions.

A Scheme to Protect Cuban Slavery

Perhaps reflecting British pressure to do something about the slave trade, the Spanish government appointed Marqués de la Pezuela as captain-general of Cuba in December 1853. Although he was viewed in Spain as a conservative, he held antislavery views. For two years, he had served as governor of Puerto Rico, where he pursued antislavery policies. He was determined to suppress the Cuban slave trade. He began by writing articles discussing slavery for *Diario de la Marina,* insisting that Spain must uphold its treaty obligations. He announced that persons importing slaves to Cuba would be fined and expelled from the island and that slaves who had been freed by the British Royal Navy but subsequently enslaved in Cuba should be set free. Cuban officials who failed to cooperate with antislavery policies would be dismissed. On May 3, 1854, he issued a decree that authorized police to enter plantation property and search for slaves who might have been brought into Cuba illegally. Pezuela's policies marked the first serious attempt by the Spanish government to curb slavery in Cuba.

Slaveholders were outraged. There was much talk about separating Cuba from Spain and becoming part of the United States, where slavery appeared to be politically secure. This idea didn't come out of the blue. It had been much discussed in the United States. President James K. Polk (1845–1849) had promoted the idea of Manifest Destiny: that the United States should extend from the Atlantic to the Pacific and, it seemed, be on the lookout for any additional territory. Polk had acquired the Oregon Territory from Great Britain and more than a million miles of the American Southwest from Mexico. In May 1848 Polk had proposed buying Cuba, and three in his cabinet—Secretary of State James Buchanan, Secretary of the Treasury Robert Walker and Secretary of the Navy John Y. Mason—agreed. Buchanan authorized the U.S. ambassador to Spain, Romulus M.

Sanders, to pay up to $100 million for Cuba but Sanders bungled the negotiations.[8]

American interest in Cuba persisted because the South was eager to expand the number of slave states as a strategy for assuring the future of slavery. In New Orleans, Cuban rebel Narciso López recruited adventurers, including veterans of the Mexican-American War, and promised each recruit $1,000 and 160 acres in Cuba if they were successful in seizing power. The U.S. government broke up the scheme as a violation of U.S. neutrality policy, but the plotting continued. López organized another expedition, 600 strong, that invaded Cuba in May 1850. But when Cubans didn't rally to his banner, he fled to Key West. In August he sailed again for Cuba, this time with 400 men. At about that time, there were two revolts in Cuba, both crushed. López landed at Bahí Honda, but was caught and garroted. His men were shipped across the Atlantic to work in Spain's mercury mines. Cuban planters withheld their support from such adventurers because they became wary of a war for independence. They were interested in being bought out.

When a new Spanish government came to power, Pezuela was dismissed and replaced as captain-general by Gutiérrez de la Concha, who ordered a retreat from Pezuela's policies. He had served as captain-general a few years before, when he supported the view that slavery was necessary to assure Spanish rule in Cuba. His main concern was to calm down the slaveholders.[9] Mollified by Concha's appointment and less concerned that Spain might undermine Cuban slavery, the planters lost interest in being annexed to the United States.

A Cuban Abolitionist Movement Begins

Slowly antislavery opinions gained more support in Spain and in the Spanish Caribbean. There were more teachers, authors and others who, in many cases having been educated in the United States or Europe, embraced liberal ideas. They were embarrassed by the endemic corruption of the Spanish government and its tolerance of uncivilized practices.

Francisco de Arango y Parreño was a persuasive witness. Back in 1789, as the intendant or colonial administrator of Havana, he had persuaded the Spanish government to open up Cuba to slave traders

from many nations. When Spain's Cortes debated the slave trade in 1811, he had defended it. As a member of the Council of the Indies, a colonial governing body for Spain's Caribbean colonies, he opposed proposals to abolish the slave trade. Yet he had come to acknowledge the horrors of slavery and tried to win over other Spanish officials. He dedicated what years he had left to suppressing the slave trade.[10]

In 1855, a few members of the Cortes spoke out against slavery: The principal abolitionists there were Nicolás María Rivero, Emilio Castelar and Laureano Figuerola.[11] In 1857 Rivero's newspaper, *La Discusión,* declared that the time had come to abolish slavery.

General Francisco Serrano succeeded Concha as captain-general in 1859, and he was instructed to encourage reforms that somehow would pacify dissidents without inflaming slaveholders. Believing that people in Cuba were entitled to the same political rights as people in Spain, he relaxed restrictions against political agitation for reform. Serrano was followed by Domingo Dulce in 1862, and he continued a policy of political liberalization. Reformers started publishing *El Siglio,* a newspaper that helped launch public debates about issues.

There were more antislavery voices in the 1860s. Among the most important was the Creole Julio Vizcarrondo (1830–1889). Born in Puerto Rico, the son of a slaveholder, he attended high school on the island and continued his studies in the United States. It isn't known which college he attended, but many slaveholders in Puerto Rico and Cuba sent their sons to the United States for more education, where, like Vizcarrondo, they picked up ideas of nationalism, independence and emancipation.[12]

It was easier for antislavery views to develop in Puerto Rico than in Cuba because it had a sizable number of small farmers who, without slaves, grew coffee, tobacco, fruits and vegetables. Unlike in Cuba, sugar never dominated the Puerto Rican economy and consequently, slaveholders had less political clout in Puerto Rico.

Julio Vizcarrondo married an American woman, Harriet Brewster, believed to be a Quaker. Vizcarrondo emancipated the slaves he had inherited and began promoting the abolition of slavery in Puerto Rico. But the colonial government censored the press and he was thwarted. For a while he worked as a teacher and wrote a book, *Elementos de Historia y Geografía de Puerto Rico* (1862), to help children learn about the history and geography of Puerto Rico. He and his wife opened a school for poor children.

Vizcarrondo brooded about slavery, though, and he decided to try advancing the abolitionist cause in Madrid, where decisions about a colony like Puerto Rico (or Cuba) would be made. On December 7, 1864, Vizcarrondo organized the Sociedad Abolicionista Espanõla (Spanish Abolitionist Society). He adopted the same symbol, an African slave on a bended knee ("Am I Not A Man And A Brother?"), that porcelain entrepreneur Josiah Wedgewood had created for the British abolitionist movement in the late eighteenth century. His principal associates were fellow Puerto Ricans Joaquín Sanromá and José J. Acosta. The Havana-born Rafael María de Labra, whose mother was Creole and whose father was an officer in the Spanish army, emerged as a leading Spanish abolitionist. Emilio Castelar and Laureano Figuerola were also important members of the new abolitionist group. Vizcarrondo's wife organized a chapter for women while he helped launch its newspaper, *El Abolicionista Espanol* and organized abolitionist meetings in theaters around Spain. Vizcarrondo and his associates wrote articles expressing abolitionist views in other newspapers such as *La Discusión, La Democracia* and *La Propaganda.* Sanromá remarked that Vizcarrondo was "the soul. . . . He began the movement, organized it, united us, encouraged us, he looked after the publications of pamphlets and the *Abolicionista,* and he did all this with a deal, diligence, and a practical sense that betrayed his Anglo-American education."

Meanwhile, a half-dozen rich planters who had supported annexation with the United States started meeting at the Havana Reform Club. They wanted more say in how Cuba was governed by Spain. In particular, they wanted representation in Spain's Cortes and limits on the power of the captain-general. These men began to envision different ways of organizing the sugar business. With the construction of Cuban railroads, it was possible to ship sugar cane longer distances. This created the possibility of having sugar mills serve many plantations, which meant it would no longer be necessary for each plantation to invest in and manage its own mill. The development of such specialized factories suggested the possibility of importing factory labor, the kind of free laborers who manned factories in Europe, Great Britain and the United States. Importing free white laborers might help keep Cuba Spanish and reduce the fear of revolts that accompanied the importation of black slaves. These reformers came to the conclusion that Cuba would be better off without the slave trade.[13]

Meanwhile, sugar prices declined as a result of expanding sugar cane production and new supplies of sugar from sugar beet cultivation in Europe, which put pressure on Cuban planters. Britain's Royal Navy disrupted the slave trade enough that buying slaves became more costly. Slavery could not be made to function more efficiently, based as it was mainly on hand labor with simple tools.

In 1865 slaves at two plantations, Miguel Aldama's Unión and Julián de Zulueta's Alava, went on strike, refusing to continue working without compensation. They declared that since they had been imported to Cuba after 1820, they were legally free. Although there was no violence, the planters summoned militia forces to compel the strikers to resume work. But the spectacle of slaves going on strike had revolutionary implications.

White factory workers began to establish mutual aid societies, collecting a part of each member's pay to help those who became sick. Such societies operated on a parish by parish basis. Free black workers began to establish similar mutual aid societies. People began to help themselves in other ways, too. A newspaper was established to publish information helpful for workers. In some tobacco factories, those who were literate read books to groups of workers. In other words, ordinary people were starting to educate themselves.

Cuban unrest, agitation to make Spain's colony of Santo Domingo independent, and the victory of the North in the U.S. Civil War were events pressuring the Spanish government. In November 1865, the government agreed that Cuba should elect representatives to serve on a commission that would go to Spain and discuss possible reforms. But before the representatives departed, local officials made it illegal for workers to educate each other, claiming that "meetings of the artisans were converted into political clubs." The books being read were "prejudicial to the weak intelligence of persons who do not possess the critical faculties and the learning necessary to judge with accuracy."[14]

The representatives hadn't reached Madrid when, on July 9, 1866, the Cortes passed a law banning the slave trade. Those who violated the law were subject to imprisonment, and anyone who resisted arrest or caused injury to slaves could be put to death. There was a revolt in the San Gil barracks (Madrid), which General Leopoldo O'Donnell, the prime minister, suppressed. Queen Isabella II dismissed him for his brutality. General Francisco Serrano, an opponent of the queen, was arrested and exiled to the Canary Islands.

The reform commission concluded its work in April 1867, and Cubans expected there would be some changes. But no reforms were forthcoming. Then General Francisco Lersundi was named captain-general of Cuba. He announced a 6 percent income tax, which could jump to 12 percent if he believed the government needed it. This income tax was on top of customs taxes and other taxes.

Big planters were reluctant to revolt against the taxes since their vast properties would probably be damaged in the violence. Many small planters in eastern Cuba, however, figured they had more to gain and less to lose. They owned little machinery, and two-thirds of their sugar mills were powered by oxen. Some of these planters had let their slaves work off their plantations for wages.

In Masonic lodges, particularly in Bayamo, eastern planters began to talk about a possible revolt. There, three members of a Masonic lodge established *Junta Revolucionaria* to have discussions with some of the big landowners in the region who supported reform. Many of these planters had sent their children to Europe or the United States for an education, and often they became interested in the liberal ideas they encountered.

Support for Slavery Erodes

On September 18, 1868, discontented Spanish liberals together with army and naval officers agreed that the corrupt monarchy must go. General Francisco Serrano came out of exile, led some soldiers into Madrid, and Queen Isabella II fled to France. A new government was headed by Serrano, who served as prime minister, with Juan Prim as minister of war. The revolutionaries hadn't worked out a program other than a desire to hold new elections for the Cortes. They did support the kinds of constitutional changes that were being adopted through much of Western Europe, including near-universal male suffrage, freedom of the press, freedom of assembly, freedom of association and freedom of religion.[15]

Since the trend in the West was to abolish slavery, the new government agreed in principle that should be done. But the commitment was for Spain only, not Spain's colonies—Cuba, Puerto Rico and the Philippines. The revolution and possible support for abolition energized abolitionists. Labra, for one, expressed the natural rights view

that individuals owned their bodies, and consequently he opposed paying compensation to slaveholders.

In eastern Cuba, on October 10, 1868, Carlos Manuel Céspedes gave a speech that became known as "Grito de Yara" (Cry of Yara). He urged Cubans to fight for independence. "Gentlemen," he said, "the power of Spain is decrepit and worm-eaten. If it still appears strong and great, it is because for over three centuries we have regarded it from our knees. Let us rise!"[16] He was certainly right that Spain was decrepit, since its government had been in turmoil amid decades of wrangling among members of the royal family, generals and politicians. It was hard to tell what any of them stood for aside from their own ambition.

About 40 businessmen from western Cuba met with Captain-General Lersundi. He blasted the rebels and refused to discuss any of the concerns Cubans had. Spanish government officials were mainly concerned to protect the flow of Cuban revenue. Since offering reforms to colonists didn't seem to have worked in the past, his idea was to force Cuba into submission. Some of the businessmen backed Lersundi. Others were alienated by his intransigence, and a number of these, including José Manuel Mestre, Morales Lemus and Miguel Aldama, began raising money for the rebels.

Rebels gained control of towns in the Oriente and Puerto Principe areas. For the time being, the rebels wouldn't say what they proposed to do about slavery. Runaway slaves weren't accepted as soldiers unless their owners approved. Although the rebels had limited resources, Lersundi's forces were busy guarding the big plantations around Cárdenas and Colón, where the sugar cane was almost ready to be harvested. Soon, however, Spanish forces mobilized against the rebels. Near Bayamo, Spanish forces fought about 4,000 rebels led by Donato Mámol, and the rebels lost half their men.

Céspedes freed his slaves, declared war against Spain and proclaimed the Republic of Cuba.[17] He was joined by 37 other planters who liberated their slaves. By November, the rebels had recruited some 12,000 soldiers. Spanish soldiers burned Bayamo, forcing the revolutionary leaders to keep moving around. Cubans resented Spanish domination of the Cuban government and their exclusion from it, and they objected to the government corruption and high taxes imposed by Spain.

The Spanish government had enough internal distractions without a Cuban war. General Serrano dispatched Domingo Dulce to

replace Lersundi as captain-general. Dulce took over on January 4,
1869, and announced that there would be freedom of the press,
freedom of assembly, and Cuba would be able to send representatives to the Cortes. He offered rebels amnesty if they came forward
within 40 days. He sent somebody to talk with Céspedes.[18]

But Dulce hadn't tried to win over the pro-Spanish planters, and
they rose up against him. They objected to dealing with rebels. They
particularly distrusted a man like Céspedes who had freed his slaves.
The planters formed militias that eventually numbered some 20,000
soldiers and 13,500 cavalry. The militias destroyed rebel meeting
places and disrupted the flow of volunteers on their way to help Céspedes. Intimidated by the militias, Dulce abandoned liberalization.
Press censorship returned, and anyone suspected of supporting the
rebels was imprisoned. Cuba's Ten Years War was underway.

The individuals who led the Cuban revolution weren't interested
in emancipating slaves, but they recognized that they probably could-
n't gain diplomatic recognition as an independent state and perhaps
secure some military or other assistance without emancipation.[19] In
addition, if there was going to be a war with Spain, the revolutionaries
would need all the help they could get, including slaves serving as loyal
soldiers. But the revolutionaries couldn't afford to alienate the slaveholders in Western Cuba. Céspedes declared, "We desire the gradual
and indemnified abolition of slavery." Later, he said, "a free Cuba is
incompatible with a slavist Cuba."

In April 1869, the rebels held a constitutional convention in
Guámairo with representatives from the areas where they had some
control. Céspedes was chosen to be president of the republic and
Manuel de Quesada, commander-in-chief. There would be a legislature—the House of Representatives. Article 24 of the draft constitution stated: "All the inhabitants of the Republic are absolutely free."
Apparently, however, it became necessary to compromise with some of
the planters on their side, and the House of Representatives later decided that former slaves must continue working on their plantations,
but they would receive pay, food and clothing. Céspedes decreed that
inciting slaves to revolt would be punishable by death. Such compromises upset some of the rebel commanders.

The Guámairo convention voted in favor of annexing Cuba to the
United States—seemingly the best hope for getting out from under
Spanish rule since the rebels hadn't been able to spark an uprising

throughout the island. The United States had recently acquired Alaska from Russia, and there was much interest in acquiring Cuba.

U.S. president Ulysses S. Grant, who had been the leading Northern general in the Civil War, wanted to promote the abolition of Cuban slavery. Destruction of American properties in Cuba added further provocation to intervene. The government had some clout, since the United States was the biggest market for Cuban products,[20] with two-thirds of Cuban sugar shipped to the United States.[21]

Grant sent a friend, General David Daniel E. Sickles, to Spain. He was a curious choice. The New York State Assembly had censured him for bringing prostitute Fanny White into its chambers. Later he went with her to England and presented her to Queen Victoria, leaving his pregnant wife, Teresa, back home. As a congressman, Sickles became involved in a larceny case. He murdered his wife's lover, Philip Barton Key (son of "Star Spangled Banner" composer Francis Scott Key), in Lafayette Park, near the White House, but was acquitted after pleading insanity. During the Civil War, he had fought for the North, lost a leg at Gettysburg and became noted for his harsh policies as a Reconstruction governor in the Carolinas.[22]

Spain's General Prim, who ruled with General Serrano, met with Sickles and his associate Paul Forbes. Prim's proposal had four elements: an amnesty for rebels who handed over their weapons; an election of Cuban representatives to the Spanish Cortes; a plebiscite to determine whether Cubans wanted independence, and if they did, they would have it; in the case of independence, Cuba would pay Spain $125 million of compensation, guaranteed by the United States. But it wasn't clear Spain would actually fulfill Prim's offer if it were accepted by Cuba and the United States, because the Spanish government was unstable and there was much Spanish opposition to the offer. Opponents were convinced that their military forces could again make Cuba a submissive generator of revenue for Spain.

Sickles offered to help resolve the war, which appeared likely to go on for a while, with four provisions: Spain would accept the independence of Cuba; Cuba would offer Spain compensation for giving up sovereignty and various government properties in Cuba; Cuba would abolish slavery; and both sides would agree to an armistice until peace negotiations were completed. If Spain refused to accept these conditions, then the United States might provide assistance to the

Cuban rebels.[23] The provision about abolishing slavery was probably enough by itself to doom this proposal.

Spain countered by demanding that the Cubans end their rebellion. Spanish officials promised to hold an election that would give Cubans an opportunity to vote on the independence question. U.S. Secretary of State Hamilton Fish expressed skepticism because Spanish officials might fix the election. Although American opinion increasingly favored the Cubans, Britain and France strongly urged the United States to refrain from supporting the Cuban rebels, as they had refrained from supporting the South during the Civil War.

If the rebel movement had been clearly and strongly for abolishing slavery, it might have secured an American connection that could have helped win the struggle against Spain. But the presence of proslavery planters among rebel ranks sent confused signals. After the Civil War, it was difficult for the U.S. government to support rebels who might tolerate slavery.

In September 1869 Manuel Beccera became Spain's colonial minister; he believed that offering enough reforms might persuade Cuba to remain a Spanish colony. To counter the rebels who offered freedom to slaves joining the rebel cause, he proposed liberating slaves who fought in the Spanish army, and he proposed freedom for slave children who were born after September 29, 1868. He said they should continue to be with their masters until age 18, unless one of their parents had purchased their freedom. These proposals were rejected because they would have alienated Cuban slaveholders who were a powerful interest group in Madrid. Acceptance of the proposals would have been viewed as an acknowledgment that the rebels had justice on their side.

Beccera resigned on April 1, 1870, but this wasn't a victory for the slaveholders—Segismundo Moret y Prendergast, a member of the Sociedad Abolicionista Españõla, became minister of the colonies.[24] He recognized that Spain couldn't defeat the rebels, and the longer the war continued, the greater was the likelihood that the United States would support the rebels. Spanish officials struggled to figure out what they could do about the turmoil in their country and the war in Cuba. Moret wrote Cuba's Captain-General Caballero de Rodas: "France and Britain will not help us while we are slave-holders, and this one word [slavery] gives North America the right to hold a suspended threat above our heads."[25]

Moret and fellow abolitionists Julio Vizcarrondo, Luis Padial and Romàn Baldorioty de Castro proposed a bill providing that children of slave mothers would be freed, without compensation to the slaveholders; children of slave mothers, born during the 18 months before the law took effect, would be bought by the government for $125; slaves over 60 years old would be freed, and their masters would be obligated to continue taking care of them; slaves owned by the Spanish government and slaves who served in the Spanish army would be liberated. Whipping would be outlawed and any slave found to have suffered excessive cruelty would be granted freedom. On July 4, 1870, the Cortes voted for the Moret bill and it became law. Once Cuban representatives joined the Cortes—which couldn't happen till the end of the war between Spain and Cuba—the Spanish government could compensate plantation owners for the loss of slaves who were emancipated.[26]

Unfortunately, slaveholders had enough clout to thwart the Moret Law. It wasn't made public for several months. Many slaves over 60 weren't liberated according to the law because they lacked proof of their age. Slaveholders held the often inadequate records or they blocked access to them. In other cases, slaves were officially liberated but didn't receive any pay for their work and continued to work without compensation as they had when officially enslaved.

Although the Moret Law didn't do much for slaves of working age or for children who were obliged to work for their masters until age 18, it was a beginning. The Moret Law was one reason the slave population started to decline. Passage of the law made clear to increasing numbers of people that emancipation was coming.

According to government estimates, 45 percent of those freed by the Moret Law were elderly, 21 percent were unregistered slaves, 19 percent died, and 12 percent gained freedom by self-purchase or manumission. The Moret Law liberated about 25,000 Cuban slaves in the half-dozen years after it was passed.[27]

The Moret Law was sweet poison for the planters. Since the principal groups of slaves affected—the very young and the very old—were the least productive, the planters didn't really lose anything, and children were under their thumb for years. But the law affirmed a decisive principle: The government that slaveholders had counted on to enforce slavery could restrict it. Once that principle prevailed, why couldn't the government further restrict or even abolish slavery?

By the 1870s, the Spanish had secured control of western Cuba where the big plantations were, but they couldn't dislodge rebels who persisted with guerrilla warfare in eastern Cuba. The rebels had 10,000 to 20,000 men, enough to continue causing trouble for the Spanish, but they didn't have enough guns, and they couldn't agree whether they would improve their position or undermine it by trying to destroy the western sugar plantations. In February 1874, Dominican-born Máximo Gómez y Báez, a former Spanish officer who became a top-ranking rebel commander, invaded western Cuba. He won a couple of battles but he withdrew because his men suffered heavy casualties and lacked the ammunition to continue.[28] In January 1875 Gómez got clearance to again attack western Cuba, and in six weeks he burned 83 plantations and freed slaves, but rebel politicians feared the risk of a disastrous confrontation with a large force of well-armed Spanish troops, and he returned to eastern Cuba. Rebels generally preferred hit-and-run attacks.

The rebels suffered from high turnover among leaders, many of whom were shot. Céspedes struggled to keep the rebel government together, but he was consumed by the conflicts within the rebel camp. Rebel planters were angry about his declarations to abolish slavery, while radicals were angry at his compromises with the planters. Stressed out, he ate little, suffered from various ailments and became more volatile. He demanded more and more power until his associates deposed him. In March 1874 he was ambushed and killed by Spanish forces in San Lorenzo. His successor as president was Salvador Cisneros Betancourt, a Camagüey cattleman whose cabinet consisted entirely of slaveholders.

There was brutality on both sides. Pro-Spanish militias shot any rebels they found. People were shot on the mere suspicion of sympathizing with the rebels. In rebel strongholds, Spanish authorities ordered solders to kill any males away from home without an acceptable reason. Women and children were marched to fortified towns that were essentially concentration camps. The houses of rebels were burned. When the Spanish captured the steamship *Virginius* in October 1873, they shot 53 people on board. General Máximo Gómez y Báez trained his men to use a machete as a military weapon. They became adept at hacking their adversaries to death, and a rebel machete charge terrified the often poorly trained Spanish conscript soldiers.

Perhaps the most daring rebel commander was Antonio de la Caridad Maceo y Grajales, the son of a Venezuelan mulatto farmer and an Afro-Cuban woman. Céspedes's "Grito de Yara" speech inspired Maceo to join the rebel army as a private. Maceo's leadership ability soon became evident, and he rose quickly through the ranks and became the second-ranking rebel commander. Nicknamed the Bronze Titan, he was noted for bold attacks and resourceful escapes. But the more successful he became, the more the white rebels feared he might try to establish some kind of black republic, like Haiti.

Captain-General Arsenio Martínez de Campos y Antón negotiated the Pact of Zanjón, which most rebel leaders signed on February 12, 1878. Since the war had been stalemated for years, these rebel leaders concluded that there wasn't any point to continuing the struggle, and the pact offered some of what they wanted. In it, the Spanish agreed to give Cuba some autonomy and to grant amnesty and freedom to slaves who had fought with the rebels (the Moret Law had already granted freedom to slaves who fought with the Spanish). On March 15, Campos met with Maceo, a holdout, in an effort to win him over. When it was clear that neither independence nor the abolition of slavery would be part of the deal, Maceo decided that he couldn't go along with it. He continued fighting a while longer, then fled to New York as an exile.

The Ten Years War ended with exhaustion on both sides. Altogether, an estimated 208,000 Spaniards and 50,000 Cubans died during the decade of war. The war was believed to have cost some $300 million (a lot of money back then). The number of slaves declined more than a third: from 363,288 recorded in the 1869 census to 227,902 in 1878. The decline reflected slave deaths due to harsh working conditions on plantations, war-related slave deaths, slaves freed by the Moret Law and slaves who simply ran away from their plantations and lived on their own in the countryside or in cities.[29]

Although the Pact of Zanjón didn't liberate Cuba's slaves, it set the stage for abolition. That so many people were fighting for abolition undoubtedly led slaves to hope that someday they would be free. They developed higher expectations and became impatient, particularly as they saw other slaves escape from their plantations. At least partially depleted of slaves, many planters began hiring free workers. These included Creole peasants and free Chinese. The war further

weakened the grip of Cuban authorities who were distracted by chronic conflicts in Spain.

Emancipation Nears

The position of the sugar planters declined. Many of them suffered serious losses when the rebels raided western Cuba and sugar production dropped. In Oriente province (eastern Cuba), rebels had destroyed more than 60 percent of the sugar mills. In Puerto Príncipe province, 99 percent of the mills were destroyed.

There was more rebellion. In 1879, Calixto García and Antonio Macea, veterans of the Ten Years War, led the Guerra Chiquita (Small War) aimed at relieving grievances not fully resolved by the Pact of Zanjón—in particular, slavery and taxes.[30] The rebellion was suppressed by sending in almost 20,000 additional Spanish soldiers, but the threat of a slave rebellion seemed to increase in eastern Cuba. Many slaves had participated in the Ten Years War and quite a few had gained their freedom. Increasing numbers of slaves abandoned their plantations, practiced passive resistance and started fires that destroyed sugar cane. Creditors restricted lending to plantations, recognizing the uncertainties they faced. In addition, the Cuban currency declined against a gold standard.

In 1879 the Cuban slave system was also jolted when lists of registered slaves were published, revealing that some 29,000 slaves hadn't been registered. Plantation owners were supposed to register their slaves and pay a tax on each one, but many plantation owners minimized taxes by not registering all their slaves. Unregistered slaves were legally free. The law hadn't been enforced in years, and the new enforcement policy meant that many slaveholders could find their slave labor forces suddenly depleted.

The Moret Law had provided that Cuba could elect representatives to the Spanish Cortes when the war was over, and there would be efforts to resolve the slavery issue. A Spanish official came up with a new name—*patronato* (patronage)—for an old idea: a legally liberated slave (*patrocinado*) who was obligated to continue working for his or her master (*patrono*). Those who supported gradual emancipation envisioned this as a status between slavery and freedom. The *patronato* was pre-

sented as a compromise to resolve conflicts of interest between slave holders and slaves.

Accordingly, in November 1879 Spain's minister of the colonies, Salvador Albacete, introduced a bill to abolish Cuban slavery. He asserted that since the Pact of Zanjón had freed slaves who fought with the rebels, it was hard to justify maintaining the slavery of those who continued to work on plantations rather than joining the rebels. The first article of the bill proclaimed the abolition of slavery, but the second article provided that slaves who were freed must continue to work on their plantations. "In this manner," the bill explained, "the production of the island will not be threatened, and fears of social upheaval will be allayed."[31] Apparently, an eight-year period of continued plantation work was intended as an alternative form of compensation to planters for the loss of their slaves since the Spanish government didn't offer any monetary compensation. Spanish abolitionists objected to this provision as well as the one that required slaves to pay a high price to buy their freedom. On January 30, 1880, a majority in the Cortes voted the bill into law. The Emancipation Act took effect on February 13, 1880.[32]

For the time being, the law didn't seem like much of a step forward for slaves. Planters still were entitled to slave labor, were entitled to have runaway slaves returned, and could punish their slaves. By contrast, there wasn't anything voluntary about being a *patrocinado* who lacked the few rights of a free worker.

But the law did establish limits on abusive treatment, and some *patrocinados* were able to obtain remedies from a local junta or court established to enforce the Emancipation Act. For example, after running away from his plantation, a slave named Crecencio was caught and sentenced to wear leg irons for two years. When the plantation overseer refused to remove the leg irons after two years, Crecencio refused to work. The plantation overseer whipped him, locked him in stocks and beat him on the head. Junta officials fined the overseer and ordered that Crecencio be transferred to another *patrono*. He was eventually freed.[33]

Most important, the Emancipation Act specified that slavery would be phased out. A quarter of the *patrocinados* would be liberated at the end of each year, in descending order by age. Come 1888, slavery would be eliminated in Cuba. In addition, the law provided procedures according

to which slaves could purchase their freedom and specified the price of freedom, which declined each year until it reached zero in 1888.

Cuban planters complained that if Spain was going to enforce the abolition of slavery, being a Spanish colony didn't do them any good, particularly since their slave-based plantation economy was under pressure in changing markets. The world supply of sugar was increasing faster than demand. American sugar producers recovered after the Civil War, and their output was up. In addition, the sugar beet business was growing rapidly with free labor; sugar beets provided about 20 percent of all sugar in 1840 and more than half of all sugar in 1884.[34] Germany emerged as the biggest beet sugar producer, and both Spanish and American farmers were beginning to grow sugar beets. Consequently, both European and American sugar producers were supplying a higher proportion of their own markets. Increased sugar production put downward pressure on sugar prices. In the London market, sugar prices reportedly fell from 24 shillings per hundredweight (hundred pounds) in 1870 to 19 shillings in 1883 and 13 shillings in 1884, and prices didn't again exceed the 1884 level until World War I.

Declining prices meant that only the most efficient, lowest-cost sugar producers could survive. Since the heaviest costs of slavery were borne by the slaves themselves, slavery had appeared cheap to the planters, who persisted with inefficient production methods—hand labor, primitive tools and oxen. Declining sugar prices forced planters to introduce more efficient tools for sugar cane cultivation and to mechanize their sugar mills. Since many planters didn't harvest enough sugar cane to justify the costs of mechanization, they had to arrange for processing with other planters willing to sell their excess milling capacity.

Cuba needed to build better roads if sugar cane was to be transported greater distances to a mill, and the roads definitely had to be better if planters were to diversify with other crops, such as citrus, that could be badly damaged on rough dirt roads. After the British inventor Henry Bessemer developed a cheaper process for making steel in 1856, the cost of steel rails fell from $166 per hundredweight in 1867 to less than $30 in the 1880s. Railroad construction in Cuba expanded dramatically, enabling planters to specialize in improving the efficiency of their crop production, while others who might be some distance away specialized in sugar milling.

As the number of Cuban slaves gradually declined, plantation owners recruited other types of workers, and the labor force became more diverse. There were indentured Asians, white and mulatto wage laborers.[35] As slaveholders found they could survive despite the decline of slavery, they became less attached to it.

The deterioration of slave plantations meant declining revenue for the Cuban government, which was struggling to stay afloat amidst war debts. The Cuban budget fell from 40 million pesos in 1878 to 30 million pesos by 1884,[36] and the government found it increasingly difficult to provide the legal and police support essential for maintaining slavery.

Meanwhile, Spanish abolitionists were winning some victories. On November 28, 1883, the Spanish government agreed to outlaw the practice of punishing slaves by putting them in stocks and irons. Minister of the Colonies Suárez Inclán declared that henceforth the only lawful methods of punishing slaves were to withhold either wages or leisure time. There wasn't much left that planters could do to keep slaves on the plantations. Perhaps more than the Spanish realized, this policy, adopted in the name of eliminating cruel treatment, brought slavery to death's door.

By 1886, there were only about 26,000 slaves remaining in Cuba, down from about 200,000 in 1880.[37] On October 7, the Spanish government abolished the provision of the 1880 Emancipation Act requiring that former slaves work on their plantations for eight years.[38] Cuban slavery was gone two years ahead of schedule, and peacefully. Especially considering how Spain had promoted slavery for centuries and how the number of Cuban slaves had soared earlier in the nineteenth century, this was a great achievement.

Brazil's Resourceful Abolitionists

By the early nineteenth century, Brazil had become the largest market for slaves.[1] Since slavery had existed there for some 300 years and had an immense influence on Brazilian society and government, Brazilians believed their country couldn't exist without slavery.[2]

Yet the revolution in Haiti in the first decade of the nineteenth century had demonstrated the explosive potential of a large population of unhappy slaves. Brazilians were understandably unnerved: an estimated two-thirds of Brazil's population was black or mulatto, most of whom were enslaved. Maintaining slavery depended on the ability of slaveholders, backed by their government, to instill fear in slaves, but if they lost their fear, what might happen next?

The mortality rate for Brazilian slaves was very high because of hazardous work, unsanitary living conditions, poor nutrition and deadly diseases such as cholera and smallpox. There were only about a quarter as many women as men, and in the circumstances they didn't bear many children. Infant mortality was high as well. Consequently, Brazil imported large numbers of slaves just to maintain the slave population.[3]

Although slavery was profitable for the plantation owners who didn't compensate the slaves for their labor and provided shamefully little in

the way of housing, food, clothing or medical care, it sustained a backward economy. The slaves, of course, had no incentive to take care of or improve any property since they wouldn't have benefited from their efforts. Plantation owners had few incentives to improve anything, and many had a shocking lack of knowledge about efficient agricultural practices. Planters didn't know how to restore nutrients to soil; when one field was exhausted, they simply ordered their slaves to clear another. Much of what the planters knew often came from their slaves or from traditions going back hundreds of years.[4]

Independent Brazil Gains Jurisdiction for Its Slavery

When the British began their efforts to suppress the Brazilian slave trade, they dealt with colonial officials in Portugal. But after Napoleon invaded Portugal in 1807 and the British helped the Portuguese royal family move to Brazil, the British began dealing with officials in Brazil. Following the defeat of Napoleon, some of the Portuguese royal family moved back to Portugal while Prince Pedro remained behind. Increasingly, the British had to deal with officials both in Portugal and Brazil, complicating and delaying efforts to abolish the slave trade.

The Portuguese Cortes, their legislature, voted to reestablish the supremacy of Portugal and the subordinate colonial status of Brazil. Brazilians had no interest in giving up their status as a copartner with Portugal, which they had enjoyed during the Napoleonic Wars. The Cortes demanded that the royal family help reassert Portugal's supremacy over Brazil but Pedro refused to cooperate. He formed a new government with José Bonifácio de Andrada e Silva, a former geology professor who was an outspoken advocate of Brazilian independence, parliamentary government and the gradual abolition of slavery. On September 7, 1822, Pedro declared independence from Portugal. Three months later, he had himself crowned Emperor Pedro I.

Military units remained loyal to the Portuguese government, not Pedro, but many towns sent him petitions vowing support for independence. To help bolster his support, Petro rode horseback to visit towns in Minas Gerais and São Paulo. Brazilians resorted to guerrilla warfare against the Portuguese forces. Moreover, Pedro hired Thomas

Alexander Cochrane, one of the most successful British naval captains during the Napoleonic Wars, who had led Chile's naval forces against Spain. Pedro also hired former French general Pierre Labatut, who had fought the Spanish in Colombia. Within a year, the rebels prevailed and Brazil was independent. This was perhaps the first time people had found support from a royal family in their quest for independence. With independence, the Brazilian government gained jurisdiction over Brazilian slavery.

Events were far from settling down. A constituent assembly drafted a constitution providing for a national government based on the British Parliament. Pedro I didn't like it. He dismissed the constituent assembly and had his own constitution drafted—a reminder that independence is no protection against arbitrary power.

There was a brief but distracting war when Brazil's southern Cisplatine province wanted to become part of Argentina. Brazilian forces were routed, Britain intervened, and the result was the new nation of Uruguay. After Portuguese King Dom João VI died in 1826, Pedro became the senior member of the Braganza dynasty, and the Portuguese demanded that he return home. Eventually he did, after naming his five-year-old son, Pedro II, as heir to the Brazilian throne.

In practice, a series of regents exercised executive power in the Brazilian government, which was split among several factions. One faction, sometimes referred to as "liberals" and based mainly in the central provinces (São Paulo, Rio de Janeiro and Minas Gerais), wanted Brazil to remain independent. Another faction wanted Pedro I to move back to Brazil and reestablish a joint kingdom with Portugal. There were also the "exaltados," who were mainly interested in more autonomy for the provinces, and some of them favored dispensing with the monarchy and making Brazil a republic. Apparently none of these factions was satisfied with the constitution, and a succession of revolts took place during the 1830s.

Pedro I's death in 1834 marked the end of the faction hoping to reunite Brazil and Portugal. Pedro II succeeded to the Brazilian throne, and he had more than enough to do presiding over the land where he had been born. The most important political issues had become somewhat simpler: those favoring more power for the imperial government formed the Conservative Party, and those favoring more power for the provinces formed the Liberal Party. Both drew support from slaveholders.

Brazilian Slavery Declines

Although slaveholders remained defiant, they gradually lost political clout as British diplomats continued to press Brazil for commitments to suppress the slave trade and as the British Royal Navy destroyed Brazilian slave ships in Brazilian territorial waters.[5] At the same time, the Brazilian government was increasingly concerned that continued high levels of slave imports—over 50,000 in 1849—threatened the stability of the country in which whites were already outnumbered by blacks.[6] Conservative Eusébio de Queiroz introduced a bill in the Chamber of Deputies to ban the importation of slaves. It was adopted on July 17, 1850; the Senate passed it on August 13; the emperor signed it on September 3.

Brazilian officials still resisted doing anything about the slave trade, however. Great Britain increased the number of Royal Navy ships patrolling the Brazilian coast. In January 1851 the British threatened to pursue Brazilian slave ships in Brazilian ports, and the Brazilian government would have been discredited by its inability to do anything about that.[7] Reluctantly, at long last, the government began to help suppress the slave trade. In 1851 slave imports dropped to about 3,000 that year, 700 in 1852, and zero in 1853.[8]

After 1850, the number of slaves in Brazil declined, but an estimated 2 million slaves remained in the country, enough to keep the plantations going for many years.[9] An unintended consequence of the ban on importing African slaves was an internal slave trade developed as prospering Brazilian coffee growers acquired more slaves from within the country, especially from sugar growers who no longer found slaves worth the cost of their maintenance. Nobody seemed to be worried about the end of Brazilian slavery itself.

During the 1860s, Brazilian slaveholders were shocked by the violence of the U.S. Civil War and the defeat of the South. The Civil War had shown that a slave-based economy wasn't as strong as it appeared, and Brazil was vulnerable with its huge slave population. Brazilians felt isolated in one of the few western societies left with slavery. They were well aware that people in advanced countries viewed slavery as backward and barbarous.[10]

The Civil War was followed by a war closer to home that had a decisive impact on the status of Brazilian slaves. In 1865 Brazil had sent some forces into Uruguay supposedly to protect its citizens living

there. In March, Paraguay countered by ordering some of its forces into Uruguay and then into the Brazilian province of Mato Grosso. Paraguay fought the triple alliance of Brazil, Argentina and Uruguay. There was much concern in Brazil that Paraguay's dictator, Francisco Solano López, might invade Brazil's most southerly province, Rio Grande do Sul, and try to provoke a slave rebellion. In addition, mobilization for the war served as a reminder that most of the people were slaves whose loyalty couldn't be counted on. For lack of enough white soldiers, the government uneasily conscripted thousands of slaves who had to be emancipated before they joined the army.

The war dragged on for five years. Paraguayan soldiers turned out to be tough guerrilla fighters. After some 60,000 of them were killed, López recruited women and boys to continue the guerrilla war. Brazil's slaves performed well, and after the war many people felt that they deserved better treatment. Although Brazil won, the war helped make the evil of slavery an issue that could no longer be ignored.[11]

Rio Branco's "Free Birth" Law

In the Brazilian Chamber of Deputies, Pimento Bueno proposed a succession of bills to promote gradual emancipation. In 1868, Zacharias de Góes Vasconcellos became the first Brazilian prime minister to support emancipation. He especially liked Bueno's proposal to free the children of slave mothers. Conservatives thwarted these efforts, and some Liberals worked to better organize their efforts by forming the Reform Club, which supported gradual emancipation. Other Liberals formed the Radical Club to promote accelerated emancipation. Liberal professional people established the Republican Club.[12]

Reformers aimed to improve living conditions for slaves. In 1869 Parliament made it illegal to separate husbands and wives and children under 15. Other proposals for helping slaves included protecting their right to save money, with which, among other things, they could buy their freedom; establishing an emancipation fund from taxes and government-run lotteries; and emancipating the children of slaves.

In 1871, Brazilian Emperor Dom Pedro named Silva Paranhos, viscount of Rio Branco, to head a ministry that would act on these proposals. A Conservative allied with slaveholders, he was more willing

to consider reforms than others in his party. The emperor subsequently went on a long European vacation, so he wouldn't be drawn into what were sure to be contentious parliamentary debates.

Although most people seemed to agree slavery should end and the principal debate was about the least painful way to do it, slaveholders objected that the most popular reform proposals would interfere with a slaveholder's right as absolute master of his slaves. Any interference, it was feared, would undermine discipline, and the whole system would collapse.

The most controversial of the reform proposals was freeing the children of slave mothers—the *ingenuos*. Slaveholders viewed this as emancipation without compensation for loss of their slave assets (the children) and feared that such a policy would be a prelude to freeing adult slaves without compensation. Moreover, freeing the children of slave mothers would thwart efforts by slaveholders to increase the number of slaves naturally. Slaveholders hoped that by improving living conditions for slaves, the mortality rate among slaves could be reduced and the birth rate among slaves would go up. If the plantation owners were successful, the number of slaves would increase without imports, securing the future of Brazilian slavery despite the ban against slave trading.

Freeing the children of slave mothers amounted to gradual emancipation, an alternative to outright abolition, which was politically impossible at the time. In 1811 Chile had passed a law emancipating the children of slaves. Gran Columbia (territory now consisting of Colombia, Ecuador, Venezuela and Panama) did it in 1821, Portugal in 1856, and Spain in 1870.[13]

It became clear that a law would pass freeing the children of slave mothers, but Brazilian plantation owners flexed their political muscles, and the proposal turned out rather differently than had been intended. In 1871 Viscount Rio Branco introduced a bill with four major provisions:

1. Slaveholders were to care for the children of slaves until age eight, after which the slaveholders had the choice of receiving government compensation in the form of 6 percent, 30-year bonds, or of having the children work until age 21.
2. Slaves would be granted the right to keep money they earned or inherited, and they could buy their freedom.

3. Government-owned slaves would be freed, along with slaves involved in unclaimed inheritances and slaves abandoned by their owners.
4. The government would establish an emancipation fund for buying the freedom of slaves throughout Brazil.[14]

Although the proposed bill included important benefits for slaveholders, opposition came from Brazil's southern provinces, the coffee-growing regions where most of the country's slaves were located. Politicians from most other regions were willing to consider some reform. There were public meetings, some of which reportedly drew thousands of people, and debate in the Senate and the Chamber of Deputies went on for many weeks. Dozens of newspapers supported the Rio Branco bill.

Slaveholders, who long dominated government policy, found it necessary to start the Club da Lavoura e do Commercio (Commercial and Agricultural Club) to defend slavery. Some opponents of the Rio Branco bill didn't deny the moral case against slavery but insisted on the traditional prerogatives of slaveholders. One senator was quoted as saying that Brazilian laws "recognize not only ownership of the slave woman, but also of the child whom she might bear." Brazil's general director of public revenue acknowledged that while the market value of slave babies was small, the Rio Branco bill would undermine all the laws enacted to enforce slavery. Their concern was that freeing some of the slaves—the newborn children—would encourage a rebellious spirit among slaves.

Critics of slavery cited a wide range of arguments to support the Rio Branco bill. They pointed out that the world was changing, and Brazil was virtually alone as a nation that permitted slavery. The Rio Branco bill gave Brazilian slaveholders eight years to adapt in a changing world, the first eight years in the lives of children born after enactment of the law. Critics of slavery denounced its immorality and the harsh living conditions that slaves had to endure. There were practical arguments as well: Free labor was more efficient than slave labor, and with slavery, a threat of rebellion was always present.

Slaveholders claimed they owned the newborn babies of slave women as farmers owned the fruit from their trees. This argument was countered by Senator Francisco Sales Torres-Homem, who denounced the enslavement of babies as "piracy carried on about the

crib." He declared that so-called property rights in human beings, "far from being founded upon natural law, is . . . its most monstrous violation."

On September 27, 1871, the Brazilian parliament approved the Rio Branco bill, also known as the Law of Free Birth (*Ventre Livre*).[15] The law made it more difficult for slaveholders to maintain or to expand their slave population. Clearly, the legislative trend was to restrict rather than promote slavery. According to the 1872 census, there were 1,510,806 slaves in Brazil.[16]

The Brazilian Abolitionist Movement

Most Brazilians were long silent about slavery. It was a traditional part of life. The work on sugar and coffee plantations was brutal, and planters couldn't imagine getting anybody to do *their* work without compulsion. Moreover, business people, clergymen, lawyers, politicians and others were dependent on support from wealthy plantation owners. Small merchants complained that the planters weren't giving them much business, preferring to spend their money in big cities, but the small merchants didn't want to jeopardize the business they had. Free blacks eked out a meager existence doing odd jobs for plantation owners, and they were concerned about losing such work.[17] For these reasons, very little was published in Brazil against slavery and the slave trade during the first half of the nineteenth century.

A notable exception to this silence was José Bonifácio de Andrada e Silva, who wrote in 1823: "By what sort of justice does a man steal another man's freedom, and worse yet, the freedom of this man's children, and of his children's children." But few Brazilians heard of Bonifácio until more than 50 years later. Castro Alves (1847–1871), one of the most important nineteenth-century Brazilian authors, became well known for his abolitionist poems, including *"Os Escravos"* ("The Slaves") and *"A Cachoeira de Paulo Afonso"* ("Paulo Afonso's Waterfall"). His novel *Navio Negreiro* (*Slave Ship*) had an impact in Brazil that might be compared with the impact of Harriet Beecher Stowe's *Uncle Tom's Cabin* in the United States.[18]

In 1879, apparently worried that discontented slaves might revolt, plantation owners lobbied the government for harsher disciplinary

measures. Since capital punishment had been outlawed, there were demands to punish rebellious slaves with longer prison sentences. In the Chamber of Deputies, Lafayette Rodrigues Pereira demanded that the most dangerous rebels be sentenced to 15-year prison sentences, the first five years in solitary confinement.[19]

Such harsh demands underscored abolitionist contentions that slavery was uncivilized. There was disillusionment with the Rio Branco law. The high death rate among newborn children reduced its impact, and children who did survive would not be emancipated until they turned 21. Slaves on government-owned estates would be liberated, but only if this didn't result in a shortage of workers for the estates.[20]

Since children of slaves technically became free, they ceased to be counted in official statistics on slavery, even though they were obligated to continue working for their masters until 21. The number of Brazilian slaves actually might have increased a bit after passage of the Rio Branco law.[21]

The emancipation fund was a disappointment, too. Between 1874 and 1883, for example, it financed the emancipation of a reported 18,900 slaves. By contrast, during this period 115,625 slaves bought their freedom, and 195,348 slaves died.[22] Moreover, the emancipation fund became a source of corruption. Some slaveholders triple-billed the government by emancipating the same slaves multiple times. Government officials steered emancipation funds to their political supporters. The older the slaves were, the more compensation was due the slaveholders, and they reportedly overstated the age of slaves to receive more compensation. Slaveholders disregarded laws aimed at improving living conditions for slaves, and spouses were sold separately, breaking up slave families contrary to the 1869 law.

Many Brazilians were outraged by all this. On March 5, 1879, Jeronymo Sodré, a Chamber of Deputies member and medical school professor from Bahia, delivered a speech asserting that the way to avoid violence was to emancipate slaves, not to treat them more harshly. He declared that the fear of slave violence would never be banished, and the Brazilian economy would never be modernized until slavery itself was abolished. Sodré went on to denounce the Rio Branco law.[23] His speech marked the beginning of the Brazilian movement to abolish slavery as quickly as possible. After this, it became increasingly difficult to discuss any reforms—whether economic, educational or electoral—without addressing slavery.[24]

Sodré's speech inspired Joaquim Nabuco to join the campaign. He was a noteworthy ally because he was the son of José Tomaz Nabuco, an influential senator and major slaveholder in northeast Brazil. Liberal senator Affonso Celso Jr. described Nabuco as "tall, well-proportioned, the head and face possessing a purity of sculptural line, magnificent eyes, an expression at once gentle and virile."[25] He was educated at some of the best schools, traveled to Europe and became increasingly uncomfortable about slavery on his family's sugar plantation in the province of Pernambuco. He practiced law with his father and contributed articles to newspapers. He was elected to the Chamber of Deputies in 1878, after his father's death.

Nabuco became Brazil's most famous antislavery orator. He had a commanding presence and a rich, powerful voice that could project to the back of large rooms. He presented coherent arguments and used dramatic images that would stir his audiences. He denounced "the rotten ship of slavery." He declared, "Slavery and labor are as repellent to each other as slavery and liberty. What is slavery if not the robbing of labor and the degradation, from the cradle, of the laborer?" He warned that stubbornly maintaining slavery would cause "the ruin and bankruptcy of everything." Asked if abolishing slavery would lead to an economic crisis in Brazil, he replied: "I fear that the destruction of slavery would affect property as much as I fear that the ending of some form of piracy would destroy commerce."[26]

In 1880 he proposed a bill that would free Brazil's slaves by January 1, 1890. He explained, "an unchangeable term would leave time for the planters to prepare for a great revolution, while it would give rise directly in the hearts of the slaves to an invaluable hope, which would render life less and less hard for them at every step and bring them nearer to freedom."[27] Slaveholders fought this bill because they feared rising expectations would make slaves impatient and increase the risk of revolt. In addition, of course, any specific date was too soon for the slaveholders, who organized marches and protests against the bill.

The bill was defeated, but Nabuco persisted in promoting the idea of abolition among his fellow deputies. He sought support from the pope and European intellectuals. He vowed to introduce an abolition bill every year until one passed. He adopted a variety of tactics such as proposing antislavery amendments to budget bills, and he proposed bills that would outlaw Brazil's interprovincial slave trade.[28]

The interprovincial slave trade boomed as sugar prices declined during the 1870s, and sugar plantations generated cash by selling more and more of their slaves to coffee plantations in south central Brazil. Most of the slaves were transported on ships and endured appalling conditions as bad as those in the transatlantic slave trade.[29]

A bill banning the interprovincial slave trade was adopted, perhaps surprisingly with the support of slaveholders. Many were concerned that as slaves became concentrated in fewer regions, slavery would lose political support, and eventually slavery might be outlawed. Slaveholders who had all the slaves they needed were for the ban because it would make it harder for their competitors to acquire more slaves. In addition, by restricting the number of slaves in the coffee-producing region, the value of slaves already there would go up, and if slaves were emancipated with compensation for slaveholders, they would get more money because their slaves were worth more.

Soon abolitionism went beyond legislative chambers and began to develop into a popular movement. At Nabuco's home in Flamengo Beach, on September 7, 1880—the fifty-eighth anniversary of Brazil's independence—a group of friends founded the Sociedade Brasileira a Escravidão (Brazilian Anti-Slavery Society) whose principal aim was to generate publicity for abolition. They published pamphlets in Portuguese, French and English. On November 1, 1880, they began issuing *O Abolicionista,* their monthly publication. They denounced politicians who appeared to ignore the cruelty of slavery, and they made patriotic appeals for abolition.[30]

Among the other societies that sprang up were the Sociedade Cearense Liberertadora (Cearense Liberator Society, 1880), Sociedade Abolicionista Ouropretana (Abolitionist Society of Ouro Prêto, 1882) and Sociedade Libertadora Bahiana (Bahian Liberator Society, 1883). In addition, the Club Abolicionista dos Empregados no Commércio (Abolitionist Club of Employees in Commerce), Club dos Libertos de Niteroy (Freedman's Club of Niteroi) and Libertadorada Escola de Medicina (Liberator of the Medical School). To help facilitate communications among abolitionist clubs around Brazil, students and teachers at Escola Polytechnica established an abolitionist society with the intention of promoting abolitionist societies at other schools in Brazil.[31]

On May 12, 1883, the Abolitionist Confederation was established in Rio de Janeiro to coordinate the activities of 12 abolitionist societies.

The confederation was led by three bold Brazilian abolitionists, João Clapp (president), André Rebouças (treasurer) and José do Patrocínio (speaker).

Clapp, whose family had come from North America, owned Clapp & Filhos, a Rio de Janeiro store that sold fine porcelain and crystal housewares. He served as a director of and teacher at a night school for free blacks. A generous philanthropist, he financed abolitionist activities and helped provide protection for runaway slaves.[32]

Rebouças, a contributor to *Gazeta da Tarde,* distinguished himself as a writer of abolitionist literature and an energetic organizer. Described as "a thin, dark, soberly dressed engineer and teacher of botany, calculus, and geometry at the Polytechnical School, writer and learned analyst of the nation's economic and social problems,"[33] he was the son of a mulatto politician. Rebouças attended a military school, earned a degree in physics and mathematics, and began his career as an engineer. When the abolitionist movement got underway in 1880, he got involved and helped establish and promote a number of abolitionist societies.[34]

Patrocínio was the most widely read black journalist. With "bulging eyes, sparse beard and moustache, corpulent face and body, unruly brown hair, and skin described as the color of a Havana cigar," the son of a slave-owning priest and a black fruit seller, he started work in a Rio de Janeiro hospital when just a boy. He got a job on the *Gazeta de Noticias,* but after 1881, it adopted more conservative views and he moved on.

With help from his father-in-law, Patrocínio acquired an abolitionist newspaper, *Gazeta da Tarde.* Gathering news about slavery from 12 abolitionist societies, he offered the most comprehensive coverage of the movement. He also condensed reports from other publications, both antislavery and proslavery. The circulation of *Gazeta da Tarde* soared from about 2,000 to about 12,000, an enormous audience expansion for that time. A prolific journalist and a charismatic speaker, Patrocínio chose the motto of the confederation for his paper: "Slavery is theft."[35]

The Abolitionist Confederation played a key role accelerating the pace of abolitionist activity and dramatically increasing the number of supporters. The principals of the confederation organized marches, held parties to celebrate the freedom of former slaves, and dispatched secret agents to the countryside to encourage slaves to revolt or leave

their plantations. They established safe houses for runaway slaves, provided false papers identifying runaways as free blacks, and hired thugs who disrupted slaveholders' efforts to catch runaway slaves.

Clapp, Rebouças and Patrocínio made sure that their exploits were well publicized. The public was captivated by these daring men and amused to see officials helpless. People were increasingly sympathetic to the abolitionist cause.[36]

It wasn't surprising that the Brazilian abolitionist movement developed mainly in cities, not in rural areas where most of the slaves worked and lived. The cities were centers of business and trade that brought people into contact with the outside world. People in cities learned about new products and ideas from other countries. They knew how free markets were rapidly expanding and how the most prosperous nations had rejected slavery. People in cities wanted to be part of the Atlantic community.[37]

Abolitionist clubs usually began their campaigns by holding conferences. Their aim was to present an intellectually respectable case. Speakers tended to be respectful of slaveholders, insisting that slavery was wrong and furthermore that slavery made it harder for plantations to modernize and grow. For instance, Nabuco contacted Henry Washington Hilliard, the American diplomatic representative in Rio de Janeiro, a southerner who supported abolition. Hilliard replied by saying that the South was economically better off for having abolished slavery. He specifically denied that the South had suffered as a result of abolition. He expressed the view that Brazil should abolish slavery within seven years and provide full compensation to slaveholders. The abolitionists organized a banquet to honor Hilliard at the popular Hotel dos Estrangeiros in Rio de Janeiro, at which he reportedly gave a stirring speech for abolition.[38] Brazilian abolitionist meetings became boisterous affairs, featuring abolitionist speakers and liberated slaves as well as singers and musicians. Performers appeared amidst a shower of rose petals.

The abolitionist cause was buoyed by the growing economy, as more people had a stake in it. Plantation owners put some of their money in city banks, insurance companies, shipping companies and other businesses. Rural people started small ventures that manufactured things for city markets, and rural people bought more products made in cities or imported from abroad. The economy was increasingly diversified as nonslave sectors became more important.

An increasing number of Brazilians came to believe that free labor was better than slave labor.

The most educated and successful people supported the abolition of slavery. Newspapers ran stories about abolitionist meetings, mentioning the names of prominent citizens who attended, including doctors, lawyers, engineers and businessmen. College students formed antislavery clubs and journalists wrote antislavery books and articles.[39]

The Brazilian abolitionist movement had its ups and downs. After a dynamic 1880 and 1881, things appear to have quieted during most of 1882. Newspaper accounts seldom mentioned attendance figures at abolitionist meetings, and there were indications that little money was raised. Abolitionists were outnumbered by those who defended slavery and those who believed in gradual emancipation. Politicians were generally most interested in the perks of power. There were more antislavery politicians in the Liberal Party than in the Conservative Party, but antislavery was a minority view in both parties. Although the prime minister was from the Liberal Party between 1878 and 1885, the party didn't do much to promote the abolition of slavery.

Then in November there was a slave revolt in São Paulo. Rebels overwhelmed local police and army forces that had been dispatched, before the revolt was finally subdued. Slaveholders again became increasingly nervous about the slave population.

Emancipation Block by Block

Around the country opposition to slavery arose spontaneously in that no official government action had caused it. When government officials were supportive, they endorsed what had already taken place. Never before in Brazil's history had such large-scale upheaval occurred.[40]

Abolitionists worked to achieve slave-free neighborhoods, then cities and counties. Some planters, recognizing the inevitable, liberated their slaves and didn't ask for compensation (which they no longer expected to get). Many slaves in the state of Rio Grande do Sul and in the city of São Paulo were liberated.[41]

In Ceará, a state in northeastern Brazil, abolitionists launched a campaign to create slave-free zones by liberating slaves block by block,

town by town, and lastly reaching into rural areas. José Mariano and his comrades in the Termite Club (Clube do Cupim) took the lead. They operated secretly with a policy "to destroy without noise." They helped runaway slaves, disguising them as sailors or porters, to escape the region on ships that delivered sugar to small towns. Joaquim Nabuco observed that the ships "receive as many passengers as their tonnage allows, even doubling it. They smuggle out the free with the same audacity that in other times the slaves were smuggled in. That was the work of the Termite Club, whose fame will live forever in the tradition of the province."

The abolitionists held subscription campaigns to raise money so slaves could buy their freedom. As the number of liberated slaves increased in an area, many slaveholders granted freedom without compensation. By March 24, 1884, all 57 of Ceará's municipalities were reportedly slave-free, though a few more slaves were identified in the state. More than 22,000 slaves had been liberated. Because the president of Ceará supported this abolitionist activity, Brazil's national government removed him from office.

Ceará soon became a destination for runaway slaves escaping from other Brazilian states. Plantation owners in other states complained that the mere existence of a slave-free Ceará threatened the stability of slavery in Brazil. Abolitionists in the southern region established the Brazilian Underground Railroad, originating in São Paulo, Minas Gerais and Rio de Janeiro, with a final destination of Ceará.[42]

Meanwhile, Goiás, in western Brazil, was also on its way to becoming a slave-free state. By 1884, João Clapp and other abolitionists organized an effort in Belém, a major city in northern Brazil, to help liberate slaves in the Amazon River valley. Then came a campaign to achieve slave-free zones in Rio de Janeiro, the capital city surrounded by coffee plantations. There were celebrations with each block that was liberated. In 1884, the city's Municipal Council established an emancipation fund for liberating slaves. But liberating the capital city was a big project, and there weren't enough abolitionists around to keep it going.[43]

Supported by Carlos de Lacerda, who owned the newspaper *Vinte e Cinco de Março,* an abolitionist campaign arose in Campos, a city in the sugar-producing area of eastern Rio de Janeiro province. His Club Abolicionista Carlos de Lacerda liberated major streets in the city.

Support for abolishing slavery grew in Amazonas, Brazil's biggest state. Although the state's provincial assembly didn't have the power to

abolish slavery, in 1884 it did appropriate funds for purchasing the freedom of slaves. Additional funds were raised privately, with many women contributing their jewelry, to make sure that all slaves in the state could be liberated. Committees were established to travel around the state, contacting all the slaveholders to liberate slaves at the least possible cost. The names of slaveholders were published, and while some asked high prices for their slaves, many others asked less, perhaps hoping to get out of slavery as quietly as possible. Brazil's national government responded to this abolitionist activity by removing the president of Amazonas, Dr. Theodureto Souto.

In Pôrto Alegre, the capital of the state of Rio Grande do Sul, Colonel Joaquim Pedro Salgado and Dr. Joaquim de Sales Torres-Homem had abolitionists go door to door, asking slaveholders to free their slaves—in most cases, a household had only one or two. The names of slaveholders who pledged to free their slaves were published as encouragement for others. Reportedly more than 2,000 slaves were liberated in a few days, and Pôrto Alegre was a virtually free city by September 7, 1884. The celebrations were grander than any that had taken place there before. Ceremonies were held at the municipal palace and at the cathedral, and there were boisterous celebrations around the city. Abolitionist clubs were formed in more and more towns, and thousands more slaves were emancipated.

All this agitation to abolish slavery resulted in falling slave prices, falling plantation values, and anxious times for plantation owners whose political clout was declining too. By 1884, in less than half of Brazil's provinces did slaves account for more than 10 percent of the population. In more than a quarter of Brazil's provinces, slaves accounted for less than 5 percent of the population.[44]

Politicians Play Catch-up

An abolitionist movement developed within the government of Rio Grande do Sul, Brazil's southernmost state. This state bordered Spanish-speaking Uruguay, Paraguay and Argentina, where slavery had been abolished, and was populated by many Italian and German immigrants who didn't like slavery. Senator Silveira Martins, who was influential in Rio Grande do Sul, urged what became this state's abolitionist approach: Slaves should be granted their freedom if they

agreed to work for three to five more years. Essentially, slavery was turned into a service contract. "You will not disorganize your work force," he told the slaveholders, "and you will have time to prepare for transition to paid labor."[45]

Neither abolitionists nor slaveholders were enthusiastic about this arrangement. Abolitionists were outraged that slaves must continue working for their masters after having already spent years at it. Some abolitionists noted that if slavery were abolished in the near future, the slaves would still be stuck with their service contracts. Slaveholders complained that a service contract denied their ownership of the slaves.

Brazil's Liberal Party, which had long talked about reform while soliciting support from slaveholders, reached a consensus to seek the abolition of slavery. Liberal Senator Manoel Dantas introduced a bill that would emancipate slaves over 60 years old without compensation for slaveholders, grant freed slaves ownership of the land they worked, and introduce a new tax providing more funds to help free slaves. Dantas's reform was mainly another compromise for gradual emancipation—not what the abolitionists were looking for. But they recognized its significance: The Liberal Party had finally committed itself to ending slavery.[46] Accordingly, Dantas's proposal was supported in newspaper articles by authors with pseudonyms such as "Garrison," "Clarkson," "Wilberforce" and "Buxton"—tributes to the great American and British abolitionists. Major newspapers published the articles in space that had been paid for by abolitionist societies.

The Dantas bill together with recent gains by abolitionists led to widespread concerns about the future of slavery. The market value of plantations declined since prospective buyers weren't sure who would do the work when slavery ended. Similarly, slave prices declined.[47]

Slaveholders denounced the abolitionists. Conservative senator Martinho Campos gave a four-hour speech in which he called the abolitionists "odious to the nation." Cristiano Ottoni warned that "All those who receive abolitionist papers will be considered suspect." Senator Andrade Figueira declared that freeing 60-year-old slaves would be "robbery."

Conservative senator Moreira de Barros offered a motion that the Dantas bill be rejected. The motion carried by a slim 55–52 majority. Conservatives subsequently passed the Saraiva-Cotegipe bill, a measure supported by slaveholders that liberated slaves over 65 years old

with compensation for slaveholders, specified steep fines for anybody who helped runaway slaves, and introduced a new tax providing funds mainly to benefit slaveholders. This became law on September 28, 1885. Then, on June 12, 1886, the government issued the "Black Regulation," making it easier to transfer slaves from regions of the country where slavery was restricted to regions with fewer restrictions.

These proslavery developments inspired abolitionists to renew and intensify their efforts. Joaquim Nabuco publicized a case involving two slaves who died after a court-ordered sentence of 300 lashes in Paraíba do Sul, a town in Brazil's coffee-growing region. Many slaves had died after being lashed before, but this time many Brazilians were aroused against slavery, and the incident was widely reported in newspapers. When the case was discussed in the Senate, Brazil's minister of justice recommended the repeal of laws that permitted whipping as a punishment. A bill to this effect was introduced and passed on October 16, 1886.

Thousands Quit the Plantations

Abolitionists began to secretly visit plantations and mingle with slaves, urging them to escape and generating a large-scale exodus. Although police captured some runaways, the exodus gained momentum. Desperate to make sure there would be enough slaves to harvest their crops, plantation owners resorted to violence, but the exodus continued. During this time, José do Patrocínio visited Santos, a port town and business center in the coffee-growing region. He gave speeches that inspired local abolitionists to end slavery in the town, and it soon became a favored destination for runaway slaves. The São Paulo province chief of police, Dr. Lopes dos Anjos, appeared with an armed force intent on capturing runaways, but when some slaves were captured, abolitionists attacked the police. There was gunfire and a captured slave escaped and was rescued by abolitionists. Fears that police might attack a local abolitionist newspaper, Diario de Santos, reportedly prompted over 1,000 people to show up to help protect it.

The most dangerous assignment given to undercover abolitionists was to work on plantations and tell slaves how they could escape, since slaveholders executed anybody caught doing that. Still, the slaves left plantations in droves. Agriculture Minister Rodrigo da Silva was

aghast at all the slaves abandoning the plantations: "They flee in all directions and, transporting themselves on the railroads, they take refuge in the city of Santos, where they consider themselves immune and free from any legal compulsion from their masters."

Violence between police and runaway slaves was not unusual. A slave named Pio led about 150 slaves away from a plantation near the town of Itu and headed for Santos. They prevailed over a band of police attackers and many eluded national government forces dispatched to the scene. Some of the slaves were hunted down in the woods, but an estimated 30 slaves reached Santos. In São Paulo, police attacked runaway slaves gathered at the church of São Francisco, and runaway slaves responded by attacking police and soldiers around the government palace. Such clashes convinced more people that the time had come to abolish slavery. Marshall Deodoro da Fonseca, who headed the influential Club Militar, urged that the army not be ordered to pursue slaves who had suffered so much already. When the government continued issuing orders for soldiers to pursue runaway slaves, they went where they were ordered but refused to do anything about the runaways.

By 1887, many slaveholders surveyed their lands without anybody to work them and realized slavery was doomed. If they didn't start recruiting voluntary, paid workers, they would be out of business. Some slaveholders promised freedom to their slaves provided they agreed to work another year or longer on the plantations. Or course, such proposals for conditional freedom didn't offer any advantages to slaves who had already gained their freedom.

When in September 1887 proslavery members of the Chamber of Deputies demanded that the government try forcing the return of runaway slaves, the proslavery newspaper publisher Antonio Prado expressed his view that such efforts were pointless. He backed the abolitionists, creating a new crisis for defenders of slavery.

On December 15, 1887, principals or representatives of more than 200 plantations, which had used some 7,000 slaves, met in São Paulo to discuss a transition from slavery to free labor. The idea was to start paying a small salary to slaves who continued to work peacefully and to abolish slavery in the province by December 1890. Planters disagreed, however, on whether emancipation should be conditional or total, and when it should take place. A few planters, including some influential families, concluded that with their plantations abandoned,

their crops in jeopardy and increasing signs of anarchy, their only realistic option was to emancipate their slaves immediately—and so they did. Not wanting to be left behind by planters who lured back their former slaves and resumed operations by offering better living conditions and pay for work, more planters announced immediate emancipation of their slaves.

Some planters negotiated with Antônio Bento, who made a radical proposal: that planters should offer to pay anybody who wants to work for them, including slaves who had worked on other plantations. This was a step toward a free labor market. Despite occasional violence, emancipation proceeded apace. An estimated 100,000 slaves were liberated in São Paulo province.

Apparently news of emancipation attracted Italian immigrants to Brazil, and they helped ease the transition to a free labor market. By March 1888, some planters acknowledged that the emancipation of slaves and the beginning of a free labor market didn't result in a labor shortage. A free labor market in São Paulo meant that slavery would soon be gone from all of Brazil.

Some proslavery interests in Rio de Janeiro, Minas Gerais and elsewhere continued to demand compensation for giving up their claims on slaves. In Rio de Janeiro province, police chief Dr. João Coelho Bastos reportedly used the forces at his disposal to return thousands of runaway slaves to their owners. Coelho Bastos banned public meetings at night, but abolitionists defied his order. Police intervened and savagely beat up participants. Police arrested abolitionists at home and dispatched them to prison, harassed abolitionist publishers and destroyed their offices.

But elsewhere—in Minas Gerais, Pará, Paraná, Santa Catarina and northeastern provinces—slaves abandoned plantations and planters quickly embraced emancipation. By March 1888, some planters in Rio de Janeiro province had begun to emancipate their slaves.

The Golden Law

On March 7, 1888, Conservative João Alfredo Corrêa de Oliveira became prime minister, and his mission was to achieve emancipation nationwide. The following day, Minister of Agriculture Rodrigo Silva presented a bill that outlawed slavery throughout Brazil.

On May 3, 1888, the General Assembly began its legislative session, and the first order of business was to do something about slavery. Antônio Prado proposed emancipation with compensation for slaveholders and an obligation for slaves to work three months, until the year's coffee crop was harvested, and to remain for six years in the region where they were emancipated. But the Liberal Party, which had a majority of the Senate, supported only immediate, unconditional emancipation. Accordingly, on May 7, Conservative leaders like Antônio Prado and Senator João Alfredo Correia de Oliveira acknowledged the inevitable and supported unconditional emancipation. In the Senate, the only serious opposition came from the Baron of Cotegipe and Paulino de Souza. The emancipation act, later known as the Golden Law, passed and was ready to be signed into law. Emperor Dom Pedro II was away, so the bill was signed by princess regent Dona Isabel on May 13, 1888.[48]

The celebrations were soon underway with parades, public demonstrations and other festivities in Rio de Janeiro and elsewhere. With much raucous jubilation, the long brutal era of chattel slavery came to a merciful end in the western hemisphere.[49]

Chapter 9

Courageous Campaign against Secret Slavery in the Congo

When Leopold succeeded his father as king of Belgium in 1865, apparently he began brooding about how he might claim some greatness for his little country. He wanted a colony, but nearly all the territory in Asia and the Americas was claimed already. The only opportunities left were in Africa. Little-known central Africa was unclaimed by any European power, and he decided to try to seize it. To avoid provoking opposition in the international community or in his own country, he wanted to keep his role very quiet. Leopold posed as a crusader against nefarious Arab slave traders.

Leopold liked the idea of recruiting Welsh-born journalist and explorer Henry Morton Stanley, the man who had tracked down the English antislavery crusader David Livingstone in 1871, to help implement the plans of the Committee for the Studies of the Upper Congo, supposedly to promote the betterment of Africa with a group of European investors. In November 1877, in one of his most candid letters, Leopold wrote Baron Solvyns, the Belgian ambassador to Britain: "I think that if I entrusted Stanley publicly with the job of taking over part of Africa in my own name, the English would stop me. If I consult them, they will again try to stop me. So I think that at first I shall

give Stanley an exploring job which will not offend anybody, and will provide us with some posts down in that region."[1]

The 36-year-old Stanley had an amazing ability to resist the treacherous hazards of Africa. He had survived for years in African jungles despite the constant threat of deadly fevers, snakes, insects, carnivores, hostile natives and dangerous terrain that doomed a high percentage of African visitors. Stanley cherished the ideal of civilizing African natives, particularly under the British flag, but he had a reputation as a ruthless adventurer. Gunfire was said to be perhaps his favorite negotiating method. He seemed unconcerned about the natives he recruited to perform brutal work in the jungles. Jules Greindl, the Belgian ambassador to Spain, complained that because Stanley got into so many fights with natives, he made it unsafe for Europeans to travel on the same routes he did.

After writing a bestselling book about his travels, *Through the Dark Continent* (1878), and trying unsuccessfully to interest British businessmen and politicians in the Congo, Stanley agreed to work for Leopold. The king renamed his seemingly philanthropic exploratory organization the International Association of the Congo.

Stanley returned to Africa, explored the Congo, identified sites for administrative posts and trading stations, and sought to acquire land. Leopold encouraged him to acquire "as much land as you can."[2] To get tribal chiefs to sign over rights to their communal land, Stanley used various tricks to convince them that he had magical powers. Stanley misrepresented the "treaties" that the chiefs signed, and the documents became the legal basis for Leopold's dubious claim to a vast, vaguely defined region in the heart of Africa. According to Sherlock Holmes author Arthur Conan Doyle,

We have no record of the exact payment made to obtain these treaties, but we have the terms of a similar transaction carried out by a Belgian officer in 1883 at Palabala. In this case, the payment made to the Chief consisted of "one coat of red cloth with gold facings, one red cap, one white tunic, one piece of white baft, one piece of red points, one box of liqueurs, four demijohns of rum, two boxes of gin, 128 bottles of gin, twenty red handkerchiefs, forty singlets and forty old cotton caps." It is clear that in making such treaties the Chief thought he was giving permission for the establishment of a station. The idea that he was actually bartering away the land was

never even in his mind, for it was held by a communal tenure for the whole tribe, and it was not his to barter.[3]

Leopold suspected that initially he couldn't gain diplomatic recognition from a European rival, so he adroitly lobbied President Chester A. Arthur, the former U.S. collector of customs who had entered politics, won the vice presidential nomination and reached the highest office following the assassination of President James A. Garfield. Arthur found Leopold's edited versions of the "treaties" acceptable, and the United States became the first nation to recognize the Congo Free State in 1884. Leopold promised Great Britain, which had become the champion of free trade, that there would be free trade in the Congo, and the British were glad to see that their rivals, the French, didn't get the Congo, so they recognized the new state. The French, for their part, were glad to keep the British out of the Congo. Germany didn't want either the British or French to have the Congo. American and European diplomatic recognition helped assure Leopold that none of the European states would interfere with his plans for the Congo.

Transferring the Congo to Leopold personally was approved at the Berlin West Africa Conference that German chancellor Otto von Bismarck held in November 1884, with representatives from 14 nations. Leopold's Congo was over 900,000 square miles, about the size of non-Russian Europe. The Congo didn't have any constitution or other limits on Leopold's power. Consequently, he made unlimited claims: that all the products of the Congo belonged to his state.[4]

He established the capital at Boma, a port town, and divided the territory into 14 administrative districts. Each was divided into zones that were divided into sectors, and these were divided into posts, with Europeans stationed throughout. Stanley supervised construction of a road through the jungle, making it possible to bring in men and equipment.

Leopold wasn't interested in the long-term development of agriculture, industry or anything else. The only apparent export product of value seemed to be ivory. He decided to grab as much as possible, paying the natives little or nothing. The scheme would work only if he were able to enforce a procurement monopoly. Otherwise, competitors would get the ivory simply by offering the natives compensation. From the very beginning, it was evident that since natives probably

wouldn't be willing to perform hard labor for little or nothing, the scheme would require forceful violence.

Leopold didn't have the resources to establish government procurement operations, so he agreed to grant procurement monopolies to private companies in the ivory-producing districts. Despite Leopold's promises about free trade, nobody in his realm could sell ivory to anyone other than the official monopoly. All private trade was suppressed.

During the 1890s a global demand for rubber arose. Scottish veterinary surgeon John Dunlop had developed rubber tires for bicycles. The electrical inventions of Thomas Edison, George Westinghouse and others had stimulated a demand for wires requiring insulation, which seemed to be best satisfied with rubber. Leopold awarded monopoly licenses for companies in the various districts where rubber could be gathered from wild rubber vines. His men more readily resorted to violent enforcement action because the demand for rubber soon became much bigger than the demand for ivory. A district commissary administrator named Baert declared: "The natives of the district of Ubangi-Welle are not authorized to gather rubber. They can only receive permission to do so on condition that they gather the produce for the exclusive benefit of the State."[5]

The king was frantic to sell as much rubber as possible while prices were high, because he knew that cultivation of rubber trees was beginning in Asia and Latin America. When they grew big enough to be tapped, the supply of rubber would surge, and rubber prices would probably stabilize or even drop.[6] With rubber as with ivory, all revenue went to Leopold, and financial information was kept confidential.

Intrepid Author Exposes Atrocities

To maintain the secrecy of his Congo operations, Leopold discouraged visitors, saying they could find out everything they needed to know from his office in Brussels. There were missionaries such as George Grenfell, of the Baptist Missionary Society of London, who saw terrible things. But if they spoke out, they could expect to be expelled, ending any hopes they might have for doing good work. Even if missionaries had spoken out, who would have cared? The days of antislavery crusaders like Thomas Clarkson and William Wilberforce

were long gone. The London *Times* editorialized that "a system of compulsion closely akin to slavery would be necessary before natives of the Congo Free State could be trained to regular voluntary labor."[7]

Sometimes, though, skeptical and courageous visitors were able to look around. One of the earliest was George Washington Williams. A black American born in Pennsylvania, he had enlisted in the Union Army during the Civil War. After the war, since his only experience was in fighting, he joined the Republic of Mexico's army, which was trying to overthrow the government, and later the U.S. Army, which was fighting the American Indians. Finally ready for a new occupation, he attended Howard University, then Newton Theological Seminary. He dabbled in politics, won election to the Ohio state legislature, and made an unsuccessful bid to serve as U.S. ambassador to Haiti. He pioneered historical writing about blacks in America with two important books: *The History of the Negro Race in America 1619–1880* (1882) and *A History of Negro Troops in the War of Rebellion* (1888).

Williams wanted to help stop the slave trade that survived mainly in Africa and the Muslim world. When he learned of plans for a conference on the slave trade in Brussels, he was determined to be there. Scheduled to begin on November 18, 1889, it would have delegates from 17 nations.[8] He persuaded S. S. McClure, the New York publishing entrepreneur who had begun to syndicate newspaper columns, to have him cover the conference. This was a coup, because McClure had retained many of the most famous authors of the day, including Arthur Conan Doyle, Henry James, Rudyard Kipling, Robert Louis Stevenson and Mark Twain. Williams had met Alfred Le Ghait, the Belgian ambassador to the United States, and he helped arrange for Williams to interview King Leopold, so he could send McClure an article about the king.

Williams gushed: "While a large man, Leopold II has all that distinguishes the student, carrying no superfluous flesh; and proved himself a good listener as well as a pleasant and entertaining conversationalist. His hair and full beard were carefully trimmed and liberally sprinkled with gray. His features were strong and clear cut and keen; and his eyes, bright and quick, flashed with intelligent interest." Williams let the king pose as a philanthropist. Asked what he expected to get from his huge investment in the Congo, the king was quoted as saying: "One [motivation] is trade and commerce, which is selfish . . . and the other is to bring the means and blessings of

Christian civilization to Africa, which is noble." The topper was this line: "I do not wish to have one franc back of all the money I have expended," Williams quoted him as saying.[9]

But when Williams made clear that he wanted to see the Congo for himself, Leopold discouraged him, as did others associated with the king. Williams insisted that he must see the Congo, which provoked the king to warn that Williams couldn't travel on Congo Free State steamships—he would have to rely on steamers run by the missionary societies. The street-savvy Williams sensed an effort to cover up something. He pitched California railroad entrepreneur Collis P. Huntington, who was a financial backer of the Hampton Institute (which became Hampton University) and had invested in a Congo railroad project, for funds to explore the Congo. Perhaps surprisingly, Huntington provided modest funding, even though Williams clearly didn't know what he was getting himself into. Belgian businessmen heard about this and began to speculate that Huntington had hired Williams to help generate business in the Congo—at their expense.

In his correspondence with Huntington, Williams expressed a critical view of the Congo early on. He spent quite a bit of time with George Grenfell, the missionary, who knew far more than he was willing to talk about publicly. Grenfell seemed to marvel at how much Williams had figured out even though he was a recent arrival. "I wonder," Grenfell wrote, "what he would say if he saw, as we did, nine slaves chained neck to neck in the State Station at Upoto and waiting for a steamer to carry them down to Bangala. . . . Or what [he] would say if he met, as we did, a big canoe with a State employee on board and were told that they were out trying to buy slaves."

Williams continued his journey, venturing deeper into the interior of the Congo. By the time he reached Stanley Falls, he had gathered together his findings on the Congo regime and began writing *An Open Letter to His Serene Majesty Leopold II, King of the Belgians and Sovereign of the Independent State of Congo.*

Williams's *Open Letter* began by making a case that the king didn't have legitimate title to the territory because Henry Morton Stanley had engaged in chicanery. For example, Williams cited "the lens act": "The white brother took from his pocket a cigar, carelessly bit off the end, held up his [magnifying] glass to the sun and complaisantly smoked his cigar to the great amazement and terror of his black brother. The white man explained his intimate relation to the sun,

and declared that if he were to request him to burn up his black brother's village it would be done." Then there was the trick involving a cap gun: "the black brother was implored to step off ten yards and shoot at his white brother to demonstrate his statement that he was a spirit and, therefore, could not be killed. . . . By such means as these, too silly and disgusting to mention, and a few boxes of gin, whole villages have been signed away to your Majesty."[10]

Most of the *Open Letter* amounted to an indictment that made 12 charges against the king's administration in the Congo. First, the king didn't have the resources to govern, starting with only about 2,300 soldiers in a territory of nearly a million square miles. Few Belgian administrators knew native languages or appeared to understand what was going on. The government didn't have a single hospital for Europeans, and three sheds were the only medical facilities for Africans. Second, the king's soldiers routinely demanded that natives provide free food, and when the natives resisted, their homes were burned and many were killed. Third, the government often failed to honor contracts with its own soldiers. Fourth, Congo courts were "unjust, partial and delinquent." Laws supposedly issued to protect blacks were "a dead letter and a fraud." Fifth, the government was "excessively cruel to its prisoners, condemning them, for the slightest offenses, to the chain gang." Sixth, the government seized or bought women as sex slaves. Seventh, the government operated tax-free business enterprises and subjected competitors to taxation. Eighth, the government disregarded treaty obligations to treat natives decently. For instance, government soldiers prevented natives from trading with white companies, fired on native canoes and seized native property. Ninth, the government hired tribes (notably, cannibals) to massacre other tribes. Tenth, the government was a major participant in the slave trade: "Your Majesty's Government gives £3 per head for able-bodied slaves for military service. . . . There are some middle-men who only get from twenty to twenty-five francs per head. Three hundred and sixteen slaves were sent down the river recently, and others are to follow. . . . The labor force at the stations of your Majesty's Government in the Upper River is composed of slaves of all ages and both sexes." Eleventh, the government obtained a contract for building military posts up to Lake Tanganyika—in Arab territory beyond the king's claims. Twelfth, Henry Morton Stanley grossly understated the difficulties of building a railroad from Matadi to Stanley Pool. Among

other things, Williams explained why it would be very difficult to find enough laborers and to feed them.[11]

Williams expanded on the last point by writing a *Report on the Proposed Congo Railway,* the venture that Collis P. Huntington had invested in. Williams pointed out that even if the railroad were completed, it might not handle enough freight to justify the cost, because freight would have to be unloaded from big European steamships at Boma and left onshore, exposed to tropical downpours, while awaiting small-draft steamers that could safely reach Matadi, before being transferred to the railroad. Natives living near the railroad route had learned to fear white men and had fled, so workers had to be brought in from other regions. Because they were poorly treated, they too fled when they had an opportunity. Originally, railroad construction was expected to be completed in four years, but Williams observed that after three years, "not one mile of the roadbed is prepared."

Williams finished writing the *Open Letter* and the *Report* on July 18, 1890. They were published as pamphlets and distributed in Europe and the United States. Distribution seems to been aided by a Dutch trading company, Nieuwe Afrikaansche Handels Vennootschap, whose executives were aggravated that Leopold was promoting monopolies rather than free trade.

Huntington was upset by Williams's criticisms of the king. Huntington wrote: "I do not like the way in which Mr. Williams speaks of King Leopold and his ministers in the Congo State, as I feel quite sure that the King, at least, is solicitous of the best welfare of the natives of that country." William Mackinnon, chief executive of the British East India Company, shared Huntington's view: "The King is the last man in the world to permit or sanction any inhumanity on the part of his officers or servants."

The *New York Herald* published a story about the *Open Letter* in April 1891, and it became clear that Williams's allegations had to be answered. Alfred Le Ghait, Belgian ambassador to the United States, protested the publication of the story. According to Lord Vivian, the British ambassador in Brussels, the king warned against Williams's "scandalous and utterly unwarranted charges." Williams was denounced in the Belgian parliament. The *Journal de Bruxelles,* a pro-Leopold newspaper, dug up dirt on Williams, in particular that he had represented himself to be a colonel in the U.S. Army when he had

never made that rank. Williams was said to be illiterate when he fought in Mexico. To be sure, Williams had some defenders. For instance, *La Réforme* countered that "If Williams was an illiterate, his present writings prove that he has ceased to be one."

Administrators of the Congo Free State hastily issued a report aimed at rebutting Williams's allegations, but in some respects at least they seem to have confirmed them. For instance, the administrators claimed that Williams was wrong when he said there were only 2,300 soldiers in the Congo—there were 3,000. But if true, this was still inadequate for the size of the territory. Although the administrators claimed Williams was wrong when he said that the Congo Free State didn't have financial resources to do a proper job, they countered by saying the financial situation would be better if the Belgian government advanced it $400,000, equivalent to half the budget! The administrators said Williams was in error when he wrote that there were only two doctors in the Congo. According to the report, there were actually eight—a single doctor in each of six towns (one of which was the capital, Leopoldville), and two doctors in another town. The administrators denied that there was any slavery in the Lower Congo and blamed Arab slave traders for slavery elsewhere.

Williams went on to write *A Report upon the Congo-State and Country to the President of the Republic of the United States of America.* The report covered his findings in more detail. For instance, he wrote that "At Stanley-Falls slaves were offered to me in broad daylight; and at night I discovered canoe loads of slaves, bound strongly together."[12] His report didn't have any effect on U.S. policy toward Belgium or the Congo, but it proved to be prophetic, anticipating revelations to come.

Williams was the first to speak out against the atrocities in the Congo Free State, and his courage cost him further financial support from Huntington. Neither missionaries nor businessmen nor foreign diplomats who knew what was going on went public with their knowledge until many years after Williams did. During the course of his travels, Williams contracted tuberculosis, which worsened after he completed his writings about the Congo. He died in Blackpool, England, at age 41. It was subsequently revealed that he had an estranged wife in the United States and had many debts. These revelations together with his earlier bogus claim to have been a colonel were cited to discredit his findings. Vindication would come later.

The Novelist in the Heart of Darkness

Another visitor to the Congo, who was there at the same time as Williams, was Teodor Jósef Konrad Korzeniowski, the son of a Polish landowner who translated English and French literature into Polish. Jósef's father was arrested for helping to organize an uprising against the Russian tsar who controlled Polish territory at the time. At 11, Jósef was an orphan. He lived for a few years with his uncle in Kraków, then at 16 became a seaman to avoid conscription in the Russian army. He ended up serving for 16 years in the British merchant marine, after which he settled in Great Britain and changed his name to Joseph Conrad.

He went to the Congo because he landed a job as captain of *Roi des Belges*, a 15-ton steamship that traveled up and down the Congo River. On his initial disorienting trip as an observer, he took copious notes about landmarks.[13]

Conrad's trip became a nightmare. He became disillusioned when it was apparent that he wouldn't actually be commanding a steamer. He suffered bouts of malaria and dysentery. Worse was the cruelty he witnessed as he approached the land of ivory and rubber. While he didn't provide much in the way of graphic description, he did refer to Leopold's Congo scheme as "the vilest scramble for loot that ever disfigured the history of human conscience and geographical exploration."[14] He expressed his outrage at Leopold's "masquerading philanthropy."

From Conrad's experience in the Congo came his novel *Heart of Darkness* (1902), about the search for Kurtz, a man who had noble ideals of doing good and went to work for a company that gathered Congo ivory for sale in Europe. Assigned to a remote collecting point, he made himself the most successful ivory agent by intimidating the natives with random violence. He became ever more irrational. The narrator of the story explains:

> He wanted to shoot me, too, one day. . . . I had a small lot of ivory the chief of the village near my house gave me. You see I used to shoot game for them. Well he [Kurtz] wanted it, and wouldn't hear reason. He declared he would shoot me unless I gave him the ivory and then cleared out of the country, because he could do so, and had a fancy for it, and there was nothing on earth to prevent him from killing whom he jolly well pleased. I gave him the ivory.[15]

Kurtz could have been based on Captain Léon Rom, an ambitious military commander and civilian official in Leopold's Congo who, like Kurtz, displayed the shrunken heads of rebels.[16] Kurtz's Inner Station was surrounded by a fence whose posts were topped with shrunken heads—as Conrad described them, "black, dried, sunken, with closed eyelids, that seemed to sleep at the top of that pole, and, with the shrunken dry lips sowing a narrow white line of the teeth, was smiling, too, smiling continuously at some endless and jocose dream of that eternal slumber."[17] Conrad chronicled a killing ground: "The population had cleared out a long time ago. Here the dwellings were gone, too. . . . I passed several abandoned villages . . . [and] the body of a middle-aged negro, with a bullet-hole in the forehead, upon which I stumbled."[18]

And, of course, there were slaves in the Congo. Wrote Conrad:

> A slight clinking behind me made me turn my head. Six black men advanced in a file, toiling up the path. They walked erect and slow, balancing small baskets full of earth on their heads, and the clink kept time with their footsteps. Black rags were wound round their loins, and the short ends behind waggled to and fro like tails. I could see every rib, the joints of their limbs were like knots in a rope; each had an iron collar on his neck, and all were connected together with a chain whose bights [loops] swung between them, rhythmically clinking.[19]

And there were slaves left to die:

> They were dying slowly—it was very clear. They were not enemies, they were not criminals, they were nothing earthly now. Nothing but black shadows of disease and starvation, lying confusedly in the greenish gloom. Brought from all the recesses of the coast in all the legality of time contracts, lost in uncongenial surroundings, fed on unfamiliar food, they sickened, because inefficient, and were then allowed to crawl away.[20]

More than a dozen years after his time in the Congo, Conrad expressed interest in learning Spanish so he could read about the conquistadors, "If only to forget all about our modern *Conquistadores*. Their achievement is monstrous enough in all conscience . . . like that of a gigantic and obscene beast. Leopold is their Pizarro."

"Black Livingstone"

In May 1890, when Conrad was in Matadi, a black Southern Presbyterian minister named William Sheppard arrived with his associate, Samuel Lapsley, a white Southern Presbyterian minister. Born in 1865, Sheppard had been educated at the Hampton Institute (which became Hampton University) and the Colored Theological Seminary, Tuscaloosa, Alabama (which became Stillman College). After serving as a minister in Montgomery and Atlanta, he decided he wanted to be a missionary in the Congo. But the Presbyterian Foreign Missions Board, headquartered in Baltimore, wouldn't send a black minister to Africa without a white minister.

Enter General Henry Shelton Sanford who had owned a shipping company that did business in the Congo. He had failed as a diplomat and a businessman until, with mounting debts, he connected with King Leopold. Sanford was retained to promote the king's interests in the United States. The Congo needed labor, so Sanford called on Washington politicians, touting the Congo as a good place to send American blacks—a variation on the colonization idea that had been favored in the United States during the early nineteenth century. The problem was that few blacks born in the United States were interested in living in Africa. They wanted to be free in the only country they knew. They had family and friends in America. Nonetheless, Alabama senator John Tyler Morgan thought that sending American blacks to the Congo was a great idea. He helped make sure that President Chester A. Arthur's administration extended diplomatic recognition to Leopold's Congo Free State, and he encouraged the Southern Presbyterian Church to send missionaries into the Congo. He encouraged his former law partner's son to offer his services as a missionary there, and so 23-year-old Samuel Lapsley became available to join Sheppard.[21]

Neither man knew much about Africa. For starters, maps of the time didn't provide details about the interior, as few explorers had ventured far inland from the coast. The length, course, origins and hazards of the rivers were unknown. If it became impossible for a ship to continue going up a river, perhaps because of rapids, it wasn't known how supplies could be transported through the jungles. Where would one be able to hire porters to carry everything? Little was known about the tropical diseases one might encounter in Africa's in-

terior and how those afflicted with such diseases might be cured. Finally, there was little information about the tribes, particularly which might be helpful and which hostile.

The two men crossed the Atlantic and spent some time in London trying to get information about Africa. Then they went to Brussels, where they met Sanford. He explained that after arriving in the Congo, they would board a steamship that would go up the Congo River as far as Matadi, which is where the river becomes rapids, making further steamship travel impossible. Sanford arranged an appointment with the Belgian king and accompanied Lapsley and Sheppard to the palace.[22]

Lapsley recalled that the king was "tall, erect and slender. . . . His hair, rather thin and gray, he parts a little to the right of the middle; his beard is long and fine, turning a little gray. . . . His expression is very kind, and his voice matches it. He wore a dark green military frock coat, epaulettes and sword, with no star or decoration whatever. His manner is both bright and gentle."[23] Leopold suggested that Lapsley and Sheppard establish a mission among the Kasai people, far in the interior of the Congo.

As directed, they took a steamship to Matadi and hired porters who carried their canned food, cooking utensils and everything else they would need for about 200 miles until they reached Stanley Pool (now Malebo Pool), where the Congo River widened into a lake about 14 miles wide and 22 miles long. This was navigable. The capital, Leopoldville (now Kinshasa), was near the lower end of Stanley Pool. Sheppard and Lapsley spent several months there as they tried to regain their strength, explored the area and thought about where they should go next.

They headed for Kasai, the least-known of the Congo Free State's 12 districts. Kasai was about the size of Virginia. Sheppard and Lapsley were interested in the Kuba people, who were believed to have developed a high level of civilization. Accordingly, the men decided to establish a mission at Luebo on the Lulua River, the junction of several trade routes, which would enable them to learn about different tribes. Congo Free State officials had told them that nobody had claimed land there. The missionaries traded 12 yards of cloth for a 9-acre site that traditionally belonged to the Kete people.[24]

Sheppard and Lapsley visited nearby villages with notebooks and compiled what amounted to dictionaries of local languages. Sheppard

was especially effective at winning friends. By turns, he played the role of a demanding customer and an entertaining comedian.[25] He drew on his skills as a hunter and chef, becoming a popular host for traders and tribesmen who passed through the area. He served buffalo burgers, python steaks and elephant roasts, among other savory dishes. Sheppard's visitors were glad to help teach him words in their languages, the names of villages and the names of tribal chiefs whom he should know.[26]

Sheppard and Lapsley endured the hazards of jungle life. Most of their possessions, in particular their clothing, were eaten by white ants. Nothing was left of a silk top hat, which Lapsley had bought for his visit to Leopold, except the wire frame. Sometimes there were clouds of mosquitoes. The rivers swarmed with crocodiles. Both men were debilitated by a succession of tropical diseases.

After a while, Sheppard and Lapsley began to notice signs that all was not well in the Congo. Lapsley, for instance, had a conversation with the missionary George Grenfell who reported that villagers around Grenfell's station were forced to supply Belgian "state men" with food, fuel and labor without compensation. In January 1891, when Sheppard and Lapsley were exploring the Kwango River, two starving men appeared from out of the grass by the shore. They said they had escaped brutal working conditions on the steamship *Peace*. Sheppard and Lapsley invited them into their canoes and shared some of their food.[27] On another occasion, they had encountered friendly natives in Boleke, a fishing village, but when the missionaries returned to the area later, the natives went into hiding. Sheppard and Lapsley were told that a steamship had stopped there, and the crewmen had stolen firewood. When the natives resisted, the whites burned the village. But because the natives seemed terrified, the missionaries suspected the whites must have done something worse than stealing wood. As they continued down the river, they passed more burned villages. Finally, the story came out: A Belgian force led by Guillaume Van Kerckhoven had passed through the area, and when he encountered resistance, he ordered a massacre and rewarded his men with five brass rods for each severed head they brought back.

Again and again, Sheppard displayed phenomenal courage. He got to know the Zappo-Zap tribe, fierce cannibals involved in the slave trade. One girl, who appeared to be about six years old, had been cap-

tured, and the Zappo-Zaps killed her mother, cooked her and forced the girl to eat her.[28]

Sheppard's partner, Lapsley, was less adventurous and less outgoing, and he was often ill with fevers. He regretted that he didn't win any converts for the Presbyterian church, but he came to realize that his calling was really to help people, and he did much to relieve suffering of the terribly treated natives. Unfortunately, in 1892 Lapsley contracted what was known as blackwater fever and died in Boma.

Sheppard dreamed of finding Mushenge, capital of the kingdom of the Kuba. It was hidden somewhere in the highlands northeast of Luebo, surrounded by a vast maze of pathways. Some of the pathways passed through villages, but the king of the Kuba vowed that anyone who helped a foreigner find the kingdom would be killed, and maybe his entire village would be wiped out. The Belgians had failed to find the kingdom, which they believed was loaded with ivory and gold.

Rather than asking for directions to the kingdom, which would have alarmed people, Sheppard followed natives headed for the next village market, and when he reached it, he bargained for eggs, which he used for food. Then he followed somebody who seemed headed for the next village market, and so on. As Sheppard approached the kingdom, he was discovered by some of the native king's soldiers, and they announced that they would destroy the village he was in. But he explained that he found his way without anybody's help, so nobody should be punished. The soldiers were amazed that he spoke their language, and he was taken to the king, Kot aMweeky.

The king believed Sheppard must be a previous Kuba king who had come back from the dead, and he became a royal favorite. Sheppard was careful to conduct himself as a dutiful courtier and was given the run of the royal city. He made meticulous notes of everything he observed, compiling the first record of Kuba culture and noting their exceptional skill at weaving, embroidery and wood carving. His information showed that Africans were capable of achieving an advanced civilization.

After about four months, Sheppard felt he had learned about as much as he could.[29] He asked the king's permission to return home but was refused at first. The king viewed him as a prize he wished to keep. Eventually, the king agreed that Sheppard could leave for a year. He took with him not ivory or gold but hundreds of works of art that became the basis for the world's most valuable collection of Kuba art,

which Sheppard later donated to the Hampton Institute. Not least of his priorities during his year away from the Congo was to marry the woman to whom he had been long engaged: Lucy Gantt, two years younger than he was, born in Alabama. She worked as a teacher, helping blacks become literate.[30]

The couple returned to Africa, where they experienced plenty of hardships. Natives fired arrows at their steamer, because Congo Free State officers on the previous steamer had attacked them. The Sheppards passed through villages that had been burned by white traders. They found that Luebo was a mess, because the missionaries who were there in Sheppard's absence weren't capable of maintaining it. During the next couple of years, Lucy gave birth to two children, who died in infancy from tropical fevers. The Sheppards resolved that if they had more children, they would send them to America to stay with relatives, to avoid exposure to deadly diseases.

By 1895, there were enough stories circulating about Belgian atrocities in the Congo that Leopold had to respond. He established the Commission for the Protection of the Natives and staffed it with missionaries. But their missions were far apart, based in parts of the Congo away from the rubber-gathering operations. These missionaries had little firsthand knowledge of conditions and couldn't meet easily. No surprise, then, that the commission was nothing more than a public relations ploy.[31]

Sheppard handled everything on his own at the Luebo mission, where he and his wife lived, until 1897 when a missionary named William Morrison arrived to be Sheppard's boss. A Virginian, Morrison was probably accustomed to dealing with blacks as inferiors, but he knew little about the Congo, and Sheppard qualified as an expert in every way—his knowledge of local languages, of Kuba culture, and his courage in a dangerous environment. Still, Morrison hated slavery, and he suspected the worst about what King Leopold was doing in the Congo.

In 1898 soldiers commanded by a Belgian officer named Fromont plundered Luebo. Morrison protested and threatened to report the incident.[32] This seems unlikely to have fazed Fromont, since Luebo was in the middle of nowhere and Fromont could have ordered him killed without anybody finding out about it. Morrison believed he might have an impact if he could document atrocities.

Meanwhile, thanks to the rubber boom, the Kuba were no longer safely isolated. As Leopold's men stepped up the pressure to find

more and more rubber while prices were high, the Africans took shortcuts. Instead of making an incision in a stem and waiting for the sap to drip, the Africans cut completely through a stem and accelerated the flow of sap, thereby killing the vine. Because the Africans destroyed increasingly more vines, they had to venture farther and farther away, often days from their villages. Leopold's forces followed, to keep up the pressure, seizing women, killing men and destroying villages if not enough rubber was produced.[33]

In 1899 Sheppard heard that the Belgians had hired the Zappo-Zaps to destroy the entire Kuba region. Morrison realized this might be the opportunity to document what was happening, and that if anyone could gather the evidence, Sheppard could. He issued what must have seemed like a suicide order to Sheppard.

Armed with a notebook, a Kodak box camera and a rifle, and smartly dressed in his best linens and pith helmet, Sheppard went to a Pianga village where he understood some horrifying things had happened, but it was deserted. The next Pianga village was deserted, and so was the next. He came across a single survivor who reported that the Zappo-Zaps had demanded that people in the Pianga region march to stockades the Zappo-Zaps had built, supposedly to find out how much they owed in taxes. Malumba, the Zappo-Zap leader, had demanded 60 slaves, a herd of goats, baskets of corn and, most important, 2,500 balls of rubber. When the Pianga protested this was too much, the Zappo-Zaps opened fire. In the ensuing melee, the survivor escaped through a broken stockade fence.[34]

Sheppard started following trails that led to the stockade. The villages he passed were littered with corpses. Some of the corpses were carved up, the flesh presumably consumed by the Zappo-Zaps. There was a curve in the jungle trail and suddenly Sheppard faced 16 Zappo-Zaps. "They cocked their guns and took aim," Sheppard recalled. "I jumped forwards, threw up my hands and cried in a loud voice, 'Don't shoot, I am Sheppard!' The man in the lead recognized me. I had met him many times at Luebo. His name was Chebamba. [The Zappo-Zaps] let down their guns, turned them toward the bush and lowered the hammers. Chebamba walked up and caught my hand with a hearty good morning."[35]

Sheppard was introduced to Malumba, the Zappo-Zap leader. Sheppard saw piles of corpses all around, but Malumba acted like a gracious host at a party, showing Sheppard the stockade with more

corpses, many cut up, pointing to the heart that had been cut out of a Pianga chief. Some survivors were being kept as possible hostages, and Sheppard noticed the blue flag with a gold star, the flag of Leopold's Congo Free State, a sign that the Belgians had almost certainly hired the Zappo-Zaps.

Because Malumba was bragging about his killing, Sheppard concluded that Malumba assumed Sheppard, too, was working for the Belgians. Shrewdly, Sheppard played the part of an official admirer. He flourished his notebook, began to ask questions and write down the information, and took photographs. When Malumba led Sheppard to a grill holding a pile of hands over a fire, Sheppard carefully counted the hands and wrote down the number—81. Malumba explained, "I always have to cut off the right hands of those we kill in order to show the State how many we have killed." Since many days might pass before the chief could present the hands, they had to be smoked so they wouldn't rot in the tropical heat.[36]

When Sheppard had seen enough, he headed back to their missionary station in Ibaanc. He wrote his report and had some fast runners take copies to Morrison in Luebo. Morrison brought a copy to the Congo Free State offices in Leopoldville and demanded that the killing stop. Incredibly, Belgian soldiers were dispatched to the stockade, where they freed the hostages and arrested Malumba. Congo Free State officials denied that they had anything to do with this or any of the other killings.[37]

Morrison believed that the officials were definitely behind the killing, but Congo courts, manned with Belgian judges, never found Belgians guilty of any crimes against Africans. Morrison had a copy of Sheppard's report sent to London and delivered to the Aborigines Protection Society. They tried to publicize the report, but it created hardly a stir. In 1903, when Morrison was due to leave the Congo for a vacation, he went to London and arranged to give a presentation about the Congo. He prepared a lawyer's brief about treaties violated and spoke at London's Whitehall auditorium. Morrison didn't have Sheppard's charisma, but he was the first missionary to speak publicly about atrocities in the Congo, and his case was convincing enough that a resolution was introduced in Parliament to investigate what was going on.

Sheppard also decided to take some time off from the Congo. In late 1903, he returned to America with his wife and two-year-old son.

They went to Staunton, Virginia, and visited their six-year-old daughter, who didn't recognize them. The family had little time together, because the Presbyterian church wanted him to go on the lecture circuit and raise money. He was soon traveling around the country giving about one speech a day, each of which was good for several hundred dollars of contributions. Crowds came to hear about his incredible adventures, not about King Leopold's crimes. As a black Southerner, he knew there were limits to how far he could go criticizing white rulers, and the Presbyterian church didn't want to jeopardize his mainstream appeal for fundraising. As he had done on his previous speaking tours, he displayed Kuba weavings, carvings and knives. But a missionary named Lachlan Vass, an associate of Morrison, persuaded Sheppard to be more explicit about Belgian responsibility for atrocities. Sheppard did that in a speech given in Warm Springs, Virginia. As it happened, Belgium's ambassador to the United States, Ludovic Moncheur, was in the audience. Sheppard's speech about "Atrocities in the Belgian Congo" was reported in the international press, and Moncheur was outraged.

Morrison had sent a copy of Sheppard's report to Mark Twain, and in 1905, the humorist wrote "King Leopold's Soliloquy," a parody of the king's complaints about the terrible things people were saying about him: "The meddlesome missionaries! They seem to be always around, always spying, always eye-witnessing the happenings, and everything they see they commit to paper. . . . One of these missionaries saw eighty-one hands drying over a fire for transmission to my officials—and of course he must go and set it down and print it."[38]

The Sheppards returned to Ibaanc in 1906 and found that the entire region was a war zone controlled by the Belgian police, who forced all the natives to hunt for rubber. Growing food and cooking were forbidden![39] Conscripts walked as many as 20 miles through the jungle, carrying bundles of rubber to Belgian collection points. Each conscript had to wear a rope around his neck with a numbered metal disk attached, so Belgian soldiers could keep track of which conscripts were meeting their rubber quotas and which were not.[40]

When Leopold's soldiers encountered resistance in a village, the policy was to shoot everyone. Nobody was trusted. The soldiers had to account for their bullets—hence, supervisors demanded that soldiers collect ears, noses and especially hands to show what had been accomplished with the bullets.

Sheppard began to speak out. He wrote an article for the *Kasai Herald,* a Presbyterian newsletter, about how Belgian forces were oppressing and starving the people. He expressed anguish about the sophisticated Kuba culture and their great city that lay in ruins. He made clear his conviction that the Kuba people were capable of governing themselves.[41] Later, when British vice consul Wilfred Thesiger showed up in town, perhaps gathering information for a Congo investigation authorized by Parliament, Sheppard showed him around, escorting him through some 30 burned villages. Thesiger issued a report, "The Enslavement and Destruction of the Bakuba," in which he blamed Leopold's rubber monopoly, Compagnie du Kasai (CK), as well as Leopold himself for the atrocities.

Directors of the company decided to file a libel suit. They couldn't sue Thesiger since he had diplomatic immunity, but they could go after Sheppard, who obviously had influenced the report. Morrison was named in the lawsuit, too. While Morrison was eager for the publicity such a trial would probably generate, Sheppard didn't relish the prospect of prison. Congo Free State Courts were notorious for their bad decisions. In one case, for instance, a judge ruled that a Belgian officer who had killed some 60 people wasn't responsible for his actions. The judge explained, "Long residence amongst the natives must have deprived him of all sentiments of humanity."

Morrison went directly to Leopoldville, where the trial would be held, while Sheppard was asked to do the impossible: trek through Kuba land to Leopoldville and somehow find witnesses to the killings willing to appear in court, who would have to walk with him through the jungles and catch a steamer on the Kasai River—altogether, traveling about a hundred miles. Sure enough, he arrived before the court date with 20 Kuba warriors.

Even with these witnesses, Morrison and Sheppard expected to lose, but as the trial was set to begin, three men appeared, and they might have changed everything. U.S. consul William Handley and his assistant had been dispatched by American president William Howard Taft to observe the proceedings. The third man was Emile Vandervelde, a member of the Belgian Parliament, who came to defend Morrison and Sheppard without a fee. Early on, the judge rejected claims against Morrison on a technicality. Apparently, Morrison was outraged because Sheppard would be the star of the proceedings.

Vandervelde quickly demolished CK's libel case and turned to lesser claims. The company's lawyer claimed Sheppard's wife, Lucy, had sent dinner invitations and thank-you notes to Belgians, when actually she had hostile intentions. Vandervelde hooted at the idea that Lucy should be prosecuted for being nice. "If I had received letters from ladies thanking me for gifts," he declared, "it would never have occurred to me to collect these thank-you notes to be used as evidence." Vandervelde remarked that the British knew better than to ridicule nice ladies in a courtroom. He declared that the trial involved the very serious issue of the company throttling the civil rights of the natives. Even though the judge refused to permit testimony from Sheppard's warriors, Vandervelde seemed to get the better of the courtroom exchanges.

The judge desperately sought a compromise, and he decided to reject the charges against Sheppard and to rule that CK wasn't liable for harm done to the natives, while requiring the royal company to pay court costs. As a consequence of the trial and publicity, Leopold lost the monopoly, the Belgian government began allowing other companies to compete in the rubber region, and with the competition came a tendency to treat workers much better.

In the press, Sheppard was hailed as the hero of the trial with headlines like "American Negro Hero of Congo Was First to Inform World of Congo Abuses." Shortly afterward, however, he was recalled to the United States by the Presbyterian church. There were revelations that over the years he had had a mistress in the Congo with whom he had fathered a son. He resumed his career as a speaker regaling audiences with his adventures in Africa. He finished his career as minister of a small church in Louisville, Kentucky. In 1926, he was felled by a stroke. Reportedly, more than a thousand people attended his funeral.

The Shipping Supervisor and the Distinguished Diplomat

The most potent critic of King Leopold's murderous policy was an import-export supervisor with the Liverpool-based Elder Dempster shipping company, which had been granted a cargo transport monopoly by King Leopold II. Edmund Dene Morel was a big man, with a long mustache and a burning passion.[42] During the 1880s, Morel had

been assigned to Antwerp so he could be present for the arrival and departure of the company's steamships from the Congo.

Morel observed that the ships routinely unloaded ivory and then loaded rifles and ammunition. When he checked shipping records, he had the impression that they understated the quantity of weapons. Considering the large amount of ivory coming from the Congo and the apparent lack of trade goods being shipped to the Congo, he wondered how the people there were being paid for the ivory. He knew that according to King Leopold's regulations, the people weren't allowed to use money. Morel reached a shocking conclusion: Statistics on the freight going to and from the Congo were consistent with slavery. Nothing was being shipped for the people because they weren't being paid anything. Morel wrote that he was "appalled at the cumulative significance of my discoveries. It must be bad enough to stumble upon a murder. I had stumbled upon a secret society of murders with a King for a croniman."

After noting the abundance of weapons and the lack of trade goods being shipped to the Congo, he confronted Alfred Jones, president of Elder Dempster. Jones acknowledged that something improper was going on when he told Morel that King Leopold promised there would be reforms. Subsequently Morel was offered higher-paying jobs in other departments at the company, which he declined.

Liverpool businessman John Holt had confidence in Morel and helped him start an illustrated weekly newspaper, the *West African Mail*. Given the European presence in African colonies, there was unprecedented interest in the continent. Morel couldn't go to the Congo himself because Leopold barred unfriendly journalists. But he did publish reports by people who had been to the Congo. Morel interviewed concession company employees who had become uncomfortable with what was going on and had left Africa with documentary evidence. When a member of Parliament presented evidence about Leopold's horrors, Morel published it, and he printed the names of those killed in the Congo. The more material Morel published about Leopold's oppression, the more unsolicited information he received about the Congo. People sent him clippings from European newspapers, and he in turn supplied quite a bit of information to British and European newspapers.

Gradually, information about Belgian atrocities emerged from the Congo. A Belgian officer named Lacroix had a dispute with his su-

perior, Lieutenant Lothaire, who had become notorious after having arrested and summarily hanged Charles Henry Stokes in 1895. Stokes had operated trading caravans from a German base, violating the Belgian trading monopoly. Because Stokes was an Englishman, the case provoked protests in London. Lothaire was put on trial but acquitted and later promoted to Commissaire-Général.[43] In 1898 Lothaire was assigned to the Mongalla district, and subsequently rumors reached Europe about terrible massacres there. Lacroix, who carried out some of these massacres for Lothaire, couldn't bear his complicity any longer and wrote a confessional letter to the *Nieuwe Gazet,* an Antwerp newspaper that had displayed some independence from the king. The letter, published on April 10, 1900, told how Lacroix had been ordered to massacre everyone in a village that had failed to meet its quota for rubber deliveries. Lacroix wrote, "I am going to be tried for having murdered one hundred and fifty men, for having crucified women and children, and for having mutilated many men and hung the remains on the village fence."[44]

At about the same time, another independent Belgian newspaper, *Le Petit Bleu,* published a confession by an officer named Moray. He wrote, in part:

> At Ambas, we were a party of thirty, under V [Moray's superior, name withheld] who sent us into a village to ascertain if the natives were collecting rubber. We found the natives sitting peaceably. We asked them what they were doing. They were unable to reply, thereupon we fell upon them all, and killed them without mercy. An hour later we were joined by V and told him what had been done. He answered, "It is well, but you have not done enough!" He ordered us to cut off the heads of the men and hang them on the village palisades, and to hang the women and children on the palisades in the form of a cross.

A trial was scheduled, but Moray was found murdered in his room before the trial began. A witness to the massacre, Commandant Dooms, was reportedly drowned by a hippopotamus, although a Captain Baccari claimed that Dooms had been poisoned. Officer V was acquitted.

By 1903, enough evidence had been published about Leopold's atrocities that Parliament adopted a resolution stating that Congo

"natives should be governed with humanity."[45] Members of Parliament also complained that Leopold had promoted monopolies rather than free trade as he had promised. This was a start.

As a result of the resolution, Great Britain's consul in the Congo, Roger Casement, was ordered to investigate reports of murder and mayhem. Having lived in the Congo for much of two decades, Casement proved to be a key witness who could describe major changes during the period. Herbert Ward, who worked with Casement in the Congo, described him as "A tall, handsome man of fine bearing; thin, mere muscle and bone, a sun-tanned face, blue eyes and black curly hair. A pure Irishman, he is, with a captivating voice and a singular charm of manner. A man of distinction and great refinement, high-minded and courteous."[46] According to Fred Puleston, who also knew Casement during this time, "Casement's disposition and make-up was the gentlest imaginable. He was always sweet-tempered, ready to help, condemning cruelty and injustice in any form."

Casement was born at Sandycove, near Dublin. Both his parents died before he was 10, and he went to live in Ulster with his guardian from his father's family. His mother's sister had married an agent for Elder Dempster, where Morel had worked, and this uncle arranged for Casement to get a job there. He was soon assigned to the officer responsible for service to passengers on a steamship to Africa. Then he served as a volunteer working with Henry Morton Stanley.

Casement had heard about a lot of violence in the Congo, but one occasion might have been too much. In 1887 *Force Publique* officer Guillaume Van Kerckhoven bragged that he paid five brass rods for each human head his soldiers brought him.[47] In 1890 Joseph Conrad met Casement in Matadi, where they shared a room for 10 days. Years later, in London, they had dinner and long talks. Conrad wrote a friend that "He could tell you things! Things I have tried to forget, things I never did know."

In 1903, Casement spent some three and a half months investigating in the interior of the Congo. To maintain his independence, he made arrangements for his own travel, renting such boats as might be available, for instance, rather than using government-provided transportation. He inspected rubber slavery operations. He counted the number of hostages held in a village that failed to meet its rubber quotas. He graphically described evidence of atrocities, including hands and penises cut off of corpses.

Casement witnessed the imposition of heart-breaking taxes. Some natives, he reported, "had no other means of raising so large a sum they had, many of them, been compelled to sell their children and their wives. . . . A father and mother stepped out and said that they had been forced to sell their son for 1,000 [brass] rods to meet their share. . . . A widow came and declared that she had been forced, in order to meet her share, to sell her daughter, a little girl whom I judged from her description to be about ten years of age."[48] The more Casement saw, the angrier he became. Overall, he was struck by how dramatically populations had fallen at villages he had visited in 1887.

As Casement made his research trip through the Congo, he tried to enlist support from missionaries who had withheld their observations of atrocities for years. Initially, they hadn't believed reports about slavery in the Congo. When they had seen some of the horrors themselves, they were afraid to speak out, because the Belgians could have them killed and nobody would know what happened. After some missionaries passed information to missionary officials in London, the officials suppressed it out of concern that the Belgians would shut down the missionary stations.[49] Casement told missionaries that if they had submitted reports on atrocities and the reports were suppressed by higher-ups in their missionary organizations, they should report their observations to Morel, who would publicize them.

Toward the end of 1903, Casement returned to London so he could prepare his report. He finished a draft on December 12. As word spread about Casement's forthcoming report, there were efforts to tone it down. Shipping company president Alfred Jones lobbied against the report at the British Foreign Office.[50] Some officials believed Casement's findings weren't enough to justify conclusions that were critical of Leopold. How about using reports of Congo atrocities that had been accumulating in files at the Foreign Office? Henry Petty-Fitzmaurice, Britain's Foreign Secretary, didn't want to do that since the files would show that the British government had known about Congo atrocities for years and hadn't acted.[51] Casement gave newspapers inflammatory interviews, which made suppressing the reports more difficult. Still, the British Foreign Office, which didn't want a squabble with Belgium,[52] delayed publication of Casement's report. Finally, in February 1904, the report was issued. Specific names had been replaced by initials, which undercut the impact somewhat.[53]

King Leopold did everything he could to discredit Casement's report. He blamed the brutal mutilations on tribal wars and the Arab slave trade. But it was hard to find any documentation that slave traders had punished slaves by mutilating them since that would have reduced their value.[54] Casement obtained testimony from missionaries who had been in the Congo before the Belgians came, and these missionaries hadn't seen mutilation.

Leopold blamed falling Congo village populations on sleeping sickness. But the governor-general of the Congo had asked missionaries to assess the population decline, and they didn't believe sleeping sickness was the principal issue. Rev. J. Whitehead, for instance, reported that the population of his village, Lukolela, was approximately 5,000 in 1887, and it had fallen to 352 in 1903. Whitehead blamed the population decline on brutal treatment that, at the very least, left the natives more vulnerable to disease.

A court case in the Congo finally resulted in an opinion that upheld Casement's indictment of Leopold's Congo Free State. Concession agent Philippe Caudron had been charged with ordering native soldiers to destroy many villages and killing people who lived there. He was found guilty but appealed. He never denied the charges. He claimed that he was just following orders that he documented. The Boma Court of Appeals reduced his sentence because he was obligated to follow the orders, though the judges acknowledged the orders were illegal. This was Leopold's system at work.

The Conservative British government presented Casement's report to other nations that had signed the 1885 Berlin agreement—Austria-Hungary, France, Germany, Italy, the Netherlands, Portugal, Russia, Spain, Sweden and the United States—none of whom were willing to do anything about the Congo. Consequently, Great Britain did nothing as well. The most it might have done, in any case, was to somehow try to protect its own citizens in the Congo.

Morel contacted Liberal members of Parliament and alerted them to the horrors documented in Casement's report. One member, Alfred Emmett from Oldham, criticized the Foreign Office for not doing something about the Congo and other Liberal members came forward to speak about the atrocities. Suddenly, the Conservative government recommended an independent investigation.

Inevitably, Casement and Morel met and began a dynamic collaboration. Morel recalled some of the conversation they had at a Lon-

don restaurant: "I was mostly a silent listener, clutching hard upon the arms of my chair. As the monologue of horror proceeded . . . I verily believe I *saw* those hunted women clutching their children and flying panic stricken to the bush: the blood flowing from those quivering black bodies as the hippopotamus hide whip struck and struck again; the savage soldiery rushing hither and thither amid burning villages; the ghastly tally of severed hands."[55]

The men met again at Morel's house in Hawarden, a Welsh village. Casement urged Morel to establish an organization devoted to fighting injustice in the Congo. Morel resisted since there were other organizations such as the Aborigines Protection Society. But gradually he became persuaded that a specially focused campaign was needed to fight the enormous crimes being committed in the Congo. Accordingly, he helped launch the Congo Reform Association. He did many of the things that Thomas Clarkson and William Wilberforce had done a century before to launch their epic campaign against the slave trade. Morel recruited respected citizens—bishops, businessmen, members of Parliament—to lend their names. The first rally was held on March 23, 1904, in Liverpool's Philharmonic Hall.

Morel, whom Casement referred to as "Bulldog," worked like a man possessed. He continued to edit the weekly *West African Mail,* which provided his paycheck. He produced a monthly publication for the Congo Reform Association and organized their campaigns. He recruited people to start local branches of the association to raise money and generate more support in their communities. He wrote articles and books about the Congo. In *Red Rubber* (1906), he adopted William Lloyd Garrison's declaration upon launching *The Liberator:* "I will not equivocate, I will not excuse, I will not retreat a single inch; and I will be heard." Morel spent little time with his wife and five children. He confessed to Mark Twain that "My home life is reduced to microscopic proportions . . . I am at the end of my tether." But he vowed to persist because "those wretched people out there have no one but us after all. And they have the right to live."

Like the campaign against the slave trade, Morel's campaign against Congo slavery involved one public meeting after another. He spoke at hundreds. At the largest meetings he usually managed to have a bishop and a member of Parliament present to embellish the proceedings. He featured speakers who had been to the Congo, such as the missionaries John and Alice Harris, whose props included photographs, whips and

shackles—not unlike the props Thomas Clarkson had gathered to dramatize his presentations.

Morel launched a campaign in the United States by starting the American Congo Reform Association. He spoke in New York, Boston and elsewhere. He met with President Theodore Roosevelt, and he drew support from Mark Twain and Booker T. Washington. Morel proved to be a brilliant organizer and fund raiser.[56]

King Leopold counterattacked by bribing editors who could be bought and by using his considerable charm. In Belgium, Leopold had spent a great deal of money on monuments, greenhouses and other public works for which he received credit and adulation from his people.

Leopold Quits His Claim

The accumulated evidence against King Leopold couldn't be denied. According to some estimates, Leopold's secret slave regime had killed as many as 8 million people. The king was discredited, and pressure mounted for him relinquish his authority over the Congo. He resisted providing financial accounts for Congo operations. When finally he did, they showed that the more than 30 million francs he had borrowed from the Belgian government (that is, Belgian taxpayers) were missing. There weren't any eager bidders for the Congo among other colonizing nations. The only serious prospect was the Belgian government itself. Leopold demanded that it assume all of the Congo's debts, including what he personally owed Belgium, and he insisted that the government spend about 45.5 million francs to finish his construction projects. In addition, he wanted 50 million francs as gratitude for all he had done on behalf of the country. The government bought this terrible deal, perhaps just to get rid of him and the stain he had brought to the country's legitimacy. The agreement was signed in November 1908. In December 1909, as Leopold lay dying, he made his last gift to the Belgian people by signing a bill that would establish military conscription, another form of forced labor.

With Leopold no longer in control of the Congo, some of the worst practices ended. The Belgian government, however, introduced a head tax that forced Africans to work so they could pay the tax. If there was less brutality and killing, forced labor seemed to survive. By

about 1912, it was apparent that the Congo had been substantially stripped of its rubber vines and the business was unprofitable there. Moreover, cultivated rubber trees in Latin America and Southeast Asia were coming into large-scale production. The combination of a moral crusade and market economics ended one of the most monstrous chapters in the history of Western slavery.

How Did It All Work Out?

Although abolishing slavery was an essential step to achieve a free society, it wasn't enough. Without constitutional limitations on government power, without the rule of law and equal rights, it was almost impossible for a free society to develop.

The Scourge of Dictatorships

In Haiti, the inability of slaveholders and slaves to do anything other than fight each other, compounded by invasions of French, British and Spanish forces, convinced the populace that if they didn't kill, they would be killed. The greatest champions of Haitian independence, such as Toussaint L'Ouverture, were brutal military dictators. After Toussaint was captured by Napoleon, Jean-Jacques Dessalines became president-for-life until he was assassinated in 1806. There was a civil war with factions led by black generals Alexandre Péxtion and Henri Christophe. The result of all this violence was a seemingly endless succession of bloody power struggles up to the present, rather than a free society that slaves had dreamed of when they began their revolt.

Since the abolition of slavery in Haiti, the people have had to endure some 200 revolutions, coups and civil wars.[1] Endemic violence

obliterated historical information about Haiti when, for instance, fighting destroyed government properties in 1869, 1879, 1883, 1888 and 1912. The National Palace was blown up several times. Plagued with dictators to the present day, Haiti is the poorest nation in the western hemisphere and among the poorest nations on earth.

In Cuba, the episodic Ten Years War (1868–1878), an unsuccessful bid for independence, did much to exhaust the proslavery and antislavery factions alike. By the time Spain abolished Cuban slavery in 1886, the island was peaceful. Large numbers of former slaves continued to work on plantations, but now they were paid and were free to move around. Many single men lived in their barracks without locks on the doors. Other former slaves formed families, the husband working in the fields and the wife working as a domestic in the towns. Reliable statistics about Cuban living standards at the century's turn apparently don't exist, so it's hard to determine how much better off former slaves were. Mortality rates, however, didn't fall significantly below those of the slavery era until after 1900, when more effective medical treatments for cholera, smallpox and yellow fever became available.

In the century since Cuba gained independence in 1902, it has been rocked by revolutions and ruled by dictators. There has been a totalitarian communist regime for the past four decades. Although chattel slavery is gone, the Cubans have yet to limit the power of their government and to secure their freedom.

After Brazilian emancipation in 1888, plantation owners there expected the worst, and many did go bankrupt without slaves. Large numbers of former slaves returned to the plantations where they had long worked, and they were treated with more respect as free people. Plantation owners no longer feared the threat of rebellious slaves and they had greater assurance that their crops would be well tended. Former slaves migrated from economically depressed sugar-producing areas to more prosperous coffee-producing areas.

Many plantation owners diversified by investing capital in other industries such as railroads, and in shipping and manufacturing enterprises. The Golden Law made Brazil more attractive to immigrants. Plantation owners promoted immigration by establishing the *Sociedade Promotora da Imigração* (Society for Promoting Immigration) and were able to maintain their properties and agricultural production by hiring Portuguese and Italian immigrants as well as former slaves.[2]

After emancipation, Brazilian Emperor Dom Pedro II lost the political support of the plantation owners, the burgeoning urban middle class, and the military. General Deodoro da Fonseca embraced the ideal of a republican government and organized a coup that deposed Dom Pedro II in November 1889. Fonseca declared Brazil a republic, though he proceeded to establish a military regime. He dismissed civilian officials and provoked a civil war, but he resigned in November 1891. After a power struggle, a form of republican government was finally established three years later.

Ever since, however, Brazil has been buffeted by civilian dictatorships and military dictatorships. Corruption, runaway inflation and economic chaos have repeatedly derailed efforts to establish a more liberal, democratic system.

In the Congo, chattel slavery seems to have ended within a few years after the Belgian government took control from King Leopold, but their paternalistic system treated African subjects as second-class citizens. The Belgians made it illegal for Africans to travel or to own guns without official permission. Moreover, Africans were banned from pursuing many occupations such as law and engineering.[3]

The situation worsened when, more than a half-century after King Leopold II relinquished the Congo and five years after it gained independence from Belgium, Mobutu Sese Seko became president. He changed the name of the country to Zaire, established a dictatorship, spent money lavishly on himself and bankrupted the national treasury despite the country's great wealth of natural resources. Mobutu's regime was noted for theft and fraud on an epic scale. He had mansions in a half-dozen countries and hid billions of dollars in overseas bank accounts. The regime controlled everything, and nobody's property was secure. He fled the country in 1997, leaving it more than $9 billion in debt—a reminder of how the failure to limit government power condemned people to suffer from tyrants.[4]

Controversies about the Peaceful Emancipation

In the British Caribbean, former slaves were better off following the end of transitional apprenticeship in 1838, when they were free to

choose their work. Many preferred to farm for themselves on a small scale where, they reasoned, they were likely to benefit from their labor, rather than remain on plantations where they had been abused. There was considerable social progress. More former slaves got married, husbands and wives lived together. Schools were established for former slaves and their children, and the former slaves formed self-help societies.[5]

Without question, many areas experienced labor market difficulties. Workers didn't show up or went on strike while cut canes rotted in the fields. They disrupted planters' schedules while they had prolonged holiday celebrations.[6] According to historian William A. Green, "the real cost of free labor was more than double the stipulated rate of wages." Green went on to report that "Negligence was as costly to the planters as irregularity. The abuse of equipment, destruction of carts, and the brutalization of draft animals increased in the free period. Fires caused by negligence were common. Inadequate weeding and sloppy work in boiling houses impaired the quality of plantation sugar, but managers were commonly afraid to upbraid negligent workmen for fear of losing their services during crop." However, Green was incorrect to suggest that such difficulties began with emancipation. There was plenty of sloppiness and abuse during the slavery era.

Overall, Green claimed, "free-labor sugar production had entailed higher production costs, lower output, and reduced profits." But this is utterly misleading. From an economic standpoint, what emancipation did was force all the costs into the open. During slavery, planters reported lower costs and higher profits, because substantial costs were borne by the slaves who were forced to do brutal work without compensation. The true costs of sugar production were hidden. They were revealed only in a free-labor market in which former slaves could choose what they wanted to do, plantation owners could choose what they wanted to do, and each individual was free to negotiate anywhere.

In essence, slaves were subject to a 100 percent tax on the compensation they would have earned in a free labor market, and the proceeds went to the planters. It is preposterous to suggest that true production costs went up because the 100 percent tax was abolished and workers received market-rate compensation.

The sugar business had developed in ways that didn't make any sense precisely because slavery—the 100 percent tax—concealed the

true costs of production. With the true cost of labor hidden, planters naturally wanted a lot of slaves, and it appeared cheaper to rely on slaves with primitive tools—the shovel, hoe and machete—than to invest in agricultural machinery. Finally, less productive land would not have been cultivated if planters had borne the true costs.

Ironically, even with the 100 percent tax on slave compensation many planters were in tough financial shape, chronically in debt to their suppliers, the West Indian merchants. Much of the compensation that Britain paid to the planters was used to pay down these debts rather than to invest in plantation improvements. According to an 1847 report authorized by the Jamaica Assembly, dozens of sugar plantations had been abandoned since the abolition of slavery. "Most of those properties were poorly situated," Green acknowledged. "Many had been devastated by drought. Others were 'miserable worthless places' thrown up in consequence of being plunged in debt long before the abolition of slavery."

By exposing the true production costs, emancipation forced planters to reorganize the sugar industry along more rational lines. In Trinidad, for instance, planters began adopting production methods that used fewer workers. In Jamaica, planters began using animal-drawn plows and harrows adapted for their particular soil conditions. In British Guyana, planters introduced elevators to bring cut sugar cane to mill houses and equipped sugar mills with steam engines, the same steam engines that had propelled the Industrial Revolution in the previous century.

Sometimes simple changes in production methods made a big difference. For instance, when cane plants were spaced farther apart—about six feet—there were more healthy shoots, the plants got more sunlight and could be more easily maintained, and harvesting was easier, reducing labor costs.[7]

To be sure, some places simply had a labor market that was difficult for planters. Often freedmen could grow much of their own food in the semitropical climate, and there weren't many other things to buy, so they didn't need much money. Planters couldn't pay them enough to make it worth doing the brutal hand labor that had to be done. In addition, the planters' biggest need was for seasonal work, and they couldn't offer many paying, year-round jobs. In markets with a low population density, such as Jamaica, workers were comparatively scarce and consequently hard to discipline, as they could easily

find another job. More labor market competition prevailed on densely populated Barbados, where plantations prospered with free labor and sugar production actually increased. It made sense for planting operations to contract where labor market conditions were difficult and to expand where labor market conditions were more favorable.

In an effort to increase labor market competition, many planters encouraged immigration. First, they recruited free black workers from Sierra Leone, a struggling territory founded by British evangelicals. Those who worked for five years in a Caribbean colony could have a free return ticket to Sierra Leone if they wished, and some 12,000 blacks did that. Because the number of recruits was less than hoped for, planters turned to India as a second labor source. Millions of Indians endured wretched poverty, and though indentured labor was a harsh arrangement, it seemed to be a better alternative to many. Colonial recruiters were based in Madras and Calcutta. Although the number of Indian recruits was encouraging, transporting them thousands of miles to the Caribbean was costly, and money had to be raised in Britain to fund the recruitment effort. In addition, planters had to pay a head tax for each immigrant they recruited, adding to their costs. By 1848, many planters were in debt and couldn't pay the tax or wages due the immigrant workers, and large numbers abandoned the plantations.

Some planters recruited workers from the Portuguese island of Madeira. As in Ireland, during the 1840s Madeira's main crop, potatoes, had failed. The wine crop failed too. People were starving. A few people emigrated to British Guyana and later reported they were better off, spurring further emigration. But Portuguese workers were highly susceptible to malaria and yellow fever in the Caribbean colonies.

With all these troubles, sugar production declined in the British West Indies, the opposite of what many British abolitionists thought would happen.[8] The situation alarmed them, because they realized that to achieve the international influence they wanted, British emancipation would have to be perceived as a success. But it was hard to convince many people that anything other than sugar production statistics mattered. The importance of human freedom couldn't be quantified. Nobody knew how much food former slaves were producing for their own consumption, so it didn't show up in official statis-

tics. In the United States, many Southern authors denounced British emancipation as a failure in order to help justify American slavery. The *Charleston Mercury* cited "the atmosphere of barbarism and dereliction that now pervades those once prosperous islands."[9]

Did declining sugar production really refute Adam Smith's contention that free labor was more efficient than slave labor? Not at all. As a general proposition, Smith's argument is certainly true, since market economies have outperformed command economies for thousands of years, up to the 1991 collapse of the Soviet Union and beyond. The experience of the Caribbean sugar industry confirmed that subsidies increase production of whatever is being subsidized. Sugar production had been subsidized by slaves who worked without market-rate compensation in the British West Indies. After those slaves were emancipated and paid wages, and the true production costs were no longer hidden, production was subsidized by British consumers who had to pay above-market prices for sugar, because lower-cost sugar from other sources was kept out of the British market by high tariffs.

British abolitionists split with British free traders over the sugar tariffs and found themselves in the curious position of siding with the British West Indian planters—the former slaveholders who wanted to keep high tariffs. If sugar tariffs were abolished, then the lower-priced, slave-produced sugar from Cuba and Brazil would take over the British market. The additional demand for this sugar would thereby help encourage the expansion of slavery, the last thing that abolitionists wanted.

In 1846, Parliament voted to abolish the sugar tariffs as well as tariffs on imported grain. As a result, there was a surge of imported slave-produced sugar from Brazil and Cuba. Overall exports from those sources jumped about 20 percent. Suddenly, British West Indian sugar was priced out of the market. Missionary George Blythe lamented, "The estates are now on the verge of ruin. . . . The grand experiment which has blessed these colonies with freedom must fail and the whole mass of the population will be involved in difficulties as distressing as those which lately desolated Ireland." But the plight of the West Indian planters wasn't an indictment of economic freedom. If the West Indian planters couldn't afford to pay their people market-rate compensation without being subsidized by consumers, clearly they were in the wrong business. The issue was as simple as that.

Fault Lines in American Strategy

Toward the close of the U.S. Civil War, Abraham Lincoln's conciliatory gestures had little effect because of the intense emotions stirred up by the fighting. Maryland-born actor John Wilkes Booth was among the Southerners outraged by all that the Confederacy had suffered. Booth resolved to assassinate Lincoln after he heard the president give a short speech supporting what he viewed as "nigger citizenship."[10] Booth had his chance on April 15, 1865, when Lincoln was watching a play at Ford's Theater, Washington, D.C.

Lincoln was succeeded by Vice President Andrew Johnson, a former slaveholder who had been a Democratic senator from Tennessee when the Civil War started. He was the only Southerner who remained in the Senate and sided with the Union. Lincoln had named him the military governor of Tennessee in 1862. Because Johnson was considered effective at suppressing the rebels there, Lincoln chose him as his running mate in the 1864 election. He appeared to support the North's objectives in the war.

Altogether, some 620,000 Union and Confederate soldiers died during the Civil War. Including the number of civilians killed—almost all of whom were Southerners[11]—the total probably exceeded the 700,000 American deaths in all the other wars the United States has been involved with. In many communities, entire adult populations were wiped out due to the practice of encouraging all the young men in a town to join the same fighting unit.

The financial cost of the Civil War was overwhelming. The North raised some $3 billion in taxes and loans. The Confederacy borrowed more than $2 billion.[12] Both North and South printed plenty of paper money. People in the North endured the inflation of greenbacks. In the South, there was a runaway inflation. An estimated $1 billion to $1.5 billion of property in the South was destroyed.[13]

Most of the Civil War had been fought in the South, especially Alabama, Georgia, Mississippi and Tennessee. Atlanta, Columbia, Richmond and other cities were substantially destroyed. Areas of the South that hadn't been occupied by Union troops were flooded with some 200,000 refugees. Confederacy president Jefferson Davis had suggested that people who were hungry could survive by eating rats which, he suggested, tasted better than squirrels.[14]

Union Major General Carl Schurz, traveling through the South on an 1865 fact-finding mission, reported seeing "ruin and desolation—the fences all gone; lonesome smoke stacks, surrounded by dark heaps of ashes and cinders, marking the spots where human habitations had stood; the fields along the road wildly overgrown by weeds, with here and there a sickly patch of cotton or corn cultivated by Negro squatters."[15]

Worst off were the prisoners of war. Andersonville in Georgia was among the largest Civil War prison camps, established in 1864 by the Confederacy. It held some 45,000 prisoners, of whom about 13,000 died from unsanitary conditions, malnutrition and disease. Altogether, a reported 215,000 Confederate soldiers died in Union prisons, and 195,000 Union soldiers died in Confederate prisons.[16]

Agents from the Treasury Department ranged through the conquered South, searching for assets to seize. They seized cotton and collected taxes on it.[17] The bitterness was overwhelming. Some 10,000 former slaveholders left the South, hoping to do better in the North, in Mexico, Brazil or Europe.[18] Those who remained in the South had powerful incentives to avenge their suffering. Wartime death and destruction became a huge, tragic distraction from the monstrous horrors of slavery.

On May 29, 1865, Johnson presented his plan for Reconstruction to bring the Southern states back into the Union as quickly as possible. He offered an amnesty for those who had supported the Confederacy. He affirmed the rights of planters to their land and other properties except slaves, provided that Confederates pledge their loyalty to the Union and back the abolition of slavery.[19] Confederate officials and planters with over $20,000 worth of taxable property, however, had to apply for presidential pardons individually. He insisted that when states held their constitutional conventions, they must abolish slavery, repeal the ordinances of secession and repudiate Confederate war debts.

Johnson appointed provisional governors who would start the Reconstruction process until elections were held. Except for those chosen for North Carolina and Texas, his choices were men who appealed to Southern whites. A governor had the power to fill every job in his state government, and there weren't many Southern Unionists around. Inevitably, most jobs were filled with people who had been in

state government before or during the Civil War. Consequently, Southern state governments were strongly opposed to giving blacks the right to vote.

Notably missing from Johnson's announcements was any mention of extending political rights to former slaves. He suggested that the states might take the initiative to do that, but basically he let the South go its own way. He maintained that as president he didn't have the power to tell states what they must do, and he didn't want issues involving former slaves to disrupt the process of bringing the 10 former rebel states back into the Union. In 1865 Johnson reportedly told California's Senator John Conness: "White men alone must manage the South."

Northerners who had supported the dramatic expansion of government power during the Civil War were disappointed and frightened. When Abraham Lincoln had been president, the assumption was that expanding government power would be used to do good. But his hand-picked successor turned out to be nothing like him. In the view of historian Garrett Epps, this Tennessee tailor's son who had appeared to be a supporter of Lincoln's policies was an impulsive, vindictive, racist alcoholic. At the 1865 inauguration ceremonies, Johnson reportedly had difficulty with his swearing-in as vice president, having consumed too much liquor the night before. He was said to be drunk when he delivered his speech. The day after Lincoln was assassinated, Johnson gave a speech that rambled on about his own greatness without mentioning Lincoln.[20] The presumed ally of the Republicans was actually a volatile adversary. Suddenly, a lot of people began to realize that political power can be dangerous because there's no sure way of keeping bad or incompetent people away from it.

Ex-confederates were quick to exploit Johnson's lenient policies and regain power in the South, and many won elections. Confederate colonels and generals, the Confederacy's former vice president and a half-dozen of its cabinet members, and 58 rebel congressmen gained power in 1865 and dominated southern state governments.[21] In some cases, these people wore their Confederate uniforms in government offices.

Mississippi's first postwar governor was a former Confederate brigadier general, Benjamin G. Humphreys, who gave a speech to the state legislature bristling with defiance. "Under the pressure of federal bayonets," he said, "urged on by the misdirected sympathies of the

world in behalf of the enslaved African, the people of Mississippi have abolished the institution of slavery. . . . The Negro is free, whether we like it or not; we must realize that fact now and forever. To be free, however, does not make a citizen or entitle him to social or political equality with the white man."[22] Humphreys dismissed the Civil War as "four years of cruel war conducted on principles of vandalism disgraceful to the civilization of the age."

In 1865, starting with Mississippi, southern state and local governments enacted Black Codes that restricted what former slaves could do. To be sure, there wasn't much new about these codes. They derived from all the hideous prohibitions that had supported slavery in the United States, in the British West Indies and probably elsewhere. The Black Codes severely limited the ability of former slaves to buy land, rent rooms and enter various professions. A black person wasn't permitted to go from one plantation to another without a pass. Traveling on a highway was forbidden unless a black person had his or her employer's permission. Alabama made it illegal for blacks to pursue any occupation other than farmer (the aim was to make it difficult for blacks to do work other than plantation labor).[23] Opelousas, Louisiana, made it illegal for a black person to live in town unless the individual worked as a servant. South Carolina required that blacks pay a tax of between $10 and $100 per year if they had a job other than as a field laborer or servant. In Mississippi, blacks had to provide evidence that they had a job. In Florida, whipping was the punishment for a black worker who broke a contract. Louisiana specified that blacks were to be fined for failure to obey "reasonable" orders and missing work for any reason other than illness.[24] Hunting, fishing or grazing livestock were often forbidden, since these activities helped blacks live without working on plantations.[25] Blacks were barred from serving on juries; they could be imprisoned for bringing "malicious" lawsuits against whites and could not testify against white people.[26] Blacks were excluded from schools, parks, orphanages and other public facilities.[27] Gun ownership was banned, as was interracial marriage. Any white citizen could arrest a black person. Mississippi became the first state to require that public transportation be segregated. With the Black Codes, southern governments tried to exert as much control over black people as they had had with slavery.

Planters were convinced that without compulsion, former slaves wouldn't work. Planters referred to the inherent laziness of former

slaves—the people who had done all the grunt work on plantations for decades without compensation. To prove that free labor was a failure, planters cited the experience of Saint-Domingue during the 1790s and British Jamaica during the 1830s, when large numbers of blacks quit working on plantations after the abolition of slavery.

Yet, the miracle was that so many former slaves remained on plantations. After centuries of horrifying treatment, former slaves had plenty of terrible memories. Having long labored without compensation, naturally many slaves would want to be their own bosses and work for themselves. Planters stepped up pressure on former slaves to sign labor contracts, many of which specified that blacks must not leave their plantations or hold meetings without permission. In addition, labor contracts often included restrictions on the personal lives of the former slaves, similar to those in the Black Codes.

Although the South was loaded with debt, the former Confederates who were back in power approved one spending scheme after another. They funded the construction of government buildings, bridges and railroads. They started making payments to Civil War veterans. Many of the facilities, notably government schools, were off limits to blacks. More spending required more taxes. Property taxes, sales taxes, licensing taxes and poll taxes went up. To a significant degree, blacks were taxed for things that benefited whites only.

All this provoked much revulsion in the North. The *Chicago Tribune* warned: "We tell the white men of Mississippi that the men of the North will convert the state of Mississippi into a frog pond before they will allow such laws to disgrace one foot of soil in which the bones of our soldiers sleep and over which the flag of freedom waves."[28]

The Radicals believed Congress must take charge of Reconstruction policy and force the South to do what was right. On January 31, 1865, Congress had already proposed the Thirteenth Amendment to the U.S. Constitution, abolishing slavery. By December 6, 27 states, including 7 rebel states, had ratified this amendment. It was subsequently ratified by eight more states.

The Radicals refused to seat any of the former Confederates who had been elected to Congress, which had the power to determine the qualifications of its members. Until Southern states had representatives in Congress, they couldn't rejoin the Union.

On June 13, 1866, Congress proposed the Fourteenth Amendment to the U.S. Constitution, aimed at guaranteeing that former

slaves would be American citizens, with the same rights as other American citizens. The amendment provided a broad definition of citizenship—anyone born or naturalized in the United States—and provided that "No State shall make or enforce any law which shall abridge the privileges or immunities of citizens of the United States; nor shall any State deprive any person of life, liberty, or property, without due process of law; nor deny to any person within its jurisdiction the equal protection of the laws." The amendment assured the right to vote for all male citizens over 21, except Indians. The Fourteenth Amendment was ratified by 28 states, including 6 former rebel states, by July 9, 1868. Nine more states later ratified it.

The 1866 congressional elections repudiated Johnson's Reconstruction policies and gave the Republicans a big majority. The following year, on March 3, Congress passed the first of four Reconstruction bills. It stated that there weren't any legal state governments in the former rebel states of Alabama, Arkansas, Florida, Georgia, Mississippi, North Carolina, South Carolina, Texas or Virginia. (Tennessee, which had ratified the Fourteenth Amendment, reentered the Union.) The bill designated the affected states as military districts. The president was directed to assign an officer, a brigadier general or higher, to be responsible for each district. He would be empowered to establish military tribunals for handling criminal cases. The bill required the states to hold conventions for drafting state constitutions consistent with the U.S. Constitution. Delegates to the conventions would be selected by male voters 21 years and older, resident in each state for at least a year, "of whatever race, color, or previous condition." Excluded from voting would be individuals who participated in the Confederacy or were convicted of a felony. A state could reenter the Union (1) when a proposed state constitution has been approved by Congress, (2) when the state adopted the Fourteenth Amendment, (3) when the Fourteenth Amendment actually became part of the U.S. Constitution, and (4) when Congress accepted its elected congressmen and senators. Until Congress accepted these representatives, a state government was provisional and could be revised or abolished by Congress. This bill gave Congress control of Reconstruction, and President Johnson didn't like it. He vetoed it, but Congress had the votes to override him and it became the first Reconstruction Act.

On March 23, 1867, Congress passed a supplementary bill providing what came to be known as the Ironclad Oath, which must be taken by individuals who wished to vote or hold office in the former rebel states. Oath takers had to swear, in part: "I have not been disenfranchised for participation in any rebellion or civil war against the United States, nor for felony committed against the laws of any State or of the United States, or given aid or comfort to the enemies thereof . . . I will faithfully support the Constitution."

In the border states that had sided with the Union—Delaware, Maryland, Kentucky, Missouri and West Virginia—slaveholders were bitterly opposed to the idea of liberating blacks and giving them equal rights. Resistance to abolition was strongest in Kentucky, which had more slaveholders than the other border states. When the war ended, there were still a reported 65,000 slaves in Kentucky. In Missouri, Unionists went further than restricting the right to vote: They banned anybody deemed "disloyal" from working as a teacher, lawyer or minister. West Virginia had the easiest transition, having broken away from Virginia in 1861, emancipating the few slaves in the region and joining the Union.[29]

Congress established the Freedman's Bureau, part of the War Department, to help freed slaves in the South. Initially, its principal mission was to provide food, housing and other assistance to war refugees. Soon it began to function as a court to decide on disputes involving planters' labor contracts with former slaves. The Freedman's Bureau tried to provide some protection for blacks against fraud and violence, which local government authorities didn't do. Perhaps the Freedman's Bureau had the greatest impact by providing financial support for the Hampton Institute, Howard University, Fisk University and other institutions serving blacks.[30] Altogether, the Freedman's Bureau served some 250,000 blacks in 4,300 institutions.

Radical Republicans outlawed the Black Codes and made penal codes less harsh with fewer crimes punishable by death. Farm laborers who were paid after a harvest was sold gained better liens on the crops, so they wouldn't be left with nothing after other creditors were paid.[31]

But Reconstruction benefited blacks far less than has been widely supposed. Policies of the Freedman's Bureau varied from state to state. Joseph S. Fuller, head of the Freedman's Bureau in Louisiana, ordered the arrest of New Orleans blacks who couldn't provide written evidence that they had a job. Thomas W. Cochran, head of the Freedman's Bu-

reau in Florida, directed his agents to prevent blacks from gathering in towns, at railroad stations or elsewhere, a possible sign that they aimed "to escape labor on the plantations." In 1866, planters got a boost from President Johnson's Circular 15, which ordered the Freedman's Bureau to promote labor contracts obligating former slaves to continue working on plantations. The Freedman's Bureau began ordering thousands of former slaves off abandoned or confiscated plantation properties that they had begun to cultivate for themselves.

Although Radical Republicans could determine qualifications for serving in Congress, they had a very limited impact on who served in state government. Some three-quarters of Southern white males, 18 to 45 years old, had fought for the Confederacy, and neither women nor blacks had the right to vote. Even among white southern Unionists, there was little support for giving blacks the right to vote. Whether the Radicals liked it or not, southern state governments were going to be loaded with their adversaries. Many Reconstruction policies weren't carried out in Johnson's home state of Tennessee, where former Confederates could vote and hold public office.[32] White Democrats stalled the start of Reconstruction policies in Virginia for two years, and effectively undermined those policies afterward. Georgia was even more successful derailing Reconstruction, and white Democrats substantially blocked Reconstruction in Alabama, too.

Frustrated by President Johnson's policies and in many cases denounced personally by him, Radical Republicans tried without success to have him impeached in 1867. The following year they succeeded in starting proceedings. The rationale for impeachment—Johnson's dismissal of Secretary of War Edwin Stanton—was less important than the administration's continuing efforts to thwart the Radical Reconstruction in the South. In the Senate, however, the Radicals were one vote short of the two-thirds majority needed for conviction, and the impeachment failed. Johnson subsequently lost his bid for another term, and Ulysses S. Grant won the presidential election.

In a further effort to assure that blacks had the right to vote, Congress proposed the Fifteenth Amendment on February 26, 1869. It specifically provided that "The right of citizens of the United States to vote shall not be denied or abridged by the United States or by any State on account of race, color, or previous condition of servitude." On February 3, 1870, this amendment was ratified by 29 states, including 8 former rebel states. Six more states ratified it.

The Civil War and Reconstruction involved a number of apparent conflicts with the Constitution, among them was ratification of the Thirteenth, Fourteenth and Fifteenth Amendments by former rebel states that hadn't been readmitted into the Union. The Reconstruction Act had provided that no state could be readmitted without adopting the Fourteenth Amendment. Considerable pressure was brought to bear for adopting the Fifteenth Amendment. Whether politicians in the former rebel states had any intention of abiding by these amendments was another matter.

Despite their good intentions, Radical Republicans did much harm. They promoted centralized government-supported school systems in every southern state. All the public schools were racially segregated, although New Orleans government schools were briefly integrated. Public schools had taken root in Massachusetts during the 1830s and spread throughout most of the North before the Civil War. As a consequence, whoever controlled the government controlled everybody's schools in each locality. This worked to the serious disadvantage of blacks who were excluded from schools their taxes helped pay for. Because they paid taxes for other people's children, they had fewer resources available for their own children. Much like laws of the slavery era that made it illegal to educate blacks, Reconstruction-era government school laws helped promote black illiteracy.[33]

There were violent reactions against Reconstruction. The White Brotherhood, the Red Shirts, the Knights of the White Camellia and especially the Ku Klux Klan organized efforts to intimidate blacks and Republicans alike.[34] These groups held rallies aimed at driving Northerners out of the South. Emanuel Fortune, who fled from Jackson County, Florida, reportedly remarked: "The object is to kill out the leading men of the Republican Party . . . men who have taken a prominent stand." Klan members burned black homes, schools and churches as a reminder that blacks should not challenge white supremacy. Blacks who had achieved conspicuous success were at risk. Klan members physically prevented blacks from voting. Klansmen murdered three white legislators in Georgia and forced 10 others to flee for their lives. Blacks had a hard time defending themselves from Klansmen, who ganged up on their intended victims, and state laws made it illegal for blacks to own guns. Those who intimidated or killed blacks came to be called Redeemers.

The Ku Klux Klan was particularly active in areas where whites outnumbered blacks by a wide margin, as in the Piedmont counties of South Carolina, Georgia and Louisiana. In York County, South Carolina, reportedly almost all white males were involved with the Klan, and they committed 11 murders plus hundreds of whippings. Klansmen included not just poor whites but planters, lawyers, merchants and sometimes ministers. The percentage of Klansmen convicted for their crimes was small.

Congress responded by enacting the Civil Rights Act (1871) to permit civil remedies for blacks, allowing them to file lawsuits seeking damages. Local or state officials who violated an individual's federally granted civil rights could be imprisoned. But the law had too many restrictions to be effective, and it was little-used.

The Colfax, Louisiana, courthouse massacre made clear the limitations of the ability of the North to uphold justice for blacks. On April 13, 1873, a mob of about 300 whites killed more than 70 blacks. The U.S. Department of Justice indicted 98 whites, but there were only three convictions. Two years later, the U.S. Supreme Court threw out the convictions, saying that the federal government could protect private individuals from actions by states, not from actions by other private individuals.[35]

By the mid-1870s, Reconstruction ran out of steam as Radicals died or moved on. Thaddeus Stevens had died in 1868. A former congressional ally, George W. Julian, ceased to talk about the plight of blacks and turned to other issues. Carl Schurz, the once-fiery abolitionist who had become famous for his 1859 "True Americanism" speech, which supported an inclusive view of citizenship, had been elected a U.S. senator from Missouri after he retired as a Civil War general. He devoted his energies to promoting sound money. Charles Sumner didn't seem to do much for Reconstruction after 1872. Many journalists, who had denounced Southerners during and after the Civil War, began writing about the excesses of Reconstruction.[36]

Overall, Republican efforts were limited in their ability to help blacks. Republicans faced relentless opposition from embittered Southerners, and the southern governments, largely bankrupted by the war, didn't have any money.[37] The Republicans lacked roots in the communities where they held office. They tended to be professional politicians and, without an established business or profession to fall back on, if they failed to win an election, they were without a

livelihood. Aside from a Union army occupation, they were supported only by Republican newspapers that had tiny circulations and little advertising revenue since southern businessmen were loyal to Democratic newspapers.

Republicans hit plantations with taxes intended to make them less viable, and land seized for failure to pay taxes was supposed to be divided into small plots that blacks could acquire. Millions of acres were seized, but planters drew on whatever reserves they had to pay their obligations and regain control. Often planters arranged to prevent anyone other than the owner from bidding on seized property, so he could get it back cheaply.

Republican politicians helped defeat themselves by becoming big spenders. They lavished subsidies on railroads, and state governments spent beyond their means to rebuild roads as well as other facilities destroyed during the war. The result of the spending schemes was corruption on a large scale.

The biggest American financial scandal of the nineteenth century involved Crédit Mobilier, a construction company formed to build the Union Pacific Railroad. This railroad was incorporated on July 1, 1862, soon after Congress passed the Pacific Railway Act. Crews began laying rails in Omaha, Nebraska, and headed west to meet the Central Pacific Railroad, which was laying rails east from California, forming America's first transcontinental railroad. Lavished with government subsidies, the project was intended to help bind the nation together. There wasn't any prospect of immediate profits from operating the railroad, because tracks passed through vast uninhabited regions with little freight to pick up or deliver. The principal profits came from federal subsidies appropriated for building the railroad. Crédit Mobilier distributed stock shares to congressmen who then voted for appropriations and helped promote contracts for the company. It reportedly earned a $21 million profit on $47 million worth of contracts. The Union Pacific Railroad went bankrupt during the 1870s and then again in the 1880s.

Inevitably, such huge sums of money led to corruption on a gigantic scale.[38] In North Carolina, $200,000 of bribes yielded millions of dollars of railroad subsidies. For years, bribery wasn't a crime in Louisiana. By 1870, hard-pressed states began to repeal railroad subsidies, but Republican Reconstruction had lost some of its high moral ground.

Southern Democrats strengthened their grip on their states, particularly as Republican leaders were scattered by the violence of the Ku Klux Klan. In Delaware, Democrats insisted that the state wasn't "morally bound" to have policies that complied with the postwar constitutional amendments. Delaware introduced a poll tax aimed at preventing blacks from voting, as did Georgia and Tennessee, while Maryland announced that the right to vote depended on owning a minimum amount of property, with the minimum set high enough to exclude most blacks. Virginia reduced the number of polling places in black neighborhoods and empowered the state—not the voters—to select local officials where a lot of blacks lived. Southern Democratic politicians generally motivated their supporters to get out and vote by making racist appeals. Especially in Louisiana, election campaigns were marked by chronic violence.

Grant's election to the presidency suggested that Reconstruction would continue, but he selected cabinet officers who held moderate views about the South. Since slavery had been abolished, they considered the issues substantially resolved. Perhaps they recognized the practical limits on what they could do to affect the South at the local level. Republican National Committee chairman William E. Chandler reportedly remarked, "We are bound to be overwhelmed by the new rebel combinations in every southern state."

Grant's administration had plenty of distractions from whatever it might have wanted to do in the South. Republicans promoted government spending schemes that resulted in skyrocketing taxes. Tax rates in 1870 were three or four times what they had been in 1860, even though property values had declined significantly.[39]

Grant's taxing and spending schemes generated a new wave of corruption. Government officials demanded bribes for their favors, and businessmen were usually happy to pay because there was so much loot to be had. If businessmen didn't get the hint, officials threatened to prosecute them for violating technical provisions of myriad regulations, such as those dealing with the import business or whiskey distilling.[40]

During the 1870s, in an effort to end the wartime inflation and restore the purchasing power of the American dollar, the federal government withdrew paper money—the greenbacks—from circulation. This began to affect financial markets. In 1873, Jay Cooke & Company, a Philadelphia banking firm, went bankrupt. Some 18,000 businesses failed during the next two years.

With less and less money, consumers couldn't pay what they used to for everything, and prices came down. Cotton prices fell about 50 percent during the 1870s. Businesses lost revenue, and they couldn't afford to pay workers what they used to, so wages came down. Many people had a hard time adjusting to this monetary contraction. Moreover, millions of people had become farmers, especially as land became available in the Midwest, and agricultural production increased dramatically. This put downward pressure on farm prices. Survival required that farmers not only produce but produce at a lower cost, which wasn't easy. Struggling farmers were among those who had to deal with serious issues other than the situation of former slaves.

Because of all the scandals during the Grant administration, New York state Democrat Samuel J. Tilden was favored to win the 1876 presidential election. A corporate lawyer, he entered politics as a reformer and was elected governor in 1874. He battled William M. "Boss" Tweed who fixed elections and dispensed patronage. In 1876, Tilden ran for president against the Republican candidate, former Ohio governor Rutherford B. Hayes. About 250,000 more people voted for Tilden, out of some 8.5 million votes cast, but the Constitution provided that a candidate must win a majority of electoral votes. Although Tilden carried more states, he had 184 electoral votes and needed only one more vote for an electoral majority. Hayes had 165 electoral votes. Four states with a total of 20 electoral votes had disputed election returns. The states were Oregon plus three states in the South—Florida, Louisiana and South Carolina. These were the last three states where the Union Army had occupation forces. There were reports of election fraud on both sides. Congress formed a bipartisan election commission to analyze the situation and decide on a winner. There were seven Republicans, seven Democrats and Supreme Court Justice Joseph P. Bradley (appointed by Republicans). They voted along party lines, 8–7 Republican, that Hayes should be awarded all 20 outstanding electoral votes, giving him a narrow victory.

Southern Democrats in Congress, however, threatened to block the commission's report. Apparently in exchange for the electoral votes of the three southern states that helped him win the election, Hayes agreed to withdraw federal troops from the South. The deal became known as the Compromise of 1877. Before leaving office, President Grant ordered federal troops to pull out of Florida. Hayes

ordered the withdrawal of federal troops from Louisiana and South Carolina. When federal troops left, Republican politicians left, and Democratic "Redeemers" regained control of these states, giving Democrats control of the entire South. Reconstruction was over.

The Civil War didn't persuade southerners of anything except for the military superiority of the North. The war certainly didn't persuade southerners to welcome the abolition of slavery or support the quest of the former slaves to achieve equal rights.[41]

What did the abolitionists accomplish? Clearly, they were the essential starting point in the struggle to abolish slavery. They convinced large numbers of Americans that slavery was wrong and must be eliminated. If the abolitionists hadn't risked their lives to agitate against slavery, who knows how much longer slavery might have persisted in the United States? Yet to the degree that the abolitionists demonized slaveholders—who deserved to be demonized—they probably contributed to the Civil War, and that was a disaster. The abolitionists naively assumed that if Northerners won the war, they would be willing and able to assure equal rights for the former slaves.

The North won the Civil War, but white supremacists won Reconstruction, and for almost a century they prevailed. Although the war brought the end of chattel slavery—a mighty accomplishment—the resulting death and destruction intensified the determination of former slaveholders and their allies to suppress blacks. When the Northerners who had gone South returned home after a few years, they left behind the people who lived in the South. Embittered whites had critical advantages over blacks in population numbers, in financial resources and in political connections. There was no contest as whites used their control of police to throttle black civil rights, and they used their control of government schools to throttle black education. The military strategy for abolishing slavery was no shortcut.

Conclusion

Abolishing slavery involved some difficult dilemmas. The temptation was strong to abandon all restraint when dealing with slaveholders, because they tended to be men of violence. They routinely whipped slaves. They tortured and murdered slaves. They murdered abolitionists for publishing antislavery literature, giving antislavery talks and going on plantations to tell slaves how they could escape. The more violent slaveholders were, the easier it was to support the use of force and even war against them.

War seemed even more attractive because it could destabilize slavery. When slaveholders were weakened by war, they were more vulnerable to a slave revolt. Desperate for new soldiers, belligerents often turned to slaves, who were an obvious potential source of new recruits. But slaves couldn't be trusted unless they were set free and therefore had a personal interest in seeing their liberators win. In Haiti, rebellious plantation owners liberated their slaves, and French colonial officials promised emancipation for slaves who fought with them. In Venezuela, Simón Bolívar promised that slaves would be emancipated if they joined his military campaign for independence. Amidst Cuba's Ten Years War, rebel leaders liberated their slaves and recruited many as soldiers. During the U.S. Civil War, the North offered freedom to slaves who fought on its side, and eventually the South had to do the same thing because of the massive casualties it had suffered.

Unfortunately, the savage violence of war and the inevitable backlash among losing slaveholders, made it much harder to arrive at a point where former slaveholders, former slaves and their descendants could live together peacefully in the same society. This shouldn't have been a surprise. Revenge has been a major motivation for wars that

have raged through the centuries. Napoleon's conquest of Europe triggered explosive reactions, the most serious of which occurred in Prussia. When, after World War I, Britain, France and the United States forced the vindictive Versailles Treaty on Germany, they triggered a reaction that ultimately generated political support for Hitler. In the Balkans, the Mideast, Ireland and elsewhere, wars have led to chronic violence, including the most hideous atrocities.

Why should anybody have been surprised that the North's defeat of the South during the U.S. Civil War spurred an uncontrollable lust for revenge, subverting the civil rights of blacks for another century? There never were enough Northerners down South to fill the government offices and protect the former slaves. Moreover, the Northerners were going to go home eventually, and Southerners were sure to regain full control of state and local governments—just as in our time U.S. forces went home after they got bogged down in Vietnam, and as U.S. forces began looking for ways to go home after they got bogged down in Iraq. Consequently, although the North won the Civil War, it couldn't be counted on to protect former slaves from the fury of the losers.

Moreover, the expansion of state government power extended the political clout of the embittered white majority, and they began oppressing blacks as soon as they had a chance. The idea that the federal government would protect blacks was an illusion, because they were a minority, and a minority isn't likely to control government in a democracy. The federal government itself was an interest group with its own political agenda, which was why it didn't do much about black civil rights until a century after the Civil War.

Another dilemma for abolitionists involved the timing of emancipation. William Lloyd Garrison and many other abolitionists campaigned for immediate emancipation, and who could disagree about the desirability of that? Since slavery was unjust, why should slaves have waited years before they could be free?

But there never was any such thing as "immediate emancipation." Slaveholders didn't emancipate anybody immediately. They defended slavery as long as they could. Their favorite tactic was to stall. They objected to any proposal that included a date when slavery would end, however far into the future the date might be. Attempts to forcibly emancipate slaves were forcibly resisted, so there was at least some fighting almost everywhere. Slaveholders had con-

siderable resources at their disposal, and fighting often tended to drag on much longer than participants anticipated, which delayed and complicated emancipation.

How else might slaves have been emancipated if somebody—such as Northerners in the U.S. Civil War—didn't try forcing the issue? First of all, the choice wasn't whether to do something (such as fight a war) or do nothing. Because slavery was such an entrenched institution, and slaveholders were guaranteed to resist emancipation, the process of abolishing slavery required patient, persistent efforts. Abolitionists campaigned, lobbied and negotiated for the best deal they could get at a particular time, which was often a compromise. If they were able to secure some restrictions, they came back and sought more restrictions. If they managed to get a far-out deadline for abolishing slavery, they campaigned to move it up. Abolitionists were constantly campaigning for more concessions.

No single strategy, including war, would have abolished slavery and secured equal rights, especially in the United States and Brazil, both of which had several million slaves. Multiple strategies had to be pursued for reducing the population of slaveholders and slaves, increasing the population of free blacks and the number of people who supported emancipation.

The most important antislavery strategies were:

1. slave rebellion, a reminder that slaves were able to help themselves and that slaveholding was a risky business;
2. abolitionist campaigns that involved publications and speaking tours, aimed at generating public rejection of slavery and support for emancipation;
3. campaigns aimed at electing politicians who would support restrictions, then outright bans, on the slave trade and on slavery itself;
4. encouragement and assistance for slaves who were brave enough to run away from their owners;
5. raising private funds to buy the freedom of slaves;
6. appropriating taxpayer funds for slaveholders who get out of the slavery business and emancipate their slaves.

Success with one strategy tended to improve prospects for success with others. For example, buying the freedom of slaves in one area

helped establish a slave-free zone closer to other slaves, making it easier for them to run away, and thus leading to an increase in the number of runaways. As the number of slaves declined, so did the political
clout of slaveholders, and slaveholders found themselves under economic pressure to make deals with slaves—including emancipation—so
that there would be a labor force to handle the planting and harvest.

Of the antislavery strategies listed above, undoubtedly the most
controversial was number five. Many people believed it would have
been immoral to give slaveholders money, because the slaves, not the
slaveholders, deserved compensation, which was true. If it was morally
wrong to buy the freedom of slaves, did this mean that manumission
was wrong? During World War II, René Reichmann organized Jewish
women in North Africa who shipped chocolates to secret agents near
concentration camps, who used them to bribe guards for liberating as
many Jewish children as possible. Was that wrong? Did East Germans
violate a meaningful moral standard when they bribed guards to look
the other way as they escaped into West Germany?

Using available funds to "take out" slaveholders was an important
strategy that helped achieve the top priority of freeing as many slaves as
possible as quickly as possible. Consider the advantages: (A) slaves
were emancipated, (B) the slave population was reduced, (C) the
slaveholder population was reduced and its political clout was undermined, (D) the free black population was increased, and (E) nobody
was killed, and no property was damaged, thereby reducing the risks of
an uncontrollable backlash—an important consideration since nobody
could be counted on to protect former slaves from former slaveholders motivated by revenge. As I explained, paying slaveholders to emancipate their slaves and get out of the slavery business was particularly
important for the emancipations that occurred in the British
Caribbean and in Brazil. It didn't make sense to exclude any peaceful
strategy that could help erode and abolish slavery.

Some people have objected that the United States couldn't have
bought the freedom of all the slaves, because this would have cost too
much. But buying the freedom of slaves was not more expensive than
war. Nothing is more costly than war! The costs include people killed
or disabled, destroyed property, high taxes, inflation, military expenditures, shortages, war-related famines and epidemics—plus long-
term consequences that often include more wars. The billions of
dollars of Union military expenditures during the Civil War would

have been better spent reducing the number of slaveholders and slaves, accelerating progress toward total emancipation. Initially, perhaps, such offers might have been rejected, but over time here, as elsewhere, there would have been more and more takers.

It probably wouldn't have been necessary to buy the freedom of all the slaves, because when a combination of strategies reduced the population of slaveholders and slaves down to a certain point, it would have collapsed or been abolished without a catastrophic conflict. Keep in mind that less than a third of the white people in the American South owned slaves. Slavery depended utterly on the ability of government to enforce laws making it illegal for slaves to move freely, to learn how to read, to possess a weapon and so on. When political support for governmental authorities was undermined, slavery was in trouble. By the time the slave population in Brazil got down to 1.5 million, political support for slavery had eroded to the point that it was near collapse, and it was abolished without a civil war.

Most people seem to believe that the U.S. Civil War was a shortcut to equal rights, and if the South had been permitted to secede peacefully, American slavery would have gone on indefinitely. But slavery was being eroded throughout the West by political trends and relentless agitation. The process would have continued and perhaps accelerated without the Civil War.

First, secession would almost certainly have meant the end of fugitive slave law enforcement, and free blacks and runaway slaves in the North would have been safe from Southern slave hunters. As things were in the North, runaway slaves weren't safe anywhere, and they couldn't breathe easily unless they were able to get all the way up to Canada, a daunting task. Northern mayors, governors and the president of the United States supported Southern slave hunters. But secession would have made the South—the Confederacy—a foreign country. Surely, the politics of the situation would have changed. Canadian agents weren't permitted to come into the United States and seize people, and Canadians, sensitive about the colossus along their southern border, didn't permit U.S. agents to come into their country and seize people. Likewise, if the confederacy were allowed to secede, it would have been an intolerable national affront to have agents from a foreign country come into the United States to seize and drag away peaceful people. The affront would have been especially acute since it came from the Confederacy, which had rejected and insulted

the United States by seceding. Probably even Northerners who weren't particularly sympathetic to blacks would have insisted that American sovereignty be respected. Enforcing fugitive slave laws and appearing to serve a foreign government probably would have been viewed as unpatriotic—a sure way for U.S. politicians to lose the next election.

Consequently, secession would have made it far easier for slaves to escape from the Confederacy because they would have reached safety by crossing the U.S. border, which was hundreds of miles closer than the Canadian border. The changed political situation, resulting from secession, probably would have undermined support for slavery in the border states that remained part of the Union. Even if slaveholders had enough clout for some border states to secede, runaways still would have reached safety much more easily than if they had to get to Canada.

Of course, the Confederates would have done everything they could to prevent slaves from escaping into the United States. They would have established border patrols. They might have amassed troops at key points. Perhaps they would have built barbed wire fences and cement walls. But in our own time, we have seen such efforts fail. For almost a half-century, people used many methods to escape from communist China into Hong Kong, a British colony on China's southeastern border until 1997. People bought forged papers, they tried to crash through barriers, they escaped on fishing boats, and they swam to Hong Kong. People smugglers—in what until recently was called Operation Yellowbird—did a lively business. Many Chinese made it to freedom. Similarly, communist East Germany tried to stop people from escaping, and in 1961 they built the Berlin Wall, but people never stopped trying to escape. East Germans climbed over the wall. Some hid themselves beneath cars leaving East Berlin. Many tunnels were dug from the basements of buildings near the border. Two families accumulated enough small pieces of cloth to sew them into a hot air balloon, and they waited for an opportune moment to float over the wall. Despite the wall, the barbed wire, the vicious dogs and the guards ordered to shoot on sight anybody trying to escape, thousands of East Germans made it to freedom. I doubt the Confederacy would have been able to stop the tide of slaves from crossing the border into the United States, and every runaway would have helped to undermine Confederate slavery. Publicity about Confederate troops shooting runaway slaves trying to cross the American border probably

would have helped to solidify antislavery views in the United States, undermined slavery in the border states (if they were still part of the United States) and inflamed public opinion everywhere against the Confederacy. All this would have been a huge public relations disaster, driving away whatever supporters the Confederacy had.

The Confederacy was already isolated and subject to moral pressure. As we have seen, starting in the early nineteenth century, one Western nation after another that had tolerated the slave trade for centuries passed laws banning their citizens from participating in it. Then one nation after another banned slavery itself. Those who still had a personal stake in slavery felt they had to be more discreet, and it was hard to find anybody willing to defend slavery publicly. By 1860 there were only three societies with chattel slavery in the Western Hemisphere: the United States, Cuba and Brazil. If there had been peaceful secession, the United States would have taken an important step away from slavery, though it persisted in border states, and the Confederacy would have had to bear the brunt of international criticism. Many Southerners comforted themselves by citing Biblical passages defending slavery, but they knew that increasing numbers of people viewed them as backward and barbaric. Cuba, as we know, outlawed slavery in 1886, Brazil in 1888. When Belgium's King Leopold began establishing a slave regime in the Congo during the 1880s, slavery was so unpopular that he thought it best to do his dirty deeds secretly and to conduct an elaborate public relations campaign so that if he were exposed, nobody would believe the accusations. Nonetheless, he was exposed and forced to give up his control of the Congo, and chattel slavery there ended around 1912 thanks to an abolitionist movement started in another country (England), drawing on the courageous work of a black American journalist, a black American missionary, a Polish novelist, an English shipping clerk and an Irish diplomat. Slavery was more vulnerable than it appeared to be.

Public opinion against slavery had an impact on where immigrants wanted to go and where investors wanted to deploy their capital. Immigrants generally didn't want to settle in the South, since they would have had to compete with slave labor. Moreover, many immigrants were fleeing from oppression, so they weren't comfortable living in a slave society. During the second half of the nineteenth century, millions of immigrants settled in the North and its total population surged. A larger population meant larger markets that could support

bigger industries. The majority of inventions that revolutionized American life were developed in the North. The principal centers of American finance, manufacturing and commerce were in the North. With each passing decade, the North became more prosperous than the South, and this must be counted among the significant, long-term factors working against Southern slavery.

It seems likely that the growing wealth of the North would have been a powerful magnet for whites as well as slaves. Many were loaded with debts to creditors in the North and overseas. Slavery was costly despite the fact that slaves weren't paid. An entire work force had to be maintained year-round, even though it might be needed for only a few months during the planting and harvest seasons. Because of the ever-present risk of slave rebellion, slaveholders had to maintain costly security measures. In the British Caribbean, many planters used the compensation they received to invest in machines, dispensing with slaves and security measures. Other planters got out of the difficult plantation business and entered other industries. If there had been a peaceful secession, probably quite a few Confederate slaveholders would have moved to the United States, established themselves in different businesses and participated in the prosperity there—reducing the population of Confederate slaveholders and their political clout.

More and more slaves from the Middle South were sold to the Deep South, reducing the amount of slaveholding territory and the number of whites who had a direct stake in slavery. As we have seen most dramatically in the case of Brazil, when the percentage of slaveholders in a population declined, political support for slavery declined. It's quite possible that an extensive antislavery underground might have developed in the Middle South, helping Deep South slaves escape to freedom.

In the Deep South, by 1860, the strongest political support for slavery came from a perhaps surprisingly small base: about 7 percent of whites owned some three-quarters of the slaves. Because of slave sales from the Middle South to the Deep South, slave ownership was increasingly concentrated in few hands. This was an ominous development for the future of slavery, because it utterly depended on political support for all the harsh laws that kept blacks down, making it illegal for them to move freely, own weapons, learn how to read, etc. Relaxed enforcement of these laws would have resulted in an increased number of runaway slaves.

Moreover, as the slave population and the percentage of slaves in the Deep South population increased—it was almost 50 percent in 1860—the risk of slave rebellion went up. To the extent that Deep South slaveholders succeeded in amassing more slaves, they made their wretched system more unstable. It was only a matter of time before resourceful slaves exploited their advantage in numbers. Slaveholders were doomed by their greed and brutality.

I believe there would have come a time, much sooner than most people might expect, when the combined effects of multiple antislavery strategies would have brought about the fairly peaceful collapse of Confederate slavery. If this seems doubtful, just recall how a combination of pressures led the mighty Soviet Union to collapse and vanish from the map—without a (nuclear) war.

One might argue that the multiple-strategy process of eroding slavery without war would have taken too long. Again, we need to remind ourselves that war wasn't a shortcut. Wartime massacres inevitably provoked hatred and a lust for revenge that made a bad situation worse, delaying by decades the day when the hearts and minds of people might be changed for the better. This was crucial, since nobody could be counted on to protect the former slaves and their descendants.

While one can't be sure precisely when slavery would have been abolished and civil rights would have been secured if the Civil War had been avoided, hopefully I have shown that there were powerful antislavery forces at work in the United States as elsewhere in the West. The choice wasn't to fight the Civil War or do nothing meaningful about slavery. The history of emancipation in the West clearly demonstrated there was more than one way to free the slaves. We should stop viewing the Civil War as the only way or the best way freedom could have been achieved. I believe a peaceful, persistent, multi-strategy process of eroding slavery would have made it much less difficult to arrive at a point where blacks could be both emancipated and safe, flourishing with equal rights in a free society.

Timeline of Antislavery in the Western World

1576	Publication of Jean Bodin's *Six Books of the Commonwealth*, one of the earliest works with a minor critique of slavery.
1646	Publication of English Leveller Richard Overton's pamphlet *An Arrow against all tyrants and tyranny*, which asserted an individual's most basic property right is in one's own body.
1676	Irish Quaker William Edmundson speaks out against slavery.
ca. 1679	British philosopher John Locke writes his *Second Treatise on Civil Government*, asserting the principle that a man "cannot enslave himself."
1688	Germantown (Pennsylvania) Quaker Francis Daniel Pastorious drafts the earliest known protest against African slavery.
1689	Spain's King Philip V decrees that runaway slaves from South Carolina would be free in Spanish-controlled Florida if they helped defend settlers in St. Augustine.
1693	Publication of American Quaker George Keith's *An Exhortation and Caution to Friends concerning the buying and selling of Negroes*.
1698	American Quaker William Southeby appeals to Friends in Barbados to stop sending slaves to Pennsylvania.
1700	Publication of Samuel Sewall's pamphlet *The Selling of Joseph*, attacking slavery as a breach of natural rights of man.
January 31, 1713	William Southeby petitions Pennsylvania Assembly to abolish slavery.
June 5, 1723	At a Monthly Meeting, Newport, Rhode Island, Quakers decided that it was not "agreeable to Truth" to brand a slave on the cheeks.
1729	Publication of Ralph Sandiford's pamphlet *A Brief Examination of the Practice of the Times*, an attack on slavery published by Benjamin Franklin.
1733	Publication of Elihu Coleman's pamphlet *A Testimony Against that Antichristian Practice of Making Slaves of Men*, the first criticism of slavery approved by a Quaker meeting.
1735	Georgia passes law banning the importation of African slaves.

1759	Posthumous publication of Scottish philosopher Francis Hutcheson's *A System of Moral Philosophy*, which denounced slavery.
August 24, 1759	Anthony Benezet (1715–1785) publishes *Observations on the Enslaving, Importing and Purchasing of Negroes with some Advice thereon Extracted from the Yearly Meeting Epistle of London for the present year*.
1761	British Quakers vote to expel any member who participates in the slave trade.
1769	Portugal abolishes slavery in its homeland, freeing any slave entering Portugal, but the law doesn't apply to slaves in Portugal's colonies, notably Brazil.
1769	Publication of Scottish philosopher Adam Ferguson's *Institutes of Moral Philosophy* containing denunciations of slavery, and of Granville Sharp's pamphlet *The Injustice and dangerous Tendency of tolerating Slavery in England*.
1771	Anthony Benezet establishes the Negro School of Philadelphia.
1772	Publication of Anthony Benezet's *Some Historical Account of Guinea*, which graphically portrayed horrors of slavery, and of Benjamin Rush's pamphlet *An Address to the Inhabitants of the British Settlements in America, upon Slave-Keeping*.
1772	London Quakers vote to expel members who participate in the slave trade.
June 22, 1772	In the Somerset case brought by British abolitionist Granville Sharp, Lord Chief Justice Mansfield writes: "no master was ever allowed here to take a slave by force to be sold abroad because he deserted from his service . . . ," a decision widely viewed to hold that slavery was illegal in Britain.
1774	Publication of Methodist preacher John Wesley's pamphlet *Thoughts Upon Slavery*, which denounced slavery.
March 8, 1775	Publication of Thomas Paine's essay critical of slavery, in the *Postscript to the Pennsylvania Journal and the Weekly Advertiser*.
April 1775	Anthony Benezet and fellow abolitionist John Woolman meet with other Philadelphia Quakers at the Rising Sun Tavern to form the Society for the Relief of Free Negroes Unlawfully Held in Bondage, the first antislavery organization.
March 1776	Publication of Adam Smith's *Wealth of Nations*, which among other things explains how a society is most likely to prosper with voluntary cooperation rather than compulsion.
July 4, 1776	American Continental Congress adopts the Declaration of Independence, which eloquently summarizes the ideal of individual rights and is signed by most of the delegates on August 2. The declaration's principal author, Thomas Jefferson, was a slaveholder.
1777	During the American Revolution, Vermont (with very few slaves) becomes the first British colony to outlaw slavery.
September 1780	British abolitionist William Wilberforce (1759–1833) is elected a member of Parliament.

1780	Member of Parliament Edmund Burke drafts a bill to help educate slaves for freedom but keeps it secret for 12 years, as "an abolition of the slave trade would be a very chimerical object."
April 1781	British captain Luke Collingwood orders 132 sick slaves thrown off his ship *Zong* so he can collect insurance money. The barbaric incident, publicized by Granville Sharp, Thomas Clarkson and others, helps turn British public opinion against slavery.
1784	Massachusetts slave Quock Walker runs away from his owner, Nathaniel Jennison, after a beating. A British jury subsequently awards Walker his freedom and £50 for damages.
1784	A Massachusetts judge rules that the Massachusetts Constitution outlaws slavery. Connecticut and Rhode Island (neither of which has many slaves) enact laws providing for gradual emancipation.
1784	Publication of British abolitionist James Ramsay's *Essay on the Treatment and Conversion of African Slaves in the British Sugar Colonies,* probably the first antislavery pamphlet to have an impact in Great Britain.
October 20, 1784	Six original members of the Society for the Relief of Free Negroes Unlawfully Held in Bondage form a new antislavery organization: the Pennsylvania Society for Promoting the Abolition of Slavery and the Relief of Free Negroes Unlawfully Held in Bondage.
1786	The Marquis de Lafayette and his wife, Adrienne, buy 2 plantations in French Guyana, liberate their 48 slaves, give them some land and teach them to become independent farmers.
1786	Publication of British abolitionist Thomas Clarkson's Cambridge dissertation, *An Essay on the slavery and commerce of the human species, particularly the African.*
1787	British Quakers and their allies form the Society for Effecting the Abolition of the Slave Trade.
1787	Continental Congress adopts Ordinance of 1787 covering the Northwest Territory (the region south of the Great Lakes, east of the Mississippi River and west and north of the Ohio River), providing for new states to be created from this territory (instead of expanding existing states) in which slavery would be banned.
1787	Antislavery organizer Thomas Clarkson meets Member of Parliament William Wilberforce, beginning a three-decade collaboration.
1787	The Philadelphia Society for Promoting the Abolition of Slavery reorganizes from its Pennsylvania predecessor, and two years later Benjamin Franklin becomes its president.
1789	Publication of *An Account of the Slave Trade on the Coast of Africa* by former British ship's surgeon Alexander Falconbridge, an eyewitness to the horrors of slavery.
May 12, 1789	William Wilberforce gives his first speech in Parliament about abolishing the slave trade.
August 1789	The French Revolution's National Constituent Assembly adopts the Declaration of the Rights of Man and of the Citizen, drafted in part

	by the Marquis de Lafayette; it inspires slaves in Saint-Domingue (Haiti) and elsewhere to rebellion.
1790	Benjamin Franklin presents Congress with a petition urging the emancipation of slaves; the petition was rejected.
April 1791	William Wilberforce introduces his first bill in Parliament that would make it illegal for British citizens to participate in the slave trade.
May 15, 1791	French National Assembly grants equal rights to *gens de couleur* (free blacks) born to two free parents, as well as to whites in the French colonies, an initial step to expand the application of the doctrine of individual rights.
August 21, 1791	Slave rebellion begins on Saint-Domingue (Haiti).
1792	Denmark becomes the first country to enact legislation banning its citizens from engaging in the slave trade.
1792	New York state enacts a law providing for the gradual emancipation of slaves.
January 1, 1804	After the first successful slave revolt in history, Haiti declares independence, the first black republic and the second independent country in the western hemisphere.
May 23, 1806	British Foreign Slave Trade Act takes effect, making it illegal for British citizens to be involved in shipping slaves to non-British territory.
February 23, 1807	British Royal Navy establishes the West Africa Squadron to curtail the shipment of African slaves to the western hemisphere. Between 1808 and 1860, the fleet reportedly captured some 1,600 ships and liberated some 150,000 slaves.
March 25, 1807	British Parliament passes the Slave Trade Act, banning British citizens from participation in the slave trade; but penalties are a mild £100 for each slave found on a British ship, effective May 1, 1807.
January 1, 1808	U.S. citizens prohibited from engaging in the slave trade.
1808	Mexico and Venezuela make it illegal for their citizens to participate in the slave trade.
1810	Chile makes it illegal for its citizens to engage in the slave trade.
1811	Sweden bans its citizens from participating in the slave trade.
November 28, 1811	Argentina adopts a law providing for the gradual emancipation of slaves.
July 6, 1813	The Netherlands bans its citizens from participating in the slave trade.
1814	Colombia begins a policy of gradually emancipating slaves.
1815	Great Britain, France, Prussia and Russia sign the Quadruple Alliance authorizing Great Britain's Royal Navy to stop and search suspected slave ships; though Prussia and Russia weren't factors in the slave trade, British diplomats sought their moral support against it.
February 1815	British diplomat Viscount Castlereagh persuades France, Spain and Portugal, slave-trading nations formerly allied with Great Britain

against Napoleon, to sign a general declaration against the trade, marking the start of long diplomatic efforts to restrict it.

1815	Dom João VI, king of Portugal, agrees to limit Portuguese ships to supplying only Portuguese colonies with slaves.
July 1817	Great Britain and Portugal sign a right-to-search treaty allowing each nation to stop and search ships sailing under the flag of the other and establishing "mixed courts" with a British judge and a Portuguese judge to decide maritime property disputes. An additional convention to this treaty reinforces the 1815 British agreement with Dom João VI, banning the Portuguese from providing slaves to non-Portuguese colonies.
September 13, 1817	Great Britain and Spain sign a treaty to ban the slave trade by Spanish citizens, effective May 31, 1820; in exchange, Britain loans Spain £400,000.
1818	France makes it illegal for its citizens to engage in the slave trade but doesn't stipulate penalties.
1822	Brazil declares its independence from Portugal. Consequently, Brazil gained jurisdiction over slavery in its borders, accepted British restrictions on the slave trade approved by Portugal in 1815 and 1817; and since Brazil was no longer a colony, the Portuguese could no longer ship slaves there.
1825	Abolitionist Thomas Buxton, elected in 1818, succeeds William Wilberforce as abolitionist leader in the British Parliament.
1825	Chile abolishes slavery.
1826	Brazil, as authorized by Brazilian emperor Dom Pedro, signs treaty with Great Britain, agreeing to end the Brazilian slave trade by 1830, after which the trade would be treated as piracy.
1831	Mexico, with some 10,000 slaves, abolishes slavery.
January 1831	William Lloyd Garrison begins publishing *The Liberator*.
November 1, 1831	Bolivia abolishes slavery.
August 21, 1831	Virginia slave Nat Turner leads rebellion, liberating slaves and murdering more than 50 white people before the rebellion was crushed 48 hours later.
November 1, 1831	Great Britain signs another treaty with Brazil banning the importation of slaves to Brazil, providing emancipation for any slaves brought into Brazil and serious penalties for slave traders, and exempting plantation owners from debts to slave traders.
January 1832	William Lloyd Garrison and his associates form the New England Anti-Slavery Society.
August 29, 1833	British Parliament passes law, effective August 1, 1834, providing for emancipation of an estimated 780,000 slaves in British Caribbean colonies, offers slaveholders some £20 million as compensation. Slaves had to continue working as apprentices for four years.
December 1833	American Anti-Slavery Society established in Philadelphia.

June 28, 1835	Spain signs Anglo-Spanish treaty negotiated by British foreign secretary Palmerston, authorizing the British to stop and search suspected slave ships flying the Spanish flag, subject to seizure if they had slave-trade equipment.
1835	Boston lawyer Wendell Phillips vows to fight slavery after seeing a mob nearly lynch British abolitionist George Thompson.
November 7, 1837	Elijah P. Lovejoy murdered in Alton, Illinois, for publishing a newspaper expressing abolitionist views; reports of the murder outrage Bostonians and energize the abolitionist movement.
1838	Runaway slave Frederick Douglass finds freedom in Massachusetts.
1838	Publication of Thomas Buxton's book *The Slave Trade*.
1838	Apprenticeship cut short in British Caribbean—all slaves freed.
1839	British foreign secretary Palmerston secures passage of a bill providing for seizure by Royal Navy of Portuguese ships found with slave-trade equipment, with cases to be heard by a British court.
March 12, 1839	Frederick Douglass makes his first speech against slavery, at a church meeting, and his remarks are reported in *The Liberator*.
June 1840	World Anti-Slavery Convention held in London Freemasons' Hall draws more than 5,000 abolitionists from 35 countries.
1842	Portugal signs new treaty with Great Britain, designating the slave trade as piracy and that slave ships could be seized accordingly.
(1819 and) 1842	Great Britain and the United States agree to the Ashburton Treaty, pledging their cooperation in maintaining a naval blockade of West Africa to restrict the slave trade.
1843	William Lloyd Garrison organizes 100 public antislavery gatherings in Indiana, Ohio, Pennsylvania, New York, Vermont and New Hampshire.
1845	Publication of *Narrative of the Life of Frederick Douglass, an American Slave*.
1845	William Lloyd Garrison and Frederick Douglass make speaking tour of Great Britain, meeting Daniel O'Connell, a champion of Irish freedom. British donors raise money to buy the freedom of Frederick Douglass, so that he could avoid capture and return to the South under prevailing U.S. law.
1845	British Prime Minister Robert Peel secures passage of Aberdeen Bill defining the slave trade as piracy and giving the Royal Navy greater legal authority to detain slave ships.
1848	France and Denmark emancipate slaves in their colonies.
July 1, 1850	H.M.S. *Cormorant* burns slave ships *Leonidas* and *Sereia* near Brazil.
1851	Ecuador abolishes slavery.
March 1852	Publication of Harriet Beecher Stowe's novel *Uncle Tom's Cabin*.
August 1852	U.S. Senator Charles Sumner delivers blistering attack on the fugitive slave law, declaring that it "offends against the Divine law" and that he is bound to disobey this law.

1854	Spain appoints Marqués de la Pezuela as captain-general of Cuba, and he takes action against the slave trade by announcing that Cubans who imported slaves would be expelled from the island, and that officials who fail to cooperate with antislavery policies would be fired; authorizes police to search plantations for slaves brought into Cuba illegally.
1854	Peru abolishes slavery.
1863	Venezuela abolishes slavery.
January 1, 1863	U.S. president Abraham Lincoln issues Emancipation Proclamation, establishing the abolition of slavery as a war aim.
December 1864	Puerto Rican Creole Julio Vizcarrondo goes to Spain and establishes the Sociedad Abolicionista Española (Spanish Abolitionist Society).
April 9, 1865	The Netherlands makes it illegal for people in its colonies to participate in the slave trade.
April 9, 1865	Confederate General Robert E. Lee surrenders to Union General Ulysses S. Grant at Appomattox Court House, Virginia, ending the Civil War.
December 18, 1865	The Thirteenth Amendment to the U.S. Constitution, which abolishes slavery is ratified by 27 states; eight more states later ratify it.
1867	Cuba makes it illegal for its residents to participate in the slave trade.
July 9, 1868	The Fourteenth Amendment to the U.S. Constitution, which guarantees former slaves would be American citizens with the same rights as other American citizens is ratified by 28 states; nine more states later ratify it.
October 1868	Cuban Carlos Manuel Céspedes gives his *Grito de Yara* speech urging Cubans to fight for independence, helping to launch the Ten Years War that weakened the power of planters, liberated many slaves and set the stage for slavery's abolition in Cuba.
February 3, 1870	The Fifteenth Amendment to the U.S. Constitution providing that individuals may not be denied the right to vote because of their race, color, or previous servitude is ratified by 29 states; six more states later ratify it.
July 1870	The Moret Law freed newborn children of slave mothers as well as slaves over 60. Also, slaves were freed when they helped Spain suppress Cuban rebels in the Ten Years War. Although various terms of the law were thwarted by slaveholders, it showed that the government could not be counted on to keep supporting slavery.
September 27, 1871	Brazilian parliament approves Rio Branco bill, restricting slavery by providing for "free birth"—slaveholders were to care for the children of slave mothers until age 8, after which the slaveholders had the choice of receiving government compensation in the form of bonds or having the children work until age 21; giving slaves the right to buy their freedom and retain money they earned; freeing government-owned slaves and slaves abandoned by owners or left as

unclaimed inheritances; and establishing a government emancipation fund to buy the freedom of slaves throughout Brazil.

1873 — Puerto Rico abolishes slavery.

February 12, 1878 — Pact of Zanjón basically ends Cuba's Ten Years War, during which sugar plantations and mills were largely destroyed and the number of Cuban slaves declined by more than a third.

1879 — Cuban government publishes lists of some 29,000 slaves who had been imported without being registered and who therefore were legally free.

March 5, 1879 — Jeronymo Sodré, a member of the Brazilian parliament, delivers a speech advocating the emancipation of slaves to avoid violence and modernize Brazil. The speech marked the start of the Brazilian abolition movement.

November 1879 — Spanish minister of colonies Salvador Albacete introduces bill in the Cortes to abolish slavery in Cuba, providing that emancipated slaves had to continue working on their plantations for 8 years. Bill voted on favorably January 30, 1880, to take effect February 13, 1880.

September 7, 1880 — At the home of Joaquim Nabuco in Flamengo Beach, a group of friends founds Sociedade Brasileira a Escravidão (Brazilian Anti-Slavery Society) to generate publicity for the abolition of slavery.

November 1, 1880 — Joaquim Nabuco and other Brazilian abolitionists begin publishing the monthly *O Abolicionista*.

1881 — José do Patrocínio buys an abolitionist newspaper, *Gazeta da Tarde*, offering the most comprehensive coverage of the Brazilian abolitionist movement.

May 12, 1883 — Abolitionist Confederation established in Rio de Janeiro to coordinate activities of 12 Brazilian abolitionist societies.

October 7, 1886 — Spanish government abolishes the requirement that former slaves had to continue working on plantations for 8 years, effectively ending slavery in Cuba.

May 3, 1888 — The Brazilian General Assembly passes the Golden Law abolishing slavery and giving immediate, unconditional emancipation.

July 18, 1890 — George Washington Williams finishes writing *An Open Letter to His Serene Majesty Leopold II, King of the Belgians and Sovereign of the Independent State of Congo*, a detailed indictment that reported how the king secretly used slaves to gather ivory and rubber, disregarded treaty obligations and used the Congo as his private property to enrich himself.

1902 — Publication of Joseph Conrad's novel *Heart of Darkness*, about slavery in the Congo.

December 1903 — British diplomat Roger Casement writes a report confirming that the Congo Free State ruthlessly enforced slavery; the report is issued by the British Foreign Office in February 1904.

March 1904 — Edmund Dene Morel, Roger Casement and Henry Guinness start the Congo Reform Association to publicize the horrors of slavery in

the Congo and to remove the Congo from King Leopold II's personal ownership.

November 15, 1908 Belgian Parliament annexes the Congo, buying out King Leopold II and officially ending slavery, although elements of forced labor would persist for years.

Notes

Introduction

1. Thomas Clarkson, *The History of the Rise, Progress and Accomplishment of the Abolition of the African Slave Trade by the British Parliament* (Whitefish, MT: Kessinger Publishing, 1839), 52.

2. Reginald Coupland, *The British Anti-Slavery Movement* (London: Frank Cass, 1964), 22.

3. David Richardson, "Slave Trade, Volume of Trade," in Seymour Drescher and Stanley L. Engerman, eds., *A Historical Guide to World Slavery* (New York: Oxford University Press, 1998), 387.

4. J. H. Parry, *Trade and Dominion: The European Overseas Empires in the Eighteenth Century* (New York: Praeger, 1971), 319.

5. David Eltis, *Economic Growth and the Ending of the Transatlantic Slave Trade* (New York: Oxford University Press, 1987), 59.

6. Parry, *Trade and Dominion*, 319.

7. Clarkson, *Abolition of the African Slave Trade by the British Parliament*, 285.

8. Adam Hochschild, *Bury the Chains: Prophets and Rebels in the Fight to Free an Empire's Slaves* (Boston: Houghton Mifflin, 2005), 61, 63, 65, 87.

9. Martin Ros, *Night of Fire: The Black Napoleon and the Battle for Haiti* (Rockville Center, NY: Sarpedon, 1993), 38.

10. Robert D. Heinl and Nancy G. Heinl, *Written in Blood: The Story of the Haitian People, 1492–1971* (Boston: Houghton Mifflin, 1978), 46.

11. Ralph Korngold, *Two Friends of Man: The Story of William Lloyd Garrison and Wendell Phillips and Their Relationship with Abraham Lincoln* (Boston: Little Brown, 1950), 90.

12. David Murray, *Odious Commerce: Britain, Spain and the Abolition of the Cuban Sugar Trade* (Cambridge: Cambridge University Press, 2002), 1, 2.

13. Richardson, "Slave Trade, Volume of Trade," in Drescher and Engerman, *Historical Guide to World Slavery*, 387.

14. James A. Rawley and Stephen D. Behrendt, *The Transatlantic Slave Trade* (Lincoln: University of Nebraska Press, 2005), 17.

Chapter 1

1. Herbert S. Klein, *African Slavery in Latin America and the Caribbean* (New York: Oxford University Press, 1986), 4.

2. Edwin Williamson, *The Penguin History of Latin America* (London: Penguin Press, 1992), 172.

3. Thomas E. Skidmore, *Brazil, Five Centuries of Change* (New York: Oxford University Press, 1999), 18.

4. Klein, *African Slavery in Latin America and the Caribbean*, 43.

5. James A. Rawley and Stephen D. Behrendt, *The Transatlantic Slave Trade* (Lincoln: University of Nebraska Press, 2005), 27.

6. Hugh Thomas, *The Slave Trade: The Story of the Atlantic Slave Trade: 1440–1870* (New York: Simon & Schuster, 1997), 83.

7. Klein, *African Slavery in Latin America and the Caribbean*, 35.

8. Thomas, *The Slave Trade*, 97, 98, 100.

9. Rawley and Behrendt, *The Transatlantic Slave Trade*, 54.

10. Thomas, *The Slave Trade*, 119.

11. Thomas, *The Slave Trade*, 147.

12. Thomas, *The Slave Trade*, 170.

13. Quoted in C. R. Boxer, *The Dutch Seaborne Empire, 1600–1800* (London: Penguin, 1988), 268.

14. Rawley and Behrendt, *The Transatlantic Slave Trade*, 83.

15. Thomas, *The Slave Trade*, 154.

16. Rawley and Behrendt, *The Transatlantic Slave Trade*, 94.

17. Dale Tomich and Carolyn Fick, "French Caribbean," in Seymour Drescher and Stanley L. Engerman, eds., *A Historical Guide to World Slavery* (New York: Oxford University Press, 1998), 133.

18. Tomich and Fick, "French Caribbean," in Drescher and Engerman, *Historical Guide to World Slavery*, 135.

19. Rawley and Behrendt, *The Transatlantic Slave Trade*, 209.

20. Rawley and Behrendt, *The Transatlantic Slave Trade*, 131, 132.

21. Reginald Coupland, *The British Anti-Slavery Movement* (London: Frank Cass, 1964), 20.

22. Niall Ferguson, *Empire: The Rise and Demise of the British World Order and the Lessons for Global Power* (New York: Basic Books, 2003), 80.

23. Quoted in Rawley and Behrendt, *The Transatlantic Slave Trade*, 166.

24. Quoted in Rawley and Behrendt, *The Transatlantic Slave Trade*, 175.

Chapter 2

1. For instance, in the Old Testament, Exodus, 20:17: "You shall not covet your neighbor's house; you shall not covet your neighbor's wife, or male or female slave . . ." Leviticus 25:44, 45: "As for the male and female slaves whom you may have, it is from the nations around you that you may acquire male and female slaves. You may also acquire them from among the aliens residing with you, and from their families that are with you, who have been born in your land, and they may be your property." In the New Testament, Ephesians, 6:5: "Slaves, obey your earthly masters with fear and trembling, in singleness of heart, as you obey Christ; not only while being watched, and in order to please them, but as slaves of Christ, doing the will of God from the heart." Colossians, 3:22: "Slaves, obey your earthly masters on everything."

2. See, for example, Kenneth P. Minkema, "Jonathan Edwards on Slavery and the Slave Trade," *William and Mary Quarterly*, October 1997, 823–34.

3. Albert Taylor Bledsoe, *An Essay on Liberty and Slavery* (Philadelphia: J. B. Lippincott, 1856), http://www.bible-researcher.com/bledsoe-slavery.htm, accessed 5-12-2007.

4. Jean Bodin, *Six Books of the Commonwealth*, ed. J. Tooley (Oxford: Basil Blackwell, 1955), Book One, chs. 2–5, 17.

5. Leonard W. Levy, *Constitutional Opinions* (New York: Oxford University Press, 1986), 14.

6. M. A. Gibb, *John Lilburne, the Leveller, a Christian Democrat* (London: Lindsay Drummond, 1947), 154.

7. Quoted in H. N. Brailsford, *The Levellers and the English Revolution* (Nottingham: Spokesman, 1983), 140.

8. John Locke, *Two Treatises on Government*, a critical edition with an introduction by Peter Laslett (Cambridge: Cambridge University Press, 1963), 301, 302.

9. Maurice Cranston, *John Locke: A Biography* (London: Longmans, 1957), 115.

10. Daniel J. Boorstin, *The Seekers: The Story of Man's Continuing Quest to Understand His World* (New York: Random House, 1998), 158; "Introduction," in William E. Cain, ed., *William Lloyd Garrison and the Fight against Slavery* (Boston: Bedford Books of St. Martin's, 1995), 31.

11. John Trenchard and Thomas Gordon, "An Enquiry into the Nature and Extent of Liberty; with its Loveliness and Advantages, and the Vile Effects of Slavery, January 20, 1721," in Ronald Hamowy, ed., *Cato's Letters or Essays on Liberty, Civil and Religious, and Other Important Subjects* (Indianapolis: Liberty Fund, 1995), I, 430.

12. Quoted in Arthur Herman, *How the Scots Invented the Modern World* (New York: Crown, 2001), 70.

13. Adam Ferguson, *Institutes of Moral Philosophy* (New York: Garland, 1978).

14. "The Religion of the Quakers," in William F. Fleming, trans., *The Works of Voltaire* (New York: E.R. Dumont, 1901), vol. 39, 209.

15. David Brion Davis, *The Problem of Slavery in Western Culture* (Ithaca, NY: Cornell University Press, 1966), 320.

16. Davis, *Problem of Slavery in Western Culture*, 316.

17. Hugh Thomas, *The Slave Trade: The Story of the Atlantic Slave Trade, 1440–1870* (New York: Simon & Schuster, 1997), 460.

18. Davis, *Problem of Slavery in Western Culture*, 331.

19. David Freeman Hawke, *Benjamin Rush, Revolutionary Gadfly* (Indianapolis: Bobbs-Merrill, 1971), 104.

20. Thomas Paine, "African Slavery in America," in Moncure Daniel Conway, ed., *The Writings of Thomas Paine* (New York: Burt Franklin, 1969), I, 5, 8.

21. Charles Secondat, Baron de Montesquieu, *The Spirit of the Laws* (Cambridge: Cambridge University Press, 1995), Book 15, ch.1, 246.

22. Montesquieu, *The Spirit of the Laws*, Book 15, ch. 5, 250.

23. Montesquieu, *The Spirit of the Laws*, Book 15, ch.8, 252.

24. Quoted in Thomas Clarkson, *A History of the Rise, Progress and Accomplishment of the Abolition of the African Slave Trade by the British Parliament* (Whitefish, MT: Kessinger Publishing, 2004), 72.

25. Harlow Giles Unger, *Lafayette* (New York: John Wiley, 2002), 215.

26. Laurent Dubois, *A Colony of Citizens: Revolution and Slave Emancipation in the French Caribbean, 1787–1804* (Chapel Hill: University of North Carolina Press, 2006), 70, 71.

27. Robert William Fogel, *Without Consent or Contract: The Rise and Fall of American Slavery* (New York: Norton, 1989), 203.

28. Eli F. Heckscher, *Mercantilism* (London: George Allen & Unwin, 1931), I, 29.

29. Heckscher, *Mercantilism*, I, 173

30. W. Walker Stephens, ed., *The Life and Writings of Turgot* (New York: Burt Franklin, 1971), 215.

31. Joseph A. Schumpeter, *History of Economic Analysis* (New York: Oxford University Press, 1961), ed. by Elizabeth Boody Schumpeter, 244.

32. Henry Higgs, *The Physiocrats* (New York: Augustus M. Kelley, 1989), 67.

33. Stephens, *Life and Writings of Turgot*, 27.

34. Andrew Dickson White, *Seven Great Statesmen in the Warfare of Humanity with Unreason* (New York: Century, 1919), 189.

35. Florin Aftalion, *The French Revolution: An Economic Interpretation* (Cambridge: Cambridge University Press, 1990), 15.

36. White, *Seven Great Statesmen*, 192–93.

37. Stephens, *Life and Writings of Turgot*, 34.

38. Vincent Cronin, *Louis and Antoinette* (London: Harvill Press, 1996), 95.

39. March 22, 1778, letter to Richard Price, in Stephens, *Life and Writings of Turgot*, 302.

40. Anne-Robert-Jacques Turgot, *Reflections on the Formation and Distribution of Riches* (New York: Augustus M. Kelley, 1971), 19.

41. Adam Smith, *An Inquiry into the Nature and Causes of the Wealth of Nations* (New York: Modern Library, 1965), Book I, ch. II, 14.

42. Smith, *Wealth of Nations*, Book IV, ch. V, 508.

43. Smith, *Wealth of Nations*, Book IV, ch. II, 423.

44. Smith, *Wealth of Nations*, Book III, ch. II, 366.

45. Smith, *Wealth of Nations*, Book I, ch. VIII, 81.

Chapter 3

1. David Brion Davis, *Inhuman Bondage: The Rise and Fall of Slavery in the New World* (New York: Oxford University Press, 2006), 158.

2. Martin Ros, *Night of Fire: The Black Napoleon and the Battle for Haiti* (Rockville Center, NY: Sarpedon, 1993), 19, 20.

3. Ros, *Night of Fire*, 23.

4. Ros, *Night of Fire*, 21.

5. Madison Smart Bell, *Toussaint Louverture: A Biography* (New York: Pantheon, 2007), 16.

6. Bell, *Toussaint Louverture*, 11.

7. Quoted and translated in Laurent Dubois, *A Colony of Citizens: Revolution & Slave Emancipation in the French Caribbean, 1787–1804* (Chapel Hill: University of North Carolina Press, 2004), 65.

8. Dubois, *A Colony of Citizens*, 90, 91.

9. Laurent Dubois and John D. Garrigus eds., *Slave Revolution in the Caribbean, 1789–1804: A Brief History with Documents* (New York: Palgrave Macmillan, 2006), 25.

10. Laurent Dubois, *Avengers of the New World: The Story of the Haitian Revolution* (Cambridge: Harvard University Press, 2004), 97.

11. Dubois, *Avengers of the New World*, 123.

12. Ros, *Night of Fire*, 37.

13. Dubois, *Avengers of the New World*, 126.

14. Dubois, *Avengers of the New World*, 141.

15. Bell, *Toussaint Louverture*, 93.

16. Bell, *Toussaint Louverture*, 53.

17. Dubois, *A Colony of Citizens*, 156.

18. Dubois, *Avengers of the New World*, 164.

19. Dubois and Garrigus, *Slave Revolution in the Caribbean*, 32.
20. Bell, *Toussaint Louverture*, 60.
21. Bell, *Toussaint Louverture*, 56.
22. Ros, *Night of Fire*, 58, 59.
23. Dubois, *Avengers of the New World*, 178.
24. Dubois, *Avengers of the New World*, 233.
25. Dubois, *Avengers of the New World*, 239, 240.
26. Davis, *Inhuman Bondage*, 167.
27. Dubois, *Avengers of the New World*, 248.
28. Bell, *Toussaint Louverture*, 279.
29. Dubois, *Avengers of the New World*, 292.
30. Dubois and Garrigus, *Slave Revolution in the Caribbean*, 39.
31. Dale Tomich and Carolyn Fick, "French Caribbean," in Seymour Drescher and Stanley L. Engerman eds., *A Historical Guide to World Slavery* (New York: Oxford University Press, 1998), 135. According to the 1789 census, there were 465,429 slaves on Saint-Domingue.

Chapter 4

1. Adam Hochschild, *Bury the Chains: Prophets and Rebels in the Fight to Free an Empire's Slaves* (Boston: Houghton Mifflin, 2005), 14.
2. William Blackstone, *Commentaries on the Laws of England* (Philadelphia: John Grigg, 1827), I, ch. 14, 423.
3. Reginald Coupland, *The British Antislavery Movement* (London: Frank Cass, 1964), 53.
4. Coupland, *British Antislavery Movement*, 48, 49.
5. Quoted in Coupland, *British Antislavery Movement*, 51.
6. Hochschild, *Bury the Chains*, 50.
7. Cited in Arthur Herman, *How the Scots Invented the Modern World* (New York: Crown, 2001), 89.
8. Will and Ariel Durant, *The Age of Voltaire* (New York: Simon & Schuster, 1965), 128.
9. Eric Metaxas, *Amazing Grace: William Wilberforce and the Heroic Campaign to End Slavery* (New York: HarperCollins, 2007), 9.
10. Hochschild, *Bury the Chains*, 89.
11. Robin Blackburn, *The Overthrow of Colonial Slavery, 1776–1848* (London: Verso, 2000), 137.
12. Thomas Clarkson, *The History of the Rise, Progress and Accomplishment of the Abolition of the African Slave Trade by the British Parliament* (Whitefish, MT: Kessinger Publishing Reprints, 2004), 129.
13. Clarkson, *Rise, Progress and Accomplishment of the Abolition of the African Slave Trade*, 174.
14. Quoted in Metaxas, *Amazing Grace*, 97, 98.
15. Quoted in Metaxas, *Amazing Grace*, 100.
16. Clarkson, *Rise, Progress and Accomplishment of the Abolition of the African Slave Trade*, 286.
17. Clarkson, *Rise, Progress and Accomplishment of the Abolition of the African Slave Trade*, 195, 196.
18. Clarkson, *Rise, Progress and Accomplishment of the Abolition of the African Slave Trade*, 289.
19. Coupland, *British Antislavery Movement*, 71.
20. William Hague, *William Pitt the Younger* (New York: Knopf, 2005), 112.
21. Metaxas, *Amazing Grace*, 68.
22. Coupland, *British Anti-Slavery Movement*, 73.
23. Metaxas, *Amazing Grace*, 113.

24. Robert William Fogel, *Without Consent or Contract: The Rise and Fall of American Slavery* (New York: Norton, 1989), 210.

25. Clarkson, *Rise, Progress and Accomplishment of the Abolition of the African Slave Trade*, 225.

26. Blackburn, *Overthrow of Colonial Slavery*, 139.

27. Dale H. Porter, *The Abolition of the Slave Trade in England, 1784–1807* (New York: Archon Books, 1970), 37.

28. Fogel, *Without Consent or Contract*, 212.

29. Hague, *William Pitt the Younger*, 33.

30. Hochschild, *Bury the Chains*, 304.

31. Fogel, *Without Consent or Contract*, 213.

32. Porter, *Abolition of the Slave Trade in England*, 133–35.

33. "Lord Holland," in *The Life and Works of Lord Macaulay* (London: Longman's Green, 1897), vi, 537.

34. Clarkson, *Rise, Progress and Accomplishment of the Abolition of the African Slave Trade*, 305.

35. W. E. F. Ward, *The Royal Navy and the Slavers* (New York: Pantheon, 1969), 47.

36. Howard Temperley, *British Antislavery, 1833–1870* (Columbia: University of South Carolina Press, 1972), 7.

37. William A. Green, *British Slave Emancipation: The Sugar Colonies and the Great Experiment, 1830–1865* (New York: Oxford University Press, 1991), 108.

38. Green, *British Slave Emancipation*, 105.

39. Temperley, *British Antislavery*, 10.

40. Hochschild, *Bury the Chains*, 324.

41. Temperley, *British Antislavery*, 13.

42. Green, *British Slave Emancipation*, 111.

43. Temperley, *British Antislavery*, 18.

44. Seymour Drescher, *The Mighty Experiment: Free Labor versus Slavery in British Emancipation* (New York: Oxford University Press, 2002), 137.

45. Drescher, *The Mighty Experiment*, 140.

46. Green, *British Slave Emancipation*, 118.

47. Green, *British Slave Emancipation*, 119; Temperley, *British Antislavery*, 17.

48. Green, *British Slave Emancipation*, 122.

49. Temperley, *British Antislavery*, 94.

50. Temperley, *British Antislavery*, 41.

Chapter 5

1. Leslie Bethell, *The Abolition of the Brazilian Slave Trade* (Cambridge: Cambridge University Press, 1970), 9.

2. Hugh Thomas, *The Slave Trade: The Story of the Atlantic Slave Trade, 1440–1870* (New York: Simon & Schuster, 1997), 585.

3. Reginald Coupland, *The British Antislavery Movement* (London: Frank Cass, 1964), 153.

4. Bethell, *Abolition of the Brazilian Slave Trade*, 14.

5. Coupland, *British Antislavery Movement*, 158.

6. W. E. F. Ward, *The Royal Navy and the Slavers: The Suppression of the Atlantic Slave Trade* (New York: Pantheon, 1969), 80.

7. Quoted in Thomas, *The Slave Trade*, 589.

8. Thomas, *The Slave Trade*, 620.

9. Thomas, *The Slave Trade*, 625.

10. Coupland, *British Antislavery Movement*, 159.

11. Robin Blackburn, *The Overthrow of Colonial Slavery, 1776–1844* (London: Verso, 2000), 321.

12. Thomas, *The Slave Trade*, 582.

13. Ward, *Royal Navy and the Slavers*, 83.

14. David Murray, *Odious Commerce: Britain, Spain and the Abolition of the Cuban Slave Trade* (New York: Cambridge University Press, 2002), 64.

15. Murray, *Odious Commerce*, 77.

16. Thomas, *The Slave Trade*, 608.

17. Murray, *Odious Commerce*, 81.

18. David Eltis, "The Export of Slaves from Africa, 1821–43," *Journal of Economic History*, 1977, 409–33.

19. Ward, *Royal Navy and the Slavers*, 119, 120.

20. Thomas E. Skidmore, *Brazil: Five Centuries of Change* (New York: Oxford University Press, 1999), 52.

21. Carolina Nabuco, *The Life of Joaquim Nabuco* (Stanford: Stanford University Press, 1950), xix.

22. Bethell, *Abolition of the Brazilian Slave Trade*, 71.

23. James Chambers, *Palmerston, "The People's Darling"* (London: John Murray, 2004), 310.

24. A. J. P. Taylor, "Introduction," in Denis Judd, *Palmerston* (London: Weidenfeld and Nicolson, 1975), vii, viii.

25. Quoted in Coupland, *British Antislavery Movement*, 181.

26. Chambers, *Palmerston, "The People's Darling,"* 200.

27. Ward, *Royal Navy and the Slavers*, 125.

28. Coupland, *British Antislavery Movement*, 161.

29. Robert Brent Toplin, *The Abolition of Slavery in Brazil* (New York: Atheneum, 1972), 39, 40.

30. Chambers, *Palmerston, "The People's Darling,"* 201.

31. Ward, *Royal Navy and the Slavers*, 163.

32. Nabuco, *Life of Joaquim Nabuco*, xix.

33. Chambers, *Palmerston, "The People's Darling,"* 484.

34. Nabuco, *Life of Joaquim Nabuco*, xix.

35. Bethell, *Abolition of the Brazilian Slave Trade*, 327.

36. Bethell, *Abolition of the Brazilian Slave Trade*, 330.

37. Bethell, *Abolition of the Brazilian Slave Trade*, 357.

38. Chambers, *Palmerston, "The People's Darling,"* 201.

39. Arthur Herman, *To Rule the Waves: How the British Navy Shaped the Modern World* (New York: HarperCollins, 2004), 422.

40. Coupland, *British Antislavery Movement*, 165, 166.

41. Chambers, *Palmerston, "The People's Darling,"* 200.

42. Howard Temperley, *British Antislavery, 1833–1870* (London: Longman, 1972), 182.

43. Chambers, *Palmerston, "The People's Darling,"* 201.

44. Ward, *Royal Navy and the Slavers*, 134.

45. Thomas Buxton, *The Slave Trade and Its Remedy* (London: Dawsons, 1968), 281.

46. Temperley, *British Antislavery*, 51.

47. Temperley, *British Antislavery*, 87.

48. Thomas, *The Slave Trade*, 616.

49. Ward, *Royal Navy and the Slavers*, 126.
50. Temperley, *British Antislavery*, 169.
51. Howard Jones, *Mutiny on the Amistad:, The Saga of a Slave Revolt and Its Impact on American Abolition, Law, and Diplomacy* (New York: Oxford University Press, 1987), 7.
52. W. E. B. Du Bois, *The Suppression of the African Slave Trade to the United States of America, 1638–1870* (Williamstown, MA: Corner House Publishers, 1970), 142.
53. Coupland, *British Antislavery Movement*, 171.
54. Coupland, *British Antislavery Movement*, 186, 187.
55. Coupland, *British Antislavery Movement*, 160.

Chapter 6

1. "Introduction," in William E. Cain, ed., *William Lloyd Garrison and the Fight Against Slavery, Selections from "The Liberator"* (New York: Bedford/St. Martin's, 1994), 22.
2. Robert William Fogel, *Without Consent or Contract: The Rise and Fall of American Slavery* (New York: Norton, 1989), 252.
3. Henry Mayer, *All on Fire: William Lloyd Garrison and the Abolition of American Slavery* (New York: St. Martin's, 1998), 110.
4. Mayer, *All on Fire*, 115.
5. Bliss Perry, ed., *The Heart of Emerson's Journals* (New York: Dover, 1992), 215.
6. Ralph Korngold, *Two Friends of Man; the Story of William Lloyd Garrison and Wendell Phillips and Their Relationship with Abraham Lincoln* (Boston: Little, Brown, 1950), 60.
7. Korngold, *Two Friends of Man*, 84–85.
8. John L. Thomas, *The Liberator: William Lloyd Garrison, a Biography* (Boston: Little, Brown, 1963), 415.
9. Quoted in Samuel Eliot Morison, *The Oxford History of the American People* (New York: Oxford University Press, 1965), 512.
10. "To the Public," quoted in Cain, *William Lloyd Garrison and the Fight Against Slavery*, 72.
11. Quoted in Arnold Whitridge, *No Compromise! The Story of the Fanatics Who Paved the Way to the Civil War* (New York: Farrar, Straus & Cudahy, 1960), 87.
12. Thomas, *The Liberator: William Lloyd Garrison*, 139–41.
13. Elizabeth Gray Vining, *Mr. Whittier* (New York: Viking Press, 1974), 42.
14. Korngold, *Two Friends of Man*, 69.
15. Thomas, *The Liberator: William Lloyd Garrison*, 158–63.
16. Walter M. Merrill, *Against Wind and Tide: A Biography of William Lloyd Garrison* (Cambridge: Harvard University Press, 1963), 100.
17. Whitridge, *No Compromise!*, 105.
18. Quoted in "Introduction," Cain, *William Lloyd Garrison and the Fight Against Slavery*, 50–51.
19. Thomas, *The Liberator: William Lloyd Garrison*, 227.
20. Whitridge, *No Compromise!*, 96.
21. Thomas, *The Liberator: William Lloyd Garrison*, 187.
22. Vining, *Mr. Whittier*, 61–65.
23. Merrill, *Against Wind and Tide*, 104.
24. Mayer, *All on Fire*, 200–206.
25. Korngold, *Two Friends of Man*, 116.
26. Mayer, *All on Fire*, 237, 238.
27. Merrill, *Against Wind and Tide*, 117.
28. Merrill, *Against Wind and Tide*, 122.

29.   Thomas, *The Liberator, William Lloyd Garrison,* 236–37.

30.   William S. McFeely, *Frederick Douglass* (New York: Norton, 1991), 83.

31.   William Lloyd Garrison, "Preface," in Frederick Douglass, *Narrative of the Life of Frederick Douglass, an American Slave* (New York: Library of America, 1994), 4.

32.   "Introduction," in Cain, *William Lloyd Garrison and the Fight against Slavery,* 51.

33.   Korngold, *Two Friends of Man,* 148.

34.   Whitridge, *No Compromise!* 118.

35.   Booker T. Washington, *Frederick Douglass* (New York: Argosy-Antiquarian, 1969), 79, 80.

36.   Wendell Phillips, "Letter," in Michael Meyer, ed., *Frederick Douglass, The Narrative and Selected Writings* (New York: Modern Library, 1984), 11.

37.   William Lloyd Garrison, "Preface," in *Frederick Douglass, The Narrative and Selected Writings,* 6.

38.   McFeely, *Frederick Douglass,* 142.

39.   Washington, *Frederick Douglass,* 100.

40.   McFeely, *Frederick Douglass,* 144.

41.   Merrill, *Against Wind and Tide,* 147.

42.   Thomas, *The Liberator: William Lloyd Garrison,* 221.

43.   Mayer, *All on Fire,* 217.

44.   Thomas, *The Liberator: William Lloyd Garrison,* 222.

45.   Aileen S. Kraditor, *Means and Ends in American Abolitionism: Garrison and His Critics on Strategy and Tactics, 1834–1850* (Chicago: Ivan R. Dee, 1989), 6.

46.   Quoted in Lydia Maria Child, "Immediatism," in Bernard A. Weisberger, ed., *Abolitionism: Disrupter of the Democratic System or Agent of Progress* (Chicago: Rand McNally, 1963), 21.

47.   Korngold, *Two Friends of Man,* 224.

48.   Charles Sumner, "Freedom National, Slavery Sectional," in Weisberger, *Abolitionism,* 49.

49.   "Introduction," in Cain, *William Lloyd Garrison and the Fight against Slavery,* 36.

50.   McFeely, *Frederick Douglass,* 200–208.

51.   Thomas, *The Liberator: William Lloyd Garrison,* 401.

52.   Eric Foner, *Reconstruction: America's Unfinished Revolution, 1863–1877* (New York: HarperCollins, 2002), 230.

53.   Quoted in Foner, *Reconstruction: America's Unfinished Revolution,* 229.

54.   Thomas, *The Liberator: William Lloyd Garrison,* 419.

55.   Foner, *Reconstruction: America's Unfinished Revolution,* 44.

56.   Jeffrey Rogers Hummel, *Emancipating Slaves, Enslaving Free Men: A History of the American Civil War* (Chicago: Open Court, 1996), 274.

57.   Quoted in Hodding Carter, *The Angry Scar: The Story of Reconstruction* (Garden City, NY: Doubleday, 1959), 25.

58.   General William Tecumseh Sherman to Major General Henry W. Halleck, December 24, 1864, in U.S. War Department, *The War of the Rebellion: A Compilation of the Official Records of the Union and Confederate Armies* (Washington, DC: Government Printing Office, 1880–1901), ser.1, vol. 44, 799.

59.   General William Tecumseh Sherman to Major General Ulysses S. Grant, October 4, 1862, in U.S. War Department, *The War of the Rebellion: A Compilation of the Official Records of the Union and Confederate Armies* (Washington, DC: Government Printing Office, 1880–1901), ser.1, vol.17, pt. 2, 261.

60.   Quoted in Hummel, *Emancipating Slaves, Enslaving Free Men,* 278.

61. Quoted in Carter, *The Angry Scar*, 25.
62. Herbert S. Klein, *African Slavery in Latin America and the Caribbean* (New York: Oxford University Press, 1986), 297.

Chapter 7

1. David Murray, *Odious Commerce: Britain, Spain and the Abolition of the Cuban Slave trade* (New York: Cambridge University Press, 2002), 13.
2. Murray, *Odious Commerce*, 1, 2.
3. Hugh Thomas, *Cuba: The Pursuit of Freedom* (New York: Harper & Row, 1971), 112.
4. Rebecca J. Scott, *Slave Emancipation in Cuba: The Transition To Free Labor, 1860–1899* (Princeton, NJ: Princeton University Press, 1986), 24, 25.
5. Thomas, *Cuba: The Pursuit of Freedom*, 134.
6. Thomas, *Cuba: The Pursuit of Freedom*, 142.
7. Thomas, *Cuba: The Pursuit of Freedom*, 205.
8. Thomas, *Cuba: The Pursuit of Freedom*, 213, 214.
9. Arthur F. Corwin, *Spain and the Abolition of Slavery in Cuba, 1817–1886* (Austin: University of Texas Press, 1967), 123.
10. Murray, *Odious Commerce*, 87.
11. Corwin, *Spain and Abolition of Slavery in Cuba*, 154.
12. Corwin, *Spain and Abolition of Slavery in Cuba*, 155.
13. Thomas, *Cuba: The Pursuit of Freedom*, 235.
14. Quoted in Thomas, *Cuba: The Pursuit of Freedom*, 239.
15. Corwin, *Spain and Abolition of Slavery in Cuba*, 217.
16. Quoted in Thomas, *Cuba: The Pursuit of Freedom*, 243.
17. Corwin, *Spain and Abolition of Slavery in Cuba*, 222.
18. Thomas, *Cuba: The Pursuit of Freedom*, 248.
19. Corwin, *Spain and Abolition of Slavery in Cuba*, 224.
20. Corwin, *Spain and Abolition of Slavery in Cuba*, 256.
21. Scott, *Slave Emancipation in Cuba*, 84.
22. Thomas, *Cuba: The Pursuit of Freedom*, 251, 252.
23. Corwin, *Spain and Abolition of Slavery in Cuba*, 234.
24. Corwin, *Spain and Abolition of Slavery in Cuba*, 154.
25. Quoted in Thomas, *Cuba: The Pursuit of Freedom*, 257.
26. Scott, *Slave Emancipation in Cuba*, 64.
27. Scott, *Slave Emancipation in Cuba*, 72.
28. Thomas, *Cuba: The Pursuit of Freedom*, 264.
29. Corwin, *Spain and Abolition of Slavery in Cuba*, 294; note that the 1868 census figure was down from the 1861 estimate of 370,553 slaves. See Herbert S. Klein, *African Slavery in Latin America and the Caribbean* (New York: Oxford University Press, 1986), 297.
30. Scott, *Slave Emancipation in Cuba*, 116.
31. Corwin, *Spain and Abolition of Slavery in Cuba*, 301.
32. Scott, *Slave Emancipation in Cuba*, 128.
33. Scott, *Slave Emancipation in Cuba*, 143.
34. Thomas, *Cuba: The Pursuit of Freedom*, 272.
35. Scott, *Slave Emancipation in Cuba*, 91, 99.
36. Corwin, *Spain and Abolition of Slavery in Cuba*, 310.
37. Thomas, *Cuba: The Pursuit of Freedom*, 279.
38. Corwin, *Spain and Abolition of Slavery in Cuba*, 311.

Chapter 8

1. Thomas E. Skidmore, *Brazil: Five Centuries of Change* (New York: Oxford University Press, 1999), 52.

2. Seymour Drescher and Stanley L. Engerman, eds., *A Historical Guide to World Slavery* (New York: Oxford University Press, 1998), 101.

3. Leslie Bethell, *The Abolition of the Brazilian Slave Trade: Britain, Brazil and the Slave Trade, 1807–1869* (Cambridge: Cambridge University Press, 1970), 3, 4.

4. Robert Brent Toplin, *The Abolition of Slavery in Brazil* (New York: Athenaeum, 1972), 7, 8.

5. Robert Conrad, *The Destruction of Brazilian Slavery, 1850–1888* (Berkeley: University of California Press, 1972), 21.

6. Bethell, *Abolition of the Brazilian Slave Trade,* 312.

7. Conrad, *Destruction of Brazilian Slavery,* 23.

8. W. E. F. Ward, *The Royal Navy and the Slavers* (New York: Pantheon, 1969), 165, 166.

9. Conrad, *Destruction of Brazilian Slavery,* 27.

10. Toplin, *Abolition of Slavery in Brazil,* 41, 42.

11. Carolina Nabuco, *The Life of Joaquim Nabuco* (Palo Alto, CA: Stanford University Press, 1950), xix.

12. Toplin, *Abolition of Slavery in Brazil,* 46.

13. Conrad, *Destruction of Brazilian Slavery,* 90.

14. Conrad, *Destruction of Brazilian Slavery,* 91.

15. Conrad, *Destruction of Brazilian Slavery,* 103.

16. Herbert S. Klein, *African Slavery in Latin America and the Caribbean* (New York: Oxford University Press, 1986), 297.

17. Toplin, *Abolition of Slavery in Brazil,* 35–37.

18. Skidmore, *Brazil: Five Centuries of Change,* 68.

19. Toplin, *Abolition of Slavery in Brazil,* 60.

20. Conrad, *Destruction of Brazilian Slavery,* 107.

21. Toplin, *Abolition of Slavery in Brazil,* 20, 21.

22. Toplin, *Abolition of Slavery in Brazil,* 95.

23. Conrad, *Destruction of Brazilian Slavery,* 135, 136.

24. Toplin, *Abolition of Slavery in Brazil,* 61.

25. Quoted in Conrad, *Destruction of Brazilian Slavery,* 152.

26. Nabuco, *Life of Joaquim Nabuco,* 120.

27. Quoted in Toplin, *Abolition of Slavery in Brazil,* 87.

28. Conrad, *Destruction of Brazilian Slavery,* 139.

29. Toplin, *Abolition of Slavery in Brazil,* 88, 89.

30. Conrad, *Destruction of Brazilian Slavery,* 140.

31. Conrad, *Destruction of Brazilian Slavery,* 193, 194.

32. Nabuco, *Life of Joaquim Nabuco,* 103.

33. Conrad, *Destruction of Brazilian Slavery,* 154.

34. Toplin, *Abolition of Slavery in Brazil,* 70.

35. Nabuco, *Life of Joaquim Nabuco,* 104.

36. Nabuco, *Life of Joaquim Nabuco,* 103, 104.

37. Toplin, *Abolition of Slavery in Brazil,* 63.

38. Conrad, *Destruction of Brazilian Slavery,* 142.

39. Toplin, *Abolition of Slavery in Brazil,* 65, 66.

40. Seymour Drescher, "Brazilian Abolition in Comparative Perspective," in Rebecca J. Scott, Seymour Drescher, Hebe Maria Mattos de Castro, George Reid Andrews

and Robert M. Levine, *The Abolition of Slavery and the Aftermath of Emancipation in Brazil* (Durham, NC: Duke University Press, 1988), 45.

41. Nabuco, *Life of Joaquim Nabuco*, 116.

42. Conrad, *Destruction of Brazilian Slavery*, 190.

43. Conrad, *Destruction of Brazilian Slavery*, 191–196.

44. Drescher, "Brazilian Abolition in Comparative Perspective," in *Abolition of Slavery and the Aftermath of Emancipation in Brazil*, 26.

45. Quoted in Conrad, *Destruction of Brazilian Slavery*, 205.

46. Nabuco, *Life of Joaquim Nabuco*, 106, 108.

47. Conrad, *Destruction of Brazilian Slavery*, 211.

48. Nabuco, *Life of Joaquim Nabuco*, xx.

49. Skidmore, *Brazil: Five Centuries of Change*, 70.

Chapter 9

1. Quoted in Neal Ascherson, *The King Incorporated: Leopold II and the Congo* (Garden City, NY: Doubleday, 1964), 104.

2. Ascherson, *The King Incorporated*, 15.

3. Arthur Conan Doyle, *The Crime of the Congo* (London: Hutchinson, 1909), 6.

4. Doyle, *The Crime of the Congo*, 13.

5. Doyle, *The Crime of the Congo*, 13.

6. Adam Hochschild, *King Leopold's Ghost: A Story of Greed, Terror, and Heroism in Colonial Africa* (Boston: Houghton Mifflin, 1998), 159.

7. Quoted in Ascherson, *The King Incorporated*, 242.

8. John Hope Franklin, *George Washington Williams, A Biography* (Chicago: University of Chicago Press, 1985), 183.

9. Quoted in Franklin, *George Washington Williams*, 181.

10. George Washington Williams, "An Open Letter to Léopold II," in Franklin, *George Washington Williams*, 244, 245.

11. Williams, "An Open Letter to Léopold II," in Franklin, *George Washington Williams*, 248–253.

12. Quoted in Hochschild, *King Leopold's Ghost*, 111.

13. Zdzislaw Najder, *Joseph Conrad, A Chronicle* (New Brunswick, NJ: Rutgers University Press, 1983), 134.

14. Joseph Conrad, *Last Essays* (Garden City, NY: Doubleday, Page, 1926), 17.

15. Joseph Conrad, *Heart of Darkness* (New York: Barnes & Noble Classics, 2003), 121.

16. Hochschild, *King Leopold's Ghost*, 145.

17. Conrad, *Heart of Darkness*, 123.

18. Conrad, *Heart of Darkness*, 67, 68.

19. Conrad, *Heart of Darkness*, 62.

20. Conrad, *Heart of Darkness*, 64.

21. Pagan Kennedy, *Black Livingstone, A True Tale of Adventure in the Nineteenth-Century Congo* (New York: Viking, 2002), 29.

22. Kennedy, *Black Livingstone*, 24.

23. Quoted in Kennedy, *Black Livingstone*, 26.

24. William E. Phipps, *William Sheppard, Congo's African American Livingstone* (Louisville, KY: Geneva Press, 2002), 54.

25. Kennedy, *Black Livingstone*, 50.

26. Phipps, *William Sheppard,* 69.
27. Kennedy, *Black Livingstone,* 51.
28. Kennedy, *Black Livingstone,* 69.
29. Hochschild, *King Leopold's Ghost,* 157.
30. Phipps, *William Sheppard,* 97.
31. Ascherson, *The King Incorporated,* 243.
32. Kennedy, *Black Livingstone,* 134.
33. Hochschild, *King Leopold's Ghost,* 161.
34. Kennedy, *Black Livingstone,* 136.
35. Quoted in Kennedy, *Black Livingstone,* 137, 138.
36. Hochschild, *King Leopold's Ghost,* 165.
37. Kennedy, *Black Livingstone,* 143.
38. "King Leopold's Soliloquy," in Mark Twain, *Collected Tales, Sketches, Speeches, & Essays, 1891–1910* (New York: Library of America, 1984), 667.
39. Kennedy, *Black Livingstone,* 70.
40. Hochschild, *King Leopold's Ghost,* 163.
41. Kennedy, *Black Livingstone,* 172.
42. Hochschild, *King Leopold's Ghost,* 187.
43. Ascherson, *The King Incorporated,* 242.
44. Quoted in Doyle, *The Crime of the Congo,* 29.
45. Hochschild, *King Leopold's Ghost,* 194.
46. Brian Inglis, *Roger Casement* (New York: Harcourt, 1973), 27, 28.
47. Hochschild, *King Leopold's Ghost,* 196.
48. Quoted in Doyle, *The Crime of the Congo,* 42.
49. Inglis, *Roger Casement,* 80, 81.
50. Hochschild, *King Leopold's Ghost,* 204.
51. Inglis, *Roger Casement,* 89.
52. A. J. P. Taylor, *Essays in English History* (New York: Penguin Books, 1976), 212, 213.
53. Hochschild, *King Leopold's Ghost,* 204.
54. Inglis, *Roger Casement,* 81.
55. Hochschild, *King Leopold's Ghost,* 205.
56. Cited in Hochschild, *King Leopold's Ghost,* 213.

Chapter 10

1. Robert D. Heinl and Nancy G. Heinl, *Written in Blood: The Story of the Haitian People, 1492–1971* (Boston: Houghton Mifflin, 1978), 7.
2. Edwin Williamson, *The Penguin History of Latin America* (New York: Penguin, 1992), 253.
3. George B. Ayittey, *Africa Betrayed* (New York: St. Martin's, 1992), 88.
4. See Ayittey, *Africa Betrayed,* 387, 388.
5. Howard Temperley, *British Antislavery, 1833–1870* (London: Longman, 1972), 115.
6. William A. Green, *British Slave Emancipation: The Sugar Colonies and the Great Experiment, 1830–1865* (Oxford: Oxford University Press, 1991), 195.
7. Green, *British Slave Emancipation,* 207.
8. Temperley, *British Antislavery,* 115.
9. June 4, 1853, cited in Temperley, *British Antislavery,* 117.
10. William Hanchett, *The Lincoln Murder Conspiracies* (Champaign: University of Illinois Press, 1983), 37.

11. Jeffrey R. Hummel, *Emancipating Slaves, Enslaving Free Men: A History of the American Civil War* (Chicago: Open Court, 1996), 279.

12. Samuel Eliot Morison, Henry Steel Commager and William E. Leuchtenburg, *The Growth of the American Republic* (New York: Oxford University Press, 1980), I, 719–20.

13. Hummel, *Emancipating Slaves, Enslaving Free Men*, 322.

14. Hummel, *Emancipating Slaves, Enslaving Free Men*, 279.

15. Quoted in John Hope Franklin, *Reconstruction after the Civil War* (Chicago: University of Chicago Press, 1994), 2.

16. Hummel, *Emancipating Slaves, Enslaving Free Men*, 280.

17. Franklin, *Reconstruction after the Civil War*, 39.

18. Eric Foner, *Reconstruction: America's Unfinished Revolution* (New York: HarperCollins, 2005), 135.

19. Foner, *Reconstruction: America's Unfinished Revolution*, 183.

20. Garrett Epps, *Democracy Reborn: The Fourteenth Amendment and the Fight for Equal Rights in Post–Civil War America* (New York: Henry Holt, 2006), 26–28.

21. Franklin, *Reconstruction after the Civil War*, 43.

22. Hodding Carter, *The Angry Scar: The Story of Reconstruction* (Garden City, NY: Doubleday, 1959), 52.

23. Foner, *Reconstruction: America's Unfinished Revolution*, 199.

24. Carter, *The Angry Scar*, 54.

25. Foner, *Reconstruction: America's Unfinished Revolution*, 203.

26. Carter, *The Angry Scar*, 53.

27. Foner, *Reconstruction: America's Unfinished Revolution*, 207.

28. Carter, *The Angry Scar*, 55.

29. Foner, *Reconstruction: America's Unfinished Revolution*, 38.

30. Franklin, *Reconstruction after the Civil War*, 38.

31. Foner, *Reconstruction: America's Unfinished Revolution*, 373.

32. Franklin, *Reconstruction after the Civil War*, 190.

33. See, for example, Hummel, *Emancipating Slaves, Enslaving Free Men*, 315, 316.

34. Foner, *Reconstruction: America's Unfinished Revolution*, 425; John Hope Franklin, *Reconstruction after the Civil War*, 193.

35. *U.S. v. Cruikshank*, 92 U.S. 542 (1875).

36. Franklin, *Reconstruction after the Civil War*, 192, 193.

37. Foner, *Reconstruction: America's Unfinished Revolution*, 383.

38. Foner, *Reconstruction: America's Unfinished Revolution*, 385.

39. Hummel, *Emancipating Slaves, Enslaving Free Men*, 316.

40. Foner, *Reconstruction: America's Unfinished Revolution*, 486.

41. Franklin, *Reconstruction after the Civil War*, 4.

Selected Bibliography

Articles

Anstey, Roger T. "A Re-interpretation of the Abolition of the British Slave Trade, 1806–1807." *English Historical Review* (April 1972): 302–32.

———. "Capitalism and Slavery: A Critique." *Economic History Review* (August 1968): 307–20.

Bailyn, Bernard. "Considering the Slave Trade: History and Memory." *William and Mary Quarterly* (January 2001): 245–52.

Brown, Christopher. "Empire without Slaves: British Concepts of Emancipation in the Age of the American Revolution." *William and Mary Quarterly* (April 1999): 273–306.

Cardozo, Manoel. "Slavery in Brazil as Described by Americans, 1822–1888." *The Americas* (January 1961): 241–60.

Drescher, Seymour. "Whose Abolition? Popular Pressure and the Ending of the British Slave Trade." *Past and Present* (May 1994): 136–66.

Erdem, Y. Hakan. "Slavery in the Ottoman Empire and Its Demise, 1800–1909." *International Journal of Middle East Studies* (November 1998): 574–76.

Finkelman, Paul. "Affirmative Action for the Master Class: The Creation of the Proslavery Constitution." *University of Akron Law Review* (Fall 1999): 423–70.

———. "The Kidnapping of John Davis and the Adoption of the Fugitive Slave Law of 1793." *Journal of Southern History* (August 1990): 397–422.

Fisher, Lillian Estelle. "The Intendant System in Spanish America." *Hispanic American Historical Review* (February 1928): 3–13.

Fisher, Ruth Anna. "Granville Sharp and Lord Mansfield." *Journal of Negro History* (October 1943): 381–89.

Fogel, Robert William and Stanley L. Engerman. "Philanthropy at Bargain Prices: Notes on the Economics of Gradual Emancipation." *Journal of Legal Studies* (June 1974): 377–401.

Heller, Henry. "Bodin on Slavery and Primitive Accumulation." *Sixteenth Century Journal* (Spring 1994): 53–65.

Kaufmann, Chaim D. and Robert A. Pape. "Explaining Costly International Moral Action: Britain's Sixty-Year Campaign Against the Atlantic Slave Trade." *International Organization* (October 1999): 631–68.

"Letters of Anthony Benezet." *Journal of Negro History* (January 1917): 85–95.

Martin, Percy Alvin. "Slavery and Abolition in Brazil." *Hispanic American Historical Review* (May 1933): 151–96.

——. "Causes of the Collapse of the Brazilian Empire." *Hispanic American Historical Review* (February 1921): 4–48.

Mason, Mathew. "The Battle of the Slaveholding Liberators: Great Britain, the United States, and Slavery in the Early Nineteenth Century." *William and Mary Quarterly* (July 2002): 665–96.

Minkema, Kenneth P. "Jonathan Edwards's Defense of Slavery." *Massachusetts Historical Review* vol. 4 (2002).

——. "Jonathan Edwards on Slavery and the Slave Trade." *William and Mary Quarterly* (October 1997): 823–34.

Needell, Jeffrey D. "The Abolition of the Brazilian Slave Trade in 1850: Historiography, Slave Agency, and Statesmanship." *Journal of Latin American Studies* (November 2001): 681–711.

Porter, Dorothy B. "The Negro in the Brazilian Abolition Movement." *Journal of Negro History* (January 1952): 54–80.

Putney, Martha. "The Slave Trade in French Diplomacy from 1814 to 1815." *Journal of Negro History* (July 1975): 411–27.

Reich, Jerome. "The Slave Trade at the Congress of Vienna—A Study in English Public Opinion, *Journal of Negro History* (April 1968): 129–43.

Reis, James. "The Impact of Abolitionism in Northeast Brazil: A Quantitative Approach." *Annals of the New York Academy of Sciences* (June 1977): 107–22.

Shaw, Paul Vanorden. "The Neglected Father of His Country, Brazil." *Political Science Quarterly* (March 1929): 39–53.

Shyllon, F. O. "Black Slaves in Britain." *American Journal of Legal History* (April 1976): 165–68

Sypher, Wylie. "Hutcheson and the 'Classical' Theory of Slavery." *Journal of Negro History* (July 1939): 263–80.

Books

Anderson, Eric and Alfred A. Moss. *The Facts of Reconstruction: Essays in Honor of John Hope Franklin.* Baton Rouge: Louisiana State University Press, 1991.

Anstey, Roger T. *The Atlantic Slave Trade and British Abolition, 1760–1810.* London: Macmillan, 1975.

——, Christine Bolt and Seymour Drescher, *Antislavery, Religion, and Reform: Essays in Memory of Roger Anstey.* Folkestone, UK: W. Dawson, 1980.

Armistead, Wilson. *Anthony Benezet. From the Original Memoir.* Freeport, NY: Books for Libraries Press, 1971.

Asiegbu, Johnson U. J. *Slavery and the Politics of Liberation 1787–1861: A Study of Liberated African Emigration and British Anti-Slavery Policy.* New York: Holmes & Meier, 1969.

Barclay, Oliver. *Thomas Fowell Buxton and the Liberation of Slaves.* York: William Sessions, 2001.

Beatty, Richmond Croom. *Lord Macaulay, Victorian Liberal.* Norman: University of Oklahoma Press, 1938.

Belmonte, Kevin Charles. *Hero for Humanity: A Biography of William Wilberforce.* Colorado Springs: Navpress, 2002.

Bergad, Laird W. *Slavery and the Demographic and Economic History of Minas Gerais, Brazil, 1720–1888.* New York: Cambridge University Press, 1999.

——. *The Cuban Slave Market, 1790–1880.* New York: Cambridge University Press, 1995.

Bethell, Leslie. *The Abolition of the Brazilian Slave Trade: Britain, Brazil and the Slave Trade, 1807–1869.* Cambridge: Cambridge University Press, 1970.

Blackburn, Robin. *The Making of New World Slavery: from the Baroque to the Modern, 1492–1800.* London: Verso, 1997.

———. *The Overthrow of Colonial Slavery, 1776–1848.* London: Verso, 2000.

Blackstone, William. *Commentaries on the Laws of England.* Philadelphia: John Grigg, 1827, 2 vols.

Blanchard, Peter. *Slavery and Abolition in Early Republican Peru.* Wilmington, DE: SR Books, 1992.

Booth, Charles. *Zachary Macaulay, His Part in the Abolition of the Slave Trade and of Slavery.* London: Longmans, 1934.

Brendlinger, Irv. A. *To Be Silent Would Be Criminal, The Antislavery Influence And Writings Of Anthony Benezet.* Lanham, MD: Scarecrow Press, 2006.

Brookes, George S. *Friend Anthony Benezet.* Philadelphia: University of Pennsylvania Press, 1937.

Brown, Christopher Leslie. *Moral Capital: Foundations of British Abolitionism.* Chapel Hill: University of North Carolina Press, 2006.

Brown, David. *Palmerston and the Politics of Foreign Policy, 1846–1855.* Manchester: Manchester University Press, 2002.

Brown, Ford K. *Fathers of the Victorians, the Age of Wilberforce.* Cambridge: Cambridge University Press, 1961.

Butler, Kathleen Mary. *The Economics of Emancipation: Jamaica & Barbados, 1823–1843.* Chapel Hill: University of North Carolina Press, 1995.

Buxton, Travers. *William Wilberforce, the Story of a Great Crusade.* London: Religious Tract Society, 1933.

Cadbury, Henry Joel. *Colonial Quaker Antecedents to Abolition of Slavery,* William E. Cain ed., *William Lloyd Garrison and the Fight Against Slavery, Selections from "The Liberator."* Boston: Bedford Books, 1995.

Canny, Nicholas, ed. *The Origins of Empire: British Overseas Enterprise to the Close of the Seventeenth Century.* New York: Oxford University Press, 1998.

Carey, Brycchan. *British Abolitionism and the Rhetoric of Sensibility: Writing, Sentiment, and Slavery, 1760–1807.* Basingstoke: Palgrave Macmillan, 2005.

Carter, Hodding. *The Angry Scar: The Story of Reconstruction.* Garden City, NY: Doubleday, 1959.

de Las Casas, Bartolomé. *In Defense of the Indians.* DeKalb: Northern Illinois University Press, 1992.

Chambers, James. *Palmerston, the People's Darling.* London: John Murray, 2004.

Clarkson, Thomas. *A History of the Rise, Progress and Accomplishment of the Abolition of the African Slave Trade by the British Parliament.* Whitefish, MT: Kessinger Publishing, repr. 2004.

Cheke, Marcus. *Dictator of Portugal: A Life of the Marquis of Pombal, 1688–1782.* Freeport, NY: Books for Libraries Press, 1969.

Clive, John. *Macaulay, The Shaping of the Historian.* New York: Knopf, 1973.

Colley, Linda. *Britons: Forging a Nation, 1707–1837.* New Haven: Yale University Press, 1992.

Conrad, Robert E. *The Destruction of Brazilian Slavery, 1850–1888.* Berkeley: University of California Press, 1972.

Conway, Moncure Daniel, ed. *The Writings of Thomas Paine.* New York: Burt Franklin, 1969.

Corwin, Arthur F. *Spain and the Abolition of Slavery in Cuba, 1817–1886.* Austin: University of Texas Press, 1967.

Coupland, Reginald. *Wilberforce, A Narrative.* New York: Negro Universities Press, 1968.

———. *The British Antislavery Movement.* London: Frank Cass, 1964.

Cover, Robert M. *Justice Accused: Antislavery and the Judicial Process.* New Haven, CT: Yale University Press, 1975.

Cowie, Leonard W. *William Wilberforce, 1759–1833, A Bibliography.* New York: Greenwood Press, 1992.

Craton, Michael, James Walvin, and David Wright. *Slavery, Abolition and Emancipation: Black Slaves and the British Empire, a Thematic Documentary.* London: Longmans, 1976.

Curtin, Philip D. *The Atlantic Slave Trade: A Census.* Madison: University of Wisconsin Press, 1981.

Davidson, Basil. *The African Slave Trade.* Boston: Atlantic Monthly Press, 1980.

Davis, David Brion. *Inhuman Bondage, The Rise and Fall of Slavery in the New World.* New York: Oxford University Press, 2006.

———. *The Problem of Slavery in the Age of Revolution, 1770–1823.* New York: Oxford University Press, 1999.

———. *Slavery and Human Progress.* Ithaca, NY: Cornell University Press, 1984.

———. *The Problem of Slavery in Western Culture.* Ithaca, NY: Cornell University Press, 1966.

Derry, John W. *Castlereagh.* New York: St. Martin's, 1976.

———. *Charles James Fox.* New York: St. Martin's, 1972.

DiLorenzo, Thomas J. *The Real Lincoln: A New Look at Abraham Lincoln, His Agenda, and an Unnecessary War.* New York: Crown Prima, 2002.

Drake, Thomas E. *Quakers and Slavery in America.* New Haven, CT: Yale University Press, 1950.

Drescher, Seymour. *The Mighty Experiment: Free Labor versus Slavery in British Emancipation.* New York: Oxford University Press, 2002.

———. *Econocide: British Slavery in the Era of Abolition.* Pittsburgh: University of Pittsburgh Press, 1977.

———, and Stanley L. Engerman, eds. *A Historical Guide to World Slavery.* New York: Oxford University Press, 1998.

D'Souza, Dinesh. *The End of Racism.* New York: Free Press, 1995.

Du Bois, W. E. B. *Black Reconstruction in America, 1860–1880.* Ed. David Levering Lewis. New York: Free Press, 1998.

———. *The Suppression of the African Slave-Trade in the United States of America, 1638–1870.* Williamstown, MA: Corner House Publishers, 1970.

Dubois, Laurent. *A Colony of Citizens: Revolution and Slave Emancipation in the French Caribbean, 1787–1804.* Chapel Hill: University of North Carolina Press, 2006.

———. *Avengers of the New World: The Story of the Haitian Revolution.* Cambridge, MA: Belknap Press, 2004.

———, and John G. Garrigus eds. *Slave Revolution in the Caribbean, 1789–1804: A Brief History with Documents.* New York: Palgrave Macmillan, 2006.

Edgerton, Robert. *The Troubled Heart of Africa: A History of the Congo.* New York: St. Martin's, 2002.

Eltis, David. *Economic Growth and the Ending of the Transatlantic Slave Trade.* New York: Oxford University Press, 1987.

———, and James Walvin, eds. *The Abolition of the Atlantic Slave Trade: Origins and Effects in Europe, Africa, and the Americas.* Madison: University of Wisconsin Press, 1981.

Engerman, Stanley, Seymour Drescher, and Robert Paquette, eds. *Slavery.* New York: Oxford University Press, 2001.

———, and Eugene D. Genovese, eds. *Race and Slavery in the Western Hemisphere: Quantitative Studies.* Princeton, NJ: Princeton University Press, 1975.

Epps, Garrett. *Democracy Reborn: The Fourteenth Amendment and the Fight for Equal Rights in Post—Civil War America*. New York: Henry Holt, 2006.

Ewans, Marti. *European Atrocity, African Catastrophe: Leopold II, the Congo Free State and Its Aftermath*. London: Routledge Curzon Press, 2002.

Falconridge, Alexander. *An Account of the Slave Trade on the Coast of Africa*. Ithaca, NY: Cornell University Library, 2007.

Ferguson, Adam. *Institutes of Moral Philosophy*. New York: Garland, 1978.

Finkelman, Paul. *Slavery and the Founders: Race and Liberty in the Age of Jefferson*. Armonk, NY: M. E. Sharpe, 2001.

Fisch, Audrey A. *American Slaves in Victorian England: Abolitionist Politics in Popular Literature and Culture*. New York: Cambridge University Press, 2000.

Fogel, Robert William. *Without Consent or Contract: The Rise and Fall of American Slavery*. New York: Norton, 1989.

Foner, Eric. *Slavery and Freedom in Nineteenth-Century America*. New York: Oxford University Press, 1994.

———. *Reconstruction: America's Unfinished Revolution, 1866—1877*. New York: Harper & Row, 1988.

———. *Politics and Ideology in the Age of the Civil War*. New York: Oxford University Press, 1980.

———. *Nothing But Freedom: Emancipation and Its Legacy*. Baton Rouge: Louisiana State University Press, 1976.

———, and John A. Garrity eds. *The Reader's Companion to American History*. Boston: Houghton-Mifflin, 1991.

Foner, Philip S. *Frederick Douglass, A Biography*. Boston: Beacon Press, 1964.

———. *The Life and Writings of Frederick Douglass*. New York: International Publishers, 1950—1955, 4 vols.

Fraginals, Manuel Moreno, Frank Moya Pons, and Stanley L. Engerman, eds. *Between Slavery and Free Labor: The Spanish-speaking Caribbean in the Nineteenth Century*. Baltimore, MD: Johns Hopkins University Press, 1985.

Franklin, John Hope. *George Washington Williams, A Biography*. Chicago: University of Chicago Press, 1985.

———. *From Slavery to Freedom: A History of Negro Americans*. New York: Alfred A. Knopf, 1967.

———. *The Emancipation Proclamation*. Garden City, NY: Doubleday, 1963.

———. *Reconstruction after the Civil War*. Chicago: University of Chicago Press, 1994.

———, and Loren Schweninger. *Runaway Slaves: Rebels on the Plantation*. New York: Oxford University Press, 1999.

Freedom to Be: The Abolition of Slavery in Jamaica and Its Aftermath. Jamaica: National Library of Jamaica, 1984.

Frost, Jerry William, ed. *The Quaker Origins of Antislavery*. Norwood, PA: Norwood Editions, 1980.

Fruchtman, Jack, Jr. *Thomas Paine, Apostle of Freedom*. New York: Four Walls Eight Windows, 1994.

Gaspar, David Barry and David P. Geggus eds. *A Turbulent Time: The French Revolution and the Greater Caribbean*. Bloomington: Indiana University Press, 1997.

Gates, Henry Louis, Jr. *Frederick Douglass Autobiographies*. New York: Library of America, 1994.

Geggus, David P., ed. *The Impact of the Haitian Revolution in the Atlantic World*. Columbia: University of South Carolina Press, 2001.

Gould, Philip. *Barbaric Traffic: Commerce and Antislavery in the Eighteenth-Century Atlantic World*. Cambridge, MA: Harvard University Press, 2003.

Grant, Kevin. *A Civilized Savagery: Britain and the New Slaveries in Africa, 1884–1926.* New York: Routledge, 2004.

Greaves, Richard L. *Dublin's Merchant-Quaker: Anthony Sharp and the Community of Friends, 1643–1707.* Palo Alto, CA: Stanford University Press, 1998.

Green, William A. *British Slave Emancipation: The Sugar Colonies and the Great Experiment, 1830–1865.* New York: Oxford University Press, 1991.

Griggs, Earl Leslie. *Thomas Clarkson, the Friend of Slaves.* Westport, CT: Negro Universities Press, 1970.

Grimké, Archibald H. *William Lloyd Garrison, the Abolitionist.* New York: AMS Press, 1974.

Guedalla, Philip. *Palmerston, 1784–1865.* New York: Putnam, 1927.

Hart, Richard. *Slaves Who Abolished Slavery: Blacks in Rebellion.* Barbados: University of West Indies Press, 2002.

Harvey, Robert. *Liberators:Latin America's Struggle for Independence.* Woodstock, NY: Overlook Press, 2000.

Hawke, David Freeman. *Benjamin Rush, Revolutionary Gadfly.* Indianapolis: Bobbs-Merrill, 1971.

Hazlewood, Nick. *The Queen's Slave Trader: John Hawkyns, Elizabeth I and the Trafficking in Human Souls.* New York: HarperCollins, 2004.

Hinde, Wendy. *Castlereagh.* London: Collins, 1981.

Hochschild, Adam. *Bury the Chains: Prophets and Rebels an the Fight to Free an Empire's Slaves.* Boston: Houghton Mifflin, 2005.

———. *King Leopold's Ghost: A Story of Greed, Terror and Heroism in Colonial Africa.* Boston: Houghton Mifflin, 1998.

Howard, Warren S. *American Slavers and the Federal Law, 1837–1862.* Berkeley: University of California Press, 1963.

Hutcheson, Francis. *A System of Moral Philosophy.* New York: Augustus M. Kelley, 1968.

Inglis, Brian. *Roger Casement.* New York: Harcourt, Brace, Jovanovich, 1973.

Ingram, John Kells. *A History of Slavery and Serfdom.* Boston: Adamant Media, 2000.

Inikori, Joseph E. and Stanley L. Engerman, eds. *The Atlantic Slave Trade: Effects on Economies, Societies and Peoples in Africa, the Americas and Europe.* Durham, NC: Duke University Press, 1992.

Isaacson, Walter. *Benjamin Franklin, an American Life.* New York: Simon & Schuster, 2003.

James, C. L. R. *The Black Jacobins: Toussaint L'Ouverture and the San Domingo Revolution.* New York: Dial Press, 1938.

Jeal, Tim. *Livingstone.* New York: Putnam, 1973.

Jefferson, Thomas. *Writings.* Ed. Merrill Peterson. New York: Library of America, 1984.

Jennings, Judith. *The Business of Abolishing the British Slave Trade 1783–1807.* London: Frank Cass, 1997.

Jennings, Lawrence C. *French Anti-Slavery: The Movement for the Abolition of Slavery in France, 1802–1848.* New York: Cambridge University Press, 2000.

Johnson, J. F. *Proceedings of the General Anti-Slavery Convention, called by the committee of the British and Foreign Anti-Slavery Society, and held in London, from Tuesday, June 13th, to Tuesday, June 20th, 1843.* Miami: Mnemosyne Publishing, 1969.

Judd, Denis. *Palmerston.* London: Weidenfield & Nicholson, 1975.

Keane, John. *Tom Paine, A Political Life.* Boston: Little, Brown, 1995.

Kennedy, Pagan. *Black Livingstone: A True Tale of Adventure in the Nineteenth-Century Congo.* New York: Viking, 2002.

Kettler, David. *The Social and Political Thought of Adam Ferguson.* Columbus: Ohio State University Press, 1965.

Kielstra, Paul. *The Politics of Slave Trade Suppression in Britain and France, 1814–1848.* New York: St. Martin's, 2000.

Kissinger, Henry A. *A World Restored: Metternich, Castlereagh and the Problems of Peace, 1812–1822.* Boston: Houghton Mifflin, 1973.

Kitson, Peter, et al. *Slavery, Abolition and Emancipation: Writings in the British Romantic Period.* London: Pickering and Chatto, 1999. 8 vols.

Klein, Herbert S. *African Slavery in Latin America and the Caribbean.* New York: Oxford University Press, 1986.

Korngold, Ralph. *Two Friends of Man: The Story of William Lloyd Garrison and Wendell Phillips and Their Relationship with Abraham Lincoln.* Boston: Little, Brown, 1950.

Kraditor, Aileen S. *Means and Ends in American Abolitionism: Garrison and His Critics on Strategy and Tactics, 1834–1850.* New York: Vintage, 1969.

Levy, Claude. *Emancipation, Sugar and Federalism: Barbados and the West Indies, 1833–1876.* Gainesville: University Press of Florida, 1980.

Lincove, David A., ed. *Reconstruction: An Annotated Bibliography.* Westport, CT: Greenwood Press, 2000.

Lynch, John. *Simon Bolivar, a Life.* New Haven, CT: Yale University Press, 2006.

——. *The Spanish-American Revolution, 1808–1826.* New York: Norton, 1986.

Lytton, Henry. *The Life of Henry John Temple, Viscount Palmerston.* Philadelphia: Lippincott, 1871. 2 vols.

Malone, Dumas. *Jefferson and the Rights of Man.* Boston: Little, Brown, 1951.

Mannix, Daniel. *Cargoes: A History of the Atlantic Slave Trade, 1518–1865.* New York: Viking Press, 1962.

Marques, Joao Pedro. *The Sounds of Silence, Nineteenth Century Portugal and the Abolition of the Slave Trade.* New York: Berghahn Books, 2006.

Martin, Bert Edmon. *All We Want Is Make Us Free: Amistad and the Reform Abolitionists.* Lanham, MD: University Press of America, 1986.

Masur, Gerhard. *Simon Bolivar.* Albuquerque: University of New Mexico Press, 1948.

Mayer, Henry. *All on Fire: William Lloyd Garrison and the Abolition of American Slavery.* New York: St. Martin's, 1998.

McFeely, William S. *Frederick Douglass.* New York: Norton, 1991.

McPherson, James M. *Battle Cry of Freedom: The Civil War Era.* New York: Oxford University Press, 1988.

Meltzer, Milton. *Slavery, A World History.* New York: Da Capo, 1972.

Merrill, Walter M. *Against Wind and Tide: A Biography of William Lloyd Garrison.* Cambridge, MA: Harvard University Press, 1963.

——, et al., eds. *The Letters of William Lloyd Garrison, 1822–1879.* Cambridge, MA: Harvard University Press, 1971–1981. 6 vols.

Midgley, Clare. *Women against Slavery: The British Campaigns, 1780–1870.* London: Routledge, 1992.

Monteith, Kathleen, ed. *Jamaica in Slavery and Freedom: History, Heritage and Culture.* Barbados: University of the West Indies Press, 2002.

Morel, Edmund Dene. *King Léopold's Rule In Africa.* Westport, CT: Negro Universities Press, 1970.

——. *Red Rubber, The Story Of The Rubber Slave Trade Flourishing On The Congo In The Year Of Grace 1906.* New York: Negro Universities Press, 1969.

——. *History Of The Congo Reform Movement.* Ed. William Roger Louis and Jean Stengers. Oxford: Clarendon Press, 1968.

———. *The Economic Aspect Of The Congo Problem: The Kernal Of The Question.* Liverpool: Congo Reform Association, 1908.

———. *The Congo Slave State, A Protest Against The New African Slavery; And An Appeal To The Public Of Great Britain, Of The United States And Of The Continent Of Europe.* Liverpool: J. Richardson & Sons, 1903.

Murat, Inèz. *Colbert.* Charlottesville: University Press of Virginia, 1984.

Murray, David R. *Odious Commerce: Britain, Spain, and the Abolition of the Cuban Slave Trade.* New York: Cambridge University Press, 2002.

Meyers, Jeffrey. *Joseph Conrad, a Biography.* New York: Scribner's, 1991.

Nabuco, Carolina. *The Life of Joaquim Nabuco.* Palo Alto, CA: Stanford University Press, 1950.

Nabuco, Joaquim. *Abolitionism: The Brazilian Antislavery Struggle.* Urbana: University of Illinois Press, 1977.

Nelson, Truman, ed. *Documents of Upheaval, Selections from William Lloyd Garrison's "The Liberator," 1831–1865.* New York: Hill & Wang, 1966.

Newton, John. *Out of the Depths.* Grand Rapids, MI: Kregel Publications, 2003.

Northrup, David, ed. *The Atlantic Slave Trade.* Boston: Houghton Mifflin, 2005.

Nye, Russel B. *William Lloyd Garrison and the Humanitarian Reformers.* Boston: Little, Brown, 1955.

Oldfield, J. R. *Popular Politics and British Anti-slavery: The Mobilization of Public Opinion Against the Slave Trade, 1787–1807.* Manchester: Manchester University Press, 1995.

Parkman, Thomas. *The Scramble for Africa: The White Man's Conquest of the Dark Continent.* New York: Random House, 1991.

Partridge, Michael S. and Karen E. Partridge. *Lord Palmerston, 1784–1865, A Bibliography.* Westport, CT: Greenwood Press, 1994.

Phipps, William E. *William Sheppard: Congo's African American Livingstone.* Louisville, KY.: Geneva Press, 2002.

Pollock, John Charles. *Wilberforce.* New York: St. Martin's, 1978.

Porter, Dale H. *The Abolition of the Slave Trade in England, 1784–1807.* New York: Archon Books, 1970.

Postma, Johannes. *The Dutch in the Atlantic Slave Trade, 1600–1815.* Cambridge: Cambridge University Press, 1990.

Quarles, Benjamin. *Frederick Douglass.* New York: DaCapo Press, 1997.

Rawley, James A. and Stephen D. Behrendt. *The Transatlantic Slave Trade.* Lincoln: University of Nebraska Press, 2005.

Richards, Leonard. *Antislavery Reconsidered: New Perspectives on the Abolitionists.* Baton Rouge: Louisiana State University Press, 1979.

Roberts, M. J. D. *Making English Morals: Voluntary Association and Moral Reform in England, 1787–1886.* New York: Cambridge University Press, 2004.

Rodgers, Nini. *Ireland Slavery and Anti-Slavery, 1645–1865.* New York: Palgrave Macmillan, 2006.

Rodríguez, Jaime E. *The Independence of Spanish America.* Cambridge: Cambridge University Press, 1998.

Ros, Martin. *Night of Fire: The Black Napoleon and the Battle of Haiti.* Rockville Centre, NY: Sarpedon, 1993.

Ross, Andrew C. *David Livingstone, Mission and Empire.* New York: Hambledon and London, 2002.

Saul, S. B. *Studies in British Overseas Trade, 1870–1914.* Liverpool: Liverpool University Press, 1960.

Scott, Rebecca J. *Slave Emancipation in Cuba: The Transition to Free Labor, 1860–1899.* Pittsburgh: University of Pittsburgh Press, 1985.

——, Seymour Drescher, Hebe Maria Mattos de Castro, and George Reid Andrews. *The Abolition of Slavery and the Aftermath of Emancipation in Brazil.* Durham: Duke University Press, 1988.

Shalloff, Stanley. *Reform in King Leopold's Congo.* Richmond, VA: John Knox Press, 1970.

Sheridan, Richard. *Sugar and Slavery: An Economic History of the British West Indies.* Barbados: University of West Indies Press, 2000.

Shyllon, F. O. *James Ramsay: the Unknown Abolitionist.* Edinburgh: Canongate, 1977.

Skidmore, Thomas E. *Brazil: Five Centuries of Change.* New York: Oxford University Press, 1999.

Slade, Ruth. *King Léopold's Congo.* Oxford: Oxford University Press, 1962.

Smith, Adam. *The Theory of Moral Sentiments.* Indianapolis: Liberty Classics, 1982.

——. *An Inquiry into the Nature and Causes of the Wealth of Nations.* New York: Modern Library, 1965.

Smith, Elbert B. *The Death of Slavery: the United States, 1837–65.* Chicago: University of Chicago, 1967.

Smith, Warren Thomas. *John Wesley and Slavery.* Nashville, TN: Abdingdon Press, 1986.

Solow, Barbara L. and Stanley L. Engerman, eds. *British Capitalism and Caribbean Slavery: The Legacy of Eric Williams.* New York: Cambridge University Press, 1987.

Sox, David. *John Woolman, Quintessential Quaker.* New York: Friends United Press, 1999.

Stampp, Kenneth M. *The Era of Reconstruction, 1865–1877.* New York: Knopf, 1965.

——. *The Imperiled Union: Essays on the Background of the Civil War.* New York: Oxford University Press, 1980.

——. *The Peculiar Institution: Slavery in the Antebellum South.* New York: Knopf, 1956.

——, ed. *The Causes of the Civil War.* New York: Simon & Schuster, 1991.

——, and Leon F. Litwack, ed. *Reconstruction, an Anthology of Revisionist Writings.* Baton Rouge: Louisiana State University Press, 1969.

Stanton, Elizabeth Cady, Susan B. Anthony, and Ann D. Gordon. *The Selected Papers of Elizabeth Cady Stanton and Susan B. Anthony: In the School of Anti-Slavery, 1840 to 1866. Selected Papers of Elizabeth Cady Stanton and Susan B Anthony.* New Brunswick: Rutgers University Press, 1997.

Steele, E. D. *Palmerston and Liberalism, 1855–1865.* Cambridge: Cambridge University Press, 1991.

Stephens, W. Walker, ed. *The Life and Writings of Turgot.* New York: Burt Franklin, 1971.

Stewart, James Brewer. *William Lloyd Garrison and the Challenge of Emancipation.* Arlington Heights, IL: Harlan Davidson, 1992.

Sundquist, Eric J., ed. *Frederick Douglass: New Literary and Historical Essays.* Cambridge: Cambridge University Press, 1990.

Temperley, Howard. *British Antislavery, 1833–1870.* London: Longman, 1972.

Thomas, Hugh. *The Slave Trade: The Story of the Atlantic Slave, Trade, 1440–1870.* New York: Simon & Schuster, 1997.

Thomas, John. *The Liberator: William Lloyd Garrison, a Biography.* Boston: Little, Brown, 1963.

Tomkins, Stephen. *John Wesley, A Biography.* Grand Rapids, MI: Wm. B. Eerdmans, 2003.

Toplin, Robert Brent. *The Abolition of Slavery in Brazil.* New York: Atheneum, 1972.

Trevelyan, George Otto. *The Life and Letters of Lord Macaulay.* London: Longmans, Green, 1878. 2 vols.

Tuchman, Barbara. *The March of Folly, from Troy to Vietnam.* New York: Knopf, 1984.

Turley, David. *The Culture of English Anti-Slavery: 1780–1860.* New York: Routledge, 1991.

Tyrrell, Richard. *Joseph Sturge and the Moral Radical Party in Victorian Britain.* London: C. Helm, 1987.

Unger, Harlow Giles. *Lafayette.* New York: John Wiley, 2002.

Vaucaire, Michel. *Bolivar the Liberator.* Boston: Houghton Mifflin, 1929.

Vaux, Roberts. *Memoirs of the Life of A. Benezet.* Philadelphia, 1817.

Walters, Ronald G. *The Anti-Slavery Appeal: American Abolitionism after 1830.* Baltimore, MD: Johns Hopkins Press, 1976.

Walvin, James. *Black Ivory: Slavery in the British Empire.* Oxford: Blackwell, 2001.

———. *England, Slaves and Freedom, 1776–1838.* Jackson: University Press of Mississippi, 1986.

———. *Slavery and the Slave Trade, a Short Illustrated History.* Jackson: University Press of Mississippi, 1983.

Ward, W. E. F. *The Royal Navy and the Slavers: The Suppression of the Atlantic Slave Trade.* New York: Pantheon, 1969.

Washington, Booker T. *Frederick Douglass.* Ed. Ellis Paxson Oberholtzer. New York: Argosy-Antiquarian, 1969.

Wilson, Ellen Gibson. *Thomas Clarkson, A Biography.* New York: St. Martin's Press, 1990.

Woodman, Harold D., ed. *The Legacy of the American Civil War.* New York: Wiley, 1973.

Zook, George Frederick. *The Company of Royal Adventurers Trading into Africa.* New York: Negro Universities Press, 1969.

Index